JAMES JOYCE AND THE ACT
OF RECEPTION

Reading, Ireland, Modernism

James Joyce and the Act of Reception is the first detailed account of
Joyce's own engagement with the reception of his work. It shows
how Joyce's writing, from the earliest fiction to *Finnegans Wake*,
addresses the social conditions of reading (particularly in Ireland).
Most notably, it echoes and transforms the responses of some of
Joyce's actual readers, from family and friends to key figures such as
Eglinton and Yeats. This study argues that the famous 'unreadable'
quality of Joyce's writing is a crucial feature of its historical significance. Not only does Joyce engage with the cultural contexts in
which he was read but, by inscribing versions of his own contemporary reception within his writing, he determines that his later
readers read through the responses of earlier ones. In its focus on
the local and contemporary act of reception, Joyce's work is seen to
challenge critical accounts of both modernism and deconstruction.

JOHN NASH was Lecturer in English at Trinity College Dublin until
2006. He is now Lecturer in English Studies at Durham University.

JAMES JOYCE
AND THE ACT OF RECEPTION

Reading, Ireland, Modernism

JOHN NASH

CAMBRIDGE
UNIVERSITY PRESS

CAMBRIDGE UNIVERSITY PRESS

Cambridge, New York, Melbourne, Madrid, Cape Town, Singapore, São Paulo, Delhi

Cambridge University Press

The Edinburgh Building, Cambridge CB2 8RU, UK

Published in the United States of America by Cambridge University Press, New York

www.cambridge.org

Information on this title: www.cambridge.org/9780521865760

First published 2006
Reprinted 2008

Printed in the United Kingdom at the University Press, Cambridge

A catalogue record for this publication is available from the British Library

ISBN 978-0-521-86576-0 hardback

Contents

Figures

Acknowledgements

The staff of several libraries have been of great assistance in the preparation of this book: the library of Trinity College Dublin; Special Collections at the library of University College Dublin; the National Library of Ireland; the Department of Manuscripts at the British Library; and the Department of Rare Books and Special Collections at Princeton University Library. Material from the Sylvia Beach archive is published with permission of the Princeton University Library. I would also like to thank An Post for permission to reproduce the stamps in Figures 1 and 2 and Robert Ballagh for permission to reproduce the cover image.

The anonymous readers provided by Cambridge University Press were a huge help in the preparation of the final manuscript: I am indebted to them. Two colleagues at Trinity College Dublin, Nicholas Grene and Terence Brown, commented on earlier versions of chapters 1 and 4 respectively; and Anne Fogarty offered helpful advice on a much earlier version of some material in chapter 2. Vincent Cheng and Andrew Gibson have freely given much appreciated support over the years. The incomparable John Kelly helped me with some specific points on Yeats's correspondence. Laura Weldon gave me useful advice on the Beach archive. My thanks to them all. Thanks also to the patient Ray Ryan, plus Jackie Warren, Maartje Scheltens and Caro Drake at Cambridge University Press for their help in the production of this book. Not least, I am grateful for the support of many individuals within the community of Joyce scholarship.

I write this as I am about to leave the School of English at Trinity College Dublin: my thanks to all colleagues; in particular, I'd like to acknowledge the camaraderie of Darryl Jones, Aileen Douglas, Ian Ross and Nick Daly.

Thank you to my parents and the many others who cannot be named here. My greatest debt is both personal and intellectual; this book has been hugely improved thanks to the unflinching support of Helen O'Connell. It is dedicated to her and to James Patrick.

Textual note

The following editions of Joyce's works have been cited parenthetically in the text:

CW   *The Critical Writings*, ed. Richard Ellmann and Ellsworth Mason. Ithaca: Cornell University Press, 1989.

D   *Dubliners* [1914], ed. Terence Brown. London: Penguin, 1992.

FW   *Finnegans Wake* [1939]. London: Faber and Faber, 1988. Cited by page and line number.

GJ   *Giacomo Joyce*, ed. Richard Ellmann. New York: Viking Press, 1968.

JJA   *James Joyce Archive*, ed. Michael Groden et al. New York and London: Garland Publishing, 1977–9. Cited by volume and page number.

Letters I   *Letters of James Joyce*, volume I, ed. Stuart Gilbert. New York: Viking Press, 1966.

Letters II, III   *Letters of James Joyce*, volumes II, III, ed. Richard Ellmann. New York: Viking Press, 1966.

OCPW   *Occasional, Critical and Political Writing*, ed. Kevin Barry. Translations by Conor Deane. Oxford: Oxford University Press, 2000.

P   *A Portrait of the Artist as a Young Man* [1916], ed. Seamus Deane. London: Penguin, 1992.

PE   *Poems and Exiles*, ed. J. C. C. Mays. London: Penguin, 1992.

SL   *Selected Letters of James Joyce*, ed. Richard Ellmann. London: Faber and Faber, 1975.

SH   *Stephen Hero* [1944], ed. John J. Slocum and Herbert Cahoon. London: Grafton Books, 1977.

U   *Ulysses* [1922], ed. Hans Walter Gabler et al. New York: Random House, 1986. Cited by episode and line number.

In addition, the following abbreviation has also been used in the notes:

CH I, II *James Joyce: The Critical Heritage, Volume I: 1907–1927; Volume 2: 1928–1941,* ed. Robert H. Deming. London: Routledge and Kegan Paul, 1970. (Original publications are also cited in the text in each instance.)

Introduction: writing reception

'I'll take this one,' Bloom says to the shopman. His choice of *Sweets of Sin* to fulfill his errand for Molly, at the heart of both city and novel, signals first a moment of transportation in which Bloom, as reader, nearly loses the run of himself, and then a fleeting masculine decisiveness, a 'mastering' of his 'troubled' breath (*U* 10.638-9). This act will place both Bloom and Molly within a series about which the narrator of 'Ithaca' might well have asked a question: who else has read this book? Fictionally, at least, the shopman has, but also, no one has, since *Sweets of Sin* does not exist beyond the pages of Joyce's novel. Then again, it might be as well to say that anyone who has read *Ulysses* has therefore also read *Sweets of Sin*. The invited confusion between character-as-reader and 'actual' reader renders the question 'Who has read this book?' more difficult than it might appear. In fact, the question is asked a few pages later by Stephen Dedalus, about an unnamed text at a different bookcart. 'Thumbed pages: read and read. Who has passed here before me?' (*U* 10.545-6). The identification of a readership is one of the classic problems in studies of reception, and one that is further exacerbated when the books in question overtly address this very issue.

When a question similar to Stephen's ('Who has passed here before me?') is put in 'Ithaca' – 'What preceding series?' – the 'text' is Molly's body and the 'readers' are her supposed lovers. The narrator's answer is instructive less of Molly's sexual relations than of such questions in general: 'Assuming Mulvey to be the first term of the series . . . and so on to no last term' (*U* 17.2132-42). As the narrator implies, such lists have an arbitrary starting point and no determinate conclusion. Like the lover, the reader 'is neither first nor last nor only nor alone in a series originating in and repeated to infinity' (*U* 17.2130-1). One list runs into another, forming an intertextual log of all readers. Moreover, like the Blooms' bed, such a list bears 'the imprint of a human form' (*U* 17.2125) since it is a catalogue of the compiler's own anxieties, prejudices and concerns. When

I

Dedalus asks 'Who has passed here before me?' he thus opens another 'book', the unwritten list of those readers in that 'preceding series'; his interest in *the history of that reading* is indicative of the particular significance of allusions to readers in Joyce's work in general. By recalling his earlier question on Sandymount Strand, 'Who ever anywhere will read these written words?' (*U* 3.414-15), Stephen has set up both anticipatory and reflective histories of reading: in the first case, by looking ahead to his own reception by the would-be readers of his poem; and later, at the bookcart, by placing himself as the latest in a series of readers. On this second occasion, Stephen notices the volume's 'Thumbed pages: read and read.' The words 'read and read' are suitably (and undecidably) both past and present tense, one a reflection and the other an imperative to a future reading, thus capturing both the sense of previous readers having read and at the same time the reading that is yet to come. This example again suggests a necessary qualification to any catalogue of readers: such a list is unending and is lent an almost fictional quality, which undermines a reliance solely upon the historical. The fictional can in itself provide an indication, and even suggest an implicit theory, of reception. An account of Joyce's reception should not, then, be restricted to the attempted compilation of an actual readership (and not merely a critical readership) but must also be responsible to the peculiarities of the text in question. The identification of a readership is thus not only a historical question but also a theoretical, and even textual, one.

The purpose of the present study is not, then, to offer a 'critical history' of Joyce but instead to show how – and this is the particular topic of this book – Joyce's work rewrites the responses of several actual readers and, in doing so, engages with the specific conditions of reception, notably in Ireland.[1] These actual readers to whom Joyce in turn responded ranged from family and friends to critics, writers and 'men of letters'. Of course, this became more pronounced as his career developed. On many occasions, Joyce incorporated into his writing versions of their particular responses which had been made either to his earlier work or to earlier versions of that writing. Joyce's writing of reception is thus a fiction, but a fiction that is responsible to the historical pressures of reading. Reception might well be called an act (as in the title of this book): not only for its connotations of the fictional and performative, but also for its suggestion of the social, somatic and even legal. The term might be taken to imply a stronger historical engagement than it does in Wolfgang Iser's *The Act of Reading*, a seminal work of reader-response criticism (discussed below). At the same time as implying that reading is itself a performance, the analyses that follow seek to place that action within particular contexts.[2] This book shows that Joyce's engagement with the conditions of reception – such as his tactic of incorporating within his writing variations of previous, actual responses to his work – is a matter of wider cultural significance since such issues carried particular social and political weight in Joyce's Ireland.

The question of reception is particularly germane to a reading of Joyce because his books not only have attracted countless volumes of criticism and a formidable reputation but are also in part *about* reception. Here the term 'reception' is more apt than 'reading', since it implies an institutional social discourse that envelops reading – one of publication, reviewing and cultural attitudes. Within the particular Irish contexts which it insistently invokes, Joyce's writing displays an acute recognition of its untimeliness, of being out of step with others and with expectations, of there not being an audience or 'a people' waiting for it. In this sense, it may be called modern: Joyce's work signifies its modernity in its self-conscious concern for reception.[3] The absence of a 'public' was a condition for the writing; the responses of readers the material to show this. If this is a typically modern disjunction – signalling the estrangement of a writer from possible readers – it is also one that plays out in Joyce's reception (or possible reception) in Ireland. Moreover, Joyce records and transforms that process: his is a writing of reception. Joyce's work shows a strong emphasis on the material and societal aspects of reading as well as on the inevitable 'failures' of reading. As such, it situates literary reception within particular contexts, from revivalist theatre and Catholic education to the formation of the Free State; and his rewriting of specific readers' responses (from a Trieste pupil to his mother to John Eglinton [W. K. Magee] and W. B. Yeats) exemplifies also the textual deformations that the process of reading produces.

Joyce's writing of the act of reception renders without nostalgia those lost historical moments – moments, it might be said, when reading itself was lost – as fictional indices of a cultural and aesthetic problem: the identification of a reader and the constitution of an audience. The following chapters situate those moments within broader discourses that helped shape the expectations of readers: the idea of a 'national audience' in revivalist theatre; the effect of the provision of Catholic educational institutions on strategies for reading; the institutionalisation of an 'ordinary reader'; the attempt (by Yeats in particular) to shape the cultural struggles of the Free State. Joyce thus links the personal act of reading (especially reading of his own work) to wider political forces, particularly those in Ireland. I argue that Joyce's work, in its concern with its own reception, sets out the conditions of impossibility for a determinable audience in general and for an Irish national audience in particular; at the same time, his writing exposes the various imperial and religious constraints that both enabled and closed off reading. This is the political tension of his texts: for Joyce, there can be no model of an audience, but there must of necessity be readers. The distinction – between an imagined (or actual) body of like-minded recipients and the inevitable fact of partial reading – is important; the collective audience suggests a 'readiness' that the individual reader may not have. This very distinction, it might be said, is implicit in the ending of 'The Dead' (as chapter 1 argues). So Joyce's account of the conditions of reception in Ireland, and of his own readers in particular, is not merely 'personal revenge' or 'modernist self-reflexivity' but an important cultural commentary on the social and political ramifications of reading, which continues to resonate for contemporary criticism.

Joyce's display of the disjunction between the writer and his possible readers signals in the first place the impossibility of a national audience as, for instance, ambitiously envisaged in the early days of the Revival. However, at the same time, by recording this disjunction, Joyce's writing seeks to displace the cultural practices that shaped the possibilities of reception in his Ireland. His account of the failures of his reception – the stumbling and limited responses met with by his own work – shows his commitment to reading as an inevitably partial act (that is, both incomplete and biased) and as a material, socially embedded one. In doing so, he indicates that reading was both performative (or inventive) and historical (an act undertaken in particular conditions). As with so much in Joyce, his examples were close to home: the reception of his own writing could illuminate a broad contextual terrain. It could be said that Joyce's work is addressed to the possibility of its reception in Ireland: that is to say, it recognises that a form of reading or accommodation necessarily occurs (even when not reading). The inevitability of this 'reading' in Ireland remained a lasting fascination within his writing. Yet this reception must remain at one level unachieved for Joyce; it stays at the status of the possible: the formation of an achieved reception would itself signal a cultural state that never came into being. It might be said, then, that by showing the ways in which reception was possible – by frequently alluding to his own reception, and by rewriting that reception – Joyce shows how a certain impossibility resides within the act of reading. Such an apparent 'impossibility', this book maintains, had particular political circumstances.

I

In general, readers of Joyce know two things about his reception, although little critical effort has been made to connect them. In the first place, like that of many modernist writers, Joyce's writing is thought to imply a future audience that would be sufficiently cultured to read it: Joyce remains 'ahead' of his readers. Second, it is often recognised that, in his own way, Joyce sought to extend his readership by actively promoting his work (having copies delivered to particular critics and acquaintances, thanking all for their reviews despite also exacting some comeuppance on a few). These points are exemplified by Richard Ellmann's hugely influential biography. The very first line states that 'We are still learning to be James Joyce's contemporaries', suggesting that his implied – and somehow 'best' – audience is a later, 'more educated' one than his own generation of readers. Ellmann's final page declares that 'the ingenuity with which he [Joyce] wrote his books was the same with which he forced the world to read them', and so acknowledges the author's role as a sort of ad-canvasser in his own right: he took seriously the promotion and reviewing of his work, even writing jingles for Faber's publication of two books from 'Work in Progress'.[4] Ellmann's Joyce was a revised version of the model of the aloof 'high modernist' which some earlier critics had championed: 'His [Joyce's] audience was the least of his concerns', claimed Herbert Gorman.[5] In overcoming this view of modernism, more recent critics, building on Ellmann and others, have sought to delineate the specific kinds of interaction between modernist writers and their marketplace. Lawrence Rainey argues that innovative sales methods – and *Ulysses* is typical of this – helped create a new and elite audience of reader-collectors.[6] Others have focused on the role of patrons: Joyce Piell Wexler claims that 'Joyce circumvented the need to build an audience because he attracted patrons'; specifically, she states that he 'sacrificed the Irish public he had once sought'.[7] As this book shows, Joyce's work remains an interrogation of what 'the Irish public' might be precisely because it refuses an address to such a public. While these analyses have often provided illuminating accounts of the role of authors within modernist publishing, they have also tended to ignore two important aspects: Joyce's writing itself (which, as I show, does address reception, including his own), and the particular circumstances of literary reception in Ireland.

Ellmann's observations suggest the importance of the issue of reception to an understanding of Joyce's work and its cultural placement. Yet, pinned at either end of his biography, they do little more than sketch an outline of the topic, hinting at Joyce's deep concern for his own reception and gesturing towards a number of questions raised by the work. What relationship exists between those contemporary readers and us later ones? *Is* there an appropriate audience for Joyce? Or, as Derrida would put it twenty-five years later, 'What exactly do you mean by "read Joyce"? Who can pride himself [or herself] on having "read" Joyce?'[8] The idea that Joyce's readers are somehow lagging behind him has been a lasting one. Ellmann's famous opening line itself echoes Evelyn Scott's 1920 article in *The Dial* which bore the heading 'Contemporary of the Future'.[9] More recently, Christine Froula has declared that 'we are still catching up with some of his [Joyce's] most radical aspects.'[10] Standing at either end of his monumental volume, Ellmann's remarks (and Derrida's casual echo) are symptomatic of a more general critical reluctance to connect these issues – Joyce's particular relationships with practices of reading, and his texts' apparent ability to remain ahead of readers – in analyses of the historical and textual significance of reception as his work encounters, and rewrites, it.

Modernism has also often been understood to imply a later and 'better' audience, whose shortcomings can be highlighted and corrected, one which would in time learn to read the canonical artefact. Colin MacCabe, for instance, has suggested that 'Modernism can be read as attempts to make up for the inadequacies of audiences in the present by postulating ideal audiences in the future.'[11] By contrast, the following chapters suggest that Joyce consistently grounds reading in material circumstances, which is nowhere more evident than in his depictions of actual readers and historical scenes of reading, particularly those pertaining to readings of his own work or conditions in which his work might be read. While Joyce may note the 'inadequacies' of his contemporary readership, he does so by situating it within particular circumstances. Nowhere in Joyce's work is there a model of an 'ideal reader'. This may suggest that such frustrations typify reading in general, yet this is no bland universalism but rather an insistence on the historicity of understanding and the social character of reading experiences. Joyce does not postulate a model future audience: indeed – as chapter 1 shows – his response to Revivalism in *Dubliners* in part hinges on a rejection of this notion. For Joyce, an ideal future audience would be at odds with the cultural situations and generic forms within which he worked: overt political divisions, as well as the inevitable disjunctions of textuality, did not lead Joyce to imagine a 'future ideal audience', or to reclaim one from history, but to interrogate the forms of reception in his present. In this sense, as in others, Joyce might be seen as

distinct from some of his European modernist and Irish revivalist contemporaries.[12] Indeed, his refusal to embrace a future or ideal audience,
while rewriting his contemporary readers, could be thought of as a component of his rejection of any idealised or postulated political elite while
at the same time denying the legitimacy of the status quo. Joyce's refusal
of an audience is thus quite different from, for instance, that of the editors
of *Criterion*, who kept the circulation deliberately low, for theirs is the
cultivation of an elite, like-minded audience. He also differs from Yeats,
who at various points imagines an audience either by postulating a
subservient public or by idealising specific historical figures (as discussed
in chapter 1). Unlike these, Joyce's refusal of an audience is an examination of literary reception. It might be said that Joyce's writing is addressed to the very question of an audience or a public, especially as
constituted in Ireland in the period of his work.

It is understandable that Joyce has sometimes been criticised for not
addressing a particular audience. In the 1970s, this was seen as a political
failing by MacCabe when he argued that 'Joyce's texts are politically
ineffective because they lack any definite notion of an audience to which
they are addressed.' MacCabe's solution to this failing was to fall back on
a standard supposition of early *Wake* criticism which had held that the
book could be addressed only to 'Joyce himself'.[13] Yet the problem was
more serious, as MacCabe saw it, since having deconstructed the liberal
subject, Joyce then reinscribed this immutable individuality into the text
as its addressee (i.e. himself). This could only lead to the pessimistic
conclusion that Joyce's radical linguistic, political and sexual strategies
were ultimately lost for want of an appropriate audience elsewhere.

More recently, Seamus Deane has partly concurred with MacCabe's
analysis of modernism, and Joyce's political inefficacy, arguing that 'our
incompetence is itself already incorporated into modernism's diagnosis of
"modernity". We ratify these texts by being helpless before them and then
are taught the full range of our incompetence.' Thus obscurity is canon-
ised. In this view, Joyce belittles his readers, either boring them to sleep
or bullying them into research.[14] Elsewhere, Deane suggests that Joyce's
famous lyrical endings signal a disengagement from social critique and
that this is directly related to his reception, having become a 'semisubsi-
dized bohemian for whom . . . anything other than a select audience was
an embarrassment'.[15]

There is a surprising echo of Deane's argument in John Carey's
conventionally liberalist reading of modernism, which, he contends, can
be defined as a deliberate elitism that willfully excluded ordinary readers.

This is not uncommon as a rejection of *Ulysses* and *Finnegans Wake*. 'Bloom would never and could never read a book like *Ulysses*', Carey says, since its complexity, technique and obscurity 'rigorously exclude people like Bloom from its readership'. A reader's 'sympathetic . . . solidarity' with Bloom is an 'illusion' that operates in conjunction with an irony that 'preserves the reader's – and the author's – superiority'. Carey thus accuses Joyce of 'duplicity'.[16] The implication of both Deane and Carey (despite their obvious differences) is that 'the mass audience' has been left behind and is no longer up to the task of reading: for Deane and MacCabe this signals an abandoned opportunity for a critique of imperial and class oppressions; to Carey it signals a repressive, undemocratic politics that devalues the ordinary decent individual. In each case, the presumption is that to read modernism (and Joyce in particular) requires a later, competent audience.

Carey's argument seems to presume that 'culture' and learning form a line of progress, an encoded tradition that is there simply in order to be decoded by later generations. However, such a notion as the 'competent reader' is antithetical to Joyce's texts which self-consciously open onto various linguistic and cultural forms, leading to their readers' own, necessarily partial, constructions and performances. While this is particularly the case in *Ulysses* and *Finnegans Wake*, the books about which Carey and Deane are explicitly writing, it is also true of his other texts. For Joyce's work to be an 'institutionalizing of the modern reader as a cultureless recipient' can only be the case from the point of view of that very tradition (which opposes 'possession of culture' to being cultureless) that Deane also, rightly, shows to have been exploded by Joyce.[17] A comparison might be made with the narrator of Proust's *À la Recherche du Temps Perdu*, who typically suggests 'plus tard, j'ai compris', implying that a fuller understanding would surely follow – even though it often does not.[18]

II

Many readers of Joyce have noted the paradox of a difficult text that apparently requires patient study and guidance but yet also seems to undermine all readings, thereby defeating the very idea of guidance. Myles na gCopaleen (Brian O'Nolan) hinted at this conundrum in his own fashion, suggesting that such commitment could never be successful:

Joyce has been reported as saying that he asked of his readers nothing but that they should devote their lives to reading his works. Such a method of spending a lifetime is likely to endow the party concerned with quite a unique psychic apparatus of his own. I cannot recommend it.[19]

The dilemma facing 'the party concerned' was described in slightly different terms by Jacques Derrida in perhaps the single most concerted reflection on the notion of reception as it pertains to Joyce's work (his address to the 1984 International Joyce Symposium in Paris). For Derrida, this dilemma was a tension between the competence necessarily sanctioned by the Joycean community and the undermining of this competence by the 'performativity' of Joyce's writing. In these terms, Joyce's work has 'invented' its own audience by instituting courses, conferences and an academic discourse, and yet, at the same time, that same work questions *any* reader's ability to read it. 'No truth can come from outside the Joycean community,' argues Derrida, but then 'there is no model for *Joycean* competence'.[20] Faced with this apparently irreconcilable problem, Derrida suggests that an immanent deconstruction of competence inheres already in Joyce's work.[21] The reader who is 'invented' by Joyce is thus one whose legitimacy comes from that community, but the competence thereby bestowed upon the reader is itself shaky, a performance or creative rereading. Derrida's remarks point to two significant and contradictory, but enduring, features of Joyce's critical reputation: that his work defies accommodation, remaining in an important way 'unreadable'; and that a powerful body of explication has developed containing the implicit assumption that Joyce's 'suitable', learned audience can be generated.

The trouble with the presumption of a later and better audience is, as Derrida would have it, that the competence it presumes is not possible to measure; notwithstanding all the works of exegesis that surround Joyce, his writing undermines the very idea of competence through its resistance to explication. So Derrida's interpretation of Joyce can be seen as a powerful riposte to the notion that modernism belittles its readers in order to instruct 'better' ones in the future. His analysis is valuable as a reminder of part of the significance of Joyce's 'unreadability', of the radical challenges that reading his work presents: 'everything we can say . . . has already been anticipated'.[22] The chronological inversion implied here means that the tense of one's reading is uncertain: it would be impossible for Derrida to say that Joyce 'has been read', as this would put the reader somehow ahead of the text. As he explains, 'I have the feeling that I haven't yet begun to read Joyce' – still, one might say, learning to be his contemporary.[23] Derrida's analysis thus differs from Ellmann's, despite echoing the American critic, since it highlights the extent to which reception is already written, and this is also one of the key features of Joyce's engagement with the issue. However, Derrida's emphasis on Joyce's 'anticipation' of later readers might be said to have already been overturned in Joyce's writing: by inscribing versions of specific actual readers and responses into his texts, Joyce detours those later readers back through the byways of earlier ones. This does not necessarily anticipate a later reader's reactions but it does situate those reactions in relation to a previous reader. The historicity of critical understanding is thus insisted upon even as its fictionalisation frustrates the ambitions of historical analysis. The implication is that by inscribing his faltering contemporary reception, Joyce establishes that all reading is based on previous reading. Even as we run up against the comical deflation of critical will that Joyce's writing performs, this is not a merely textual or epistemological manoeuvre, for his writing of reception points always to the local and the contextual. The 'unreadable Joyce' of deconstruction might then be complemented by a Joyce whose unreadability spoke to its own conditions of reception.

Crucially, it is impossible to ignore the fact that scholarship continually makes itself more informed and better equipped: libraries of historical, textual and biographical sources are available; new notebooks and manuscripts have been acquired by libraries 'hoping to ye public' (*FW* 313.02); relatively recent technology is capable of abetting – and changing – reading practices. There is, though, an unavoidable tension between the genuine sense of progress that exegetical and historical scholarship creates and the continuing frustrations of interpretation – which, it should be said, are sometimes only exacerbated by the expansion of critical and textual knowledge. Moreover, as the shape of the Joyce archive itself changes (the mammoth *James Joyce Archive* is now rather outdated) with the unearthing of previously hidden notebooks, so, too, the object of enquiry also changes. In this way, scholarly 'progress' often also shifts the goalposts, maintaining a sense of continual interpretive dilemmas: 'genetic' Joyce locates the sources of much of *Finnegans Wake* but it must do so in the service of interpretation.[24] On the one hand, by 'recovering' some of Joyce's contemporary readers as they echo within his texts, we elucidate our competence; and yet the 'archives' (both the fiction and the historical records) refuse to yield definitive resolutions and arguably begin to doubt the very notion of competence as it might pertain to Joyce. In its emphasis on its own reception, then, Joyce's work plays out the double bind (of authority and performativity) that Derrida identified in 1984. (In the Afterword, I will suggest that Joyce's writing of reception in fact differs in an important way from Derrida's analysis.)

Derrida's reflections bring to a head a familiar problem in Joyce criticism. From the earliest attempts to understand *Ulysses*, to the most recent genetic studies and political readings, Joyce criticism has been beset by – broadly speaking – his texts' resistance to reading and their poignant historical engagement. While some critics have found that the difficulty and self-reflexivity of Joyce's writing help make it, in an important sense, 'unreadable' (a claim with a long critical history), many others have explicated versions of his particular cultural placement, detailing the many contextual discourses to which his writing contributed. Yet it remains a persistent challenge to recent readers to place these two versions of Joyce together.[25] This study cannot offer a neat resolution to these 'historical' and 'unreadable' poles, although it does seek to bring them together into a productive tension.

If the extent to which the 'unreadable' Joyce and the 'historical' Joyce are mutually informing is gradually coming to be recognised, the question of reception might be said to clasp them together. In what particular circumstances did Joyce's work appear unreadable to his contemporaries? How did his reaction to their responses affect both his own writing and the cultural politics of their relations? It is a presupposition of this book that to read Joyce is to confront, simultaneously, the resistance of his writing to critical explication and the necessity of reading it within more-or-less determinable historical contexts. This obviously presents responsible readers with a problem. The 'solution', however, is suggested by Joyce's work itself, which consistently depicts reading as a social activity that has real cultural value: moreover, it frequently addresses actual responses and conditions of reading. As such, the resistance to reading offered by Joyce is a form of social commentary; indeed, the commonplace notion of his texts as 'unreadable' is itself a reading (or attempted accommodation) of those texts. It might be said, then, that the 'unreadable' quality of his writing is a part of what one critic calls its 'historical power' – and that power is in many ways due to Joyce's interrogation of the cultural circumstances of reading through which any text, even the most recalcitrant, is consumed.[26] By focusing on Joyce's rewriting of particular responses to his work, and the contexts enveloping them, this study attempts an interpretation of Joyce's 'unreadable' writing within particular historical conditions: it highlights some of the cultural and political forces that bore on the possible reception of his work, and reads its engagement with those forces, without presuming to be an exhaustive account of either the reception his writing encountered or the actual conditions in which it circulated. In doing so, this book places

Joyce's writing within the contexts of Revival theatre; religion and the 'university question'; and the Free State. Important but often neglected figures such as John Eglinton crop up repeatedly here; and the book opens and closes with chapters that give special attention to Yeats, first as part of the Irish Literary Theatre and later as a reader of *Ulysses*. The book also reads Joyce's developing aesthetic in relation to key contemporary discourses of critical reception such as the construct of an 'ordinary reader'. Throughout, the focus is on the cultural significance of Joyce's apparent unreadability.

The act of reception signals a 'cultural dialogic' in which Joyce inscribed versions of particular readers and their responses. One important consequence of this manoeuvre is that later readers necessarily read in and through the responses of earlier ones. Joyce's writing of reception implies, therefore, a historicity of reading. In addition, the allusion to readers' responses suggests that Joyce's work is already comprised in part from acts of reception. It can be said, then, that reception does not simply follow the text (as a 'critical history of Joyce' might presume) but that a complex chronology is at work in reading. This is not to claim that reading is the same thing as writing (or that consumption is the same as production) but it is to assert that the composition of Joyce's texts took place within (and, often, against) pre-existing pressures of reception. If their writing was already coloured by their reading, then this temporal disjunction is also replayed in those later readers who read in the responses of Joyce's contemporaries. This practice is akin to that identified by Luke Gibbons, in which spectral echoes of historical figures resurface in Joyce's writing, suggesting that the 'traditional' and the 'modern' need to be understood together, and enabling a grasp of some of the particular colonial features of Joyce's Ireland in which no unifying chronology could be said to hold sway.[27] Unlike Gibbons's historical ghosts, however, my identification of a complex chronology of reception shows how figures from Joyce's present echo in later readers. This suggests both that future readers are implicated in the conditions of Joyce's Ireland and that the historicity of reading retains a textually-performative character. As such, Joyce's writing of those historical conditions both displays and displaces them. It is just this sense of the fragile but necessary border between word and action that the act of reception signifies.

Joyce's emphasis *in* his texts on readers *of* those texts, coupled with his depiction of the unremitting materiality of reading, means that his work stands out in this respect, even from Proust and Pound, the two modernists with whom he is most often linked.[28] In fact, this feature of Joyce's work places him closer to Yeats (as discussed in chapter 1). For Joyce, the 'inadequacies' of contemporary readers, and of the social situation in which reading occurs, are both a form of political commentary and suggestive of the conditions of reading more broadly. There is then a twofold operation at work in Joyce's writing of reception: an emphasis on actual and material sites of reading, which draws attention to their various political, institutional and religious contexts; and also a questioning of the nature of reception through an insistence that later readers must also always be frustratingly mired in the actual and in the past. Joyce's work thus challenges the critical explication of modernism as dependent upon later, better audiences by introducing an 'anarchive' of its own reception, which dismantles the supposition of pre-eminence for later, 'cultured' readers. Joyce's fictionalisation of some of his actual readers serves as a caution to the later reader armed with his or her annotations: a competent reading must unearth the forms that their readings took (including at times their incompetence) and the particular conditions that both propelled and hindered them. All the while, it necessarily remains that to read Joyce is also to read (his version of) his contemporary readers.

III

This study resituates Joyce in relation to potential Irish audiences, showing that the practice of alluding to actual readers is more than an 'oppositional revenge' but is instead part of an examination of the sometimes oppressive conditions in which reading could – indeed, must – occur. Although critics have recently addressed the imbrication of Irish and (post)colonial politics in Joyce's writing, it has proved difficult to assess his complex relationship with an Irish readership and the possibility of an Irish audience. It might be thought that,

> Like other anti-colonial nationalist writers, Irish writers differ from English writers and European modernist and postmodernist writers in their sense of a double audience, one existing as an immediate community within or identified with the Irish nation, the other an outside or metropolitan readership. For the immediate community, reading is largely an act of *recognition* and bonding.[29]

However, this sense of identification is less fitting for Joyce, owing to his texts' refusal to be tied to any social group: his writing offers an implicit denial of cultural homology between text and readers even while asserting the political rights of a Catholic tradition and the inevitability of social accommodation (a point reinforced in chapter 2). At the same time, Joyce clearly shared a revivalist wariness of English audiences and, at first, an initial desire to publish in Ireland for Irish readers. No doubt partly because of the difficulty of securing an Irish publisher for his early stories, Joyce's work demonstrates a sharp awareness of the problematic appeal to a split audience that has characterised much Irish writing, especially through the nineteenth century from Edgeworth to Boucicault and beyond. Indeed, Boucicault's prominence in *Finnegans Wake* surely owes much to his address to divergent constituencies (British and Irish; popular and literary). Towards the end of his career, Joyce's work again addresses the question of his exile/emigration and the possibility of what an Irish audience might be. The complex relationship to Joyce of younger, post-Revival Irish writers such as Brian O'Nolan, Sean O'Faolain and Frank O'Connor arguably swings upon their more direct engagements with the audiences of the new State.[30] In this context, it is notable that Joyce *does* address the topic of his Irish reception in particular, in his letters as well as in his fiction. While it cannot be claimed that Joyce consistently sought Irish readers above all others (clearly he did not), or that he went so far as to model such an audience in his work, it is argued here that the conditions facing readers, and Irish ones in particular, were a primary source of material through which Joyce could explore the cultural politics of reading and audience formation.

It has sometimes been assumed that Joyce needed to leave Ireland in order to find readers. In the 1940s, Harry Levin put this case succinctly: Joyce's works 'are of Irishmen and by an Irishman, but not for Irishmen'. (This phrase evidently intrigued Joyce's friend Con Curran, who transcribed it from Levin's study into a notebook of Joyce-related material.)[31] The familiar refrain of Joycean retribution also takes shape here. In Richard Ellmann's view, derived largely from Stanislaus, Joyce's quarrels 'lost nothing from distance'; he 'kept green his memory of old injuries' in order for 'vengeance' to be greater: the sophisticated European Joyce successfully reacts against his Irish provincial 'background'.[32] From a very different perspective, and in different political terms, the editors of *Post-Structuralist Joyce* (an important milestone in Joyce studies in the 1980s) have nonetheless reiterated Levin's assertion. Whereas Dublin was the 'source of memories and material for Joyce's books, it was . . . Paris that provided the environment and the audience which those books demanded'. This argument carries the implicit assumption that an Irish (or Dublin) audience would be too 'backward' compared with its 'modern' continental counterpart, that 'shocking Paris and shockable Dublin' were 'polar opposites'.[33] To characterise Joyce's reception in this way is both historically and theoretically questionable. Joyce consistently characterises an 'audience' as a body divided by the very act of reading; to imply a cultural 'fit' between Joyce, Paris and his 'demanded' audience is highly dubious. It is disconcertingly close to the colonialist position to imply that Joyce's 'appropriate audience' would somehow later be 'achieved' in Europe (be it through *transition* or deconstruction) and that an Irish reading public was necessarily forsaken or non-existent. On the contrary, Joyce's work, as this book shows, frequently refers back to its consumption in Ireland. Whereas this reception is often problematic – an attempted political appropriation or censorship, for instance – Joyce suggests that this environment continues to condition his reception. By referring to some of his actual readers in Ireland, Joyce maintains that later readers must read through the responses of his contemporaries, thus establishing that the social conditions of his Irish reception remain a part of his work. Of course, this is not to celebrate those contemporary readers nor is it to offer instead a counter-version of a suitable audience. On these grounds it is also questionable to assume that Joyce requires an Irish reader, as writers and critics such as Frank O'Connor and Brian O'Nolan did in the Free State period in their misplaced endeavour to read Joyce as a (repressed or perverted) Catholic writer.[34]

These questions over Joyce's relationship with his reception are at the heart of the political tensions in his writing, for they touch on the charge of 'provincialism'. In this respect, it is interesting to recall a remark made by Joyce to the effect that 'some day, way off in Tibet or Somaliland, some boy or girl reading that little book [*Anna Livia Plurabelle*] would be pleased to come upon the name of his or her own river'.[35] If this dream smacks of a Eurocentric attitude, it is also indicative, perversely perhaps, of Joyce's continued provincialism (into the late 1920s). Stuart Gilbert privately dismissed Joyce's humour in 'Work in Progress' as that of 'The provincial Dubliner. Foreign is funny.'[36] The defence against this charge, made by Ezra Pound and popularised by Hugh Kenner, was that Joyce persisted in raising the local to the level of the universal: readers, it seemed, need not have any Irish knowledge after all. According to Pound – who successfully 'Europeanised' his protégé – even though Joyce possessed the provincialism of one who drags in obscure allusions, still 'the imaginary Chinaman or denizen of the forty-first century could without works of reference gain a very good idea of the scene and habits portrayed'.[37] In grounding his work in the local, however, Joyce also asserted the specific importance of his own background, split as it was between the partial 'provincialism' of the Irish

Catholic (and sometime nationalist) and the uncomfortable 'centrality' of the middle-class Dubliner (and British citizen). Joyce's famous 'universalism' might just as well be seen as a self-conscious strategy in his writing which, rather than simply 'collapsing' the particular into the universal, or the social into the aesthetic, reinscribes that problematic within the question of reception: Joyce's later readers are grounded in his contemporaries whose responses, and whose social conditions of reception, continue to echo in his writing. Readers are torn between, on the one hand, the will to explicate the names of 'obscure' rivers and, on the other hand, the realisation that Joyce's text challenges the assumptions of cultural centrality or standardisation that can lie behind such exegesis. Readers are thus invited into forms of recognition but are refused a homely sense of 'belonging'.[38] Provincialism is not necessarily to be dismissed by a metropolitan audience that thinks it has arrived; it might also speak to the dissonance of modernity. The example of Joyce (and, indeed, of Yeats) demonstrates to European modernism and its criticism that the question of reception is politically charged: the historicity of reception undermines, even as it leads to, the presumptions of a later, better audience.

IV

Reception theory does not have a primary role in this study because, in general, it fails to offer a model whereby actual readers' responses can be gauged within a particular cultural framework. Instead, the question of reception requires a more thoroughgoing historical (and textual) analysis than is available in the liberal models of reader-response criticism and even its more historicist antecedent, *rezeptionsästhetik*. Despite a renewed interest in reception, it has remained a problematic area in literary theory and criticism since Walter Benjamin's famous declaration in 1923 that 'In the appreciation of a work of art or an art form, consideration of the receiver never proves fruitful.'[39] It is perhaps not surprising that the questions 'who writes, and for whom?' have been called 'naïve' by a prominent Joyce critic.[40] Both remarks point to problems of empiricism and historical identification. There may indeed be a certain hopefulness in compiling any list of readers, as *Ulysses* itself (and the history of the first edition) suggests, but surely the question 'for whom?' is always – textually and politically – important and inescapable. As Derrida – more known for his refusal of reception theory – puts it, 'one must indeed receive the address of the other at a particular address and in a singular language; otherwise we would not receive it'.[41] That question is, more-over, of particular significance to an understanding of Joyce given his difficulty in publishing, the 'unreadable' nature of his work, and the sheer volume of references to readers and reading in his writing. It may be less a naïve question than a difficult one.

The notion of reception risks becoming polarised between complex forms of historical archiving and a textual aestheticism that is inherent in both *rezeptionästhetik* and a particular version of post-structuralism. It is an informing premise of this study that a trans-historical reflection on reading – a theory of reading – is impossible and that, instead, any notion of reception must be part of an immanent analysis of particular works in particular circumstances. Joyce is particularly significant in this regard because of the emphasis on reading as cultural practice and as textual process within and for his writing. In short, his work itself suggests a conceptual and social analysis of reception while being at the same time a particularly rewarding case for such a study.

In much of Joyce's work the fictional and the historical sit side-by-side, sometimes frustrating the distinction between them and so rendering it impossible to police the border between the 'serious' and the 'nonserious' which speech-act theorists such as John Searle have tried to enforce. Searle's taxonomy leads to some confusion and simplification, for instance his claim that 'the Russia of *War and Peace* is the real Russia'. Is the Dublin of *Ulysses* the real Dublin? What does 'of' mean here? What is 'the real Russia' or 'the real Dublin'?[42] The *rezeptionästhetik* model developed by Hans Robert Jauss and others in the 1970s, as well as the closely related reader-response theory of Wolfgang Iser, are in many ways reactions against speech-act philosophy. Working within the phenomeno-logical tradition, Jauss takes Edmund Husserl's study of the psychology of perception and translates it into a notion of reading that is framed by a 'horizon of expectations'. If, as Hans-Georg Gadamer says, the work of art is 'an experience changing the person experiencing it', then so too is the history of that work a history of its readings.[43] This constitutes a challenge by Jauss to 'historical objectivism' (in which Jauss includes critical histories of works and authors) providing instead a welcome emphasis on the experience of reading as a constitutive element in literary history. It is also an attempt to replace ontological arguments in speech-act theory about 'the logical status of fictional discourse' (as Searle dryly puts it) with what Iser sees as a more 'functional' (or pragmatic) account of reading as it is framed by both personal experience and social expect-ations. By this token, reading is recognised as a worldly activity in which the constitution of the reading subject is open to change. However, reader-response theory in general has tended to ignore the specific historical conditions attending reading in any instance, being content to allow for reading only as a form of textual affect. Even when Jauss discusses the conditions that delimit the 'horizon' of possible readings, he does so in a manner that presumes the prior recognition of 'great works'. Although he uses the Russian formalists' preferred example of *Tristram Shandy*, Jauss could just as well have discussed *Ulysses*, for his measure of aesthetic value is the extent to which a text is able to reflect on and modify generic tradition so that it subverts readers' expectations and generates an awareness of the literary and social conditions under which their interpretation labours. Such 'ideal' texts 'objectify' the horizon of expectations. Jauss thus relies upon a formalist model of 'defamiliarization' which is unfortunately circular: the critic reconstructs the 'horizon of expectations' from the text itself, not from societal, or even critical, sources.[44] This study seeks to avoid that pitfall by reading Joyce's inscription of moments of actual responses in tandem with key cultural and political formations as well as contemporary responses and reviews.

Although Iser's work, and reader-response criticism as a whole, has the advantage of showing how readers simultaneously construct the text and are constructed by it, thus avoiding a naïve empiricism, it remains profoundly troubled by reading as a historical act or by representations of actual acts of reading. *Ulysses*, of course, often crops up in Iser's criticism to exemplify the putative reader's involvement in the construction of the text; but it is the status of the example, not the example itself, that is interesting. Just as *Ulysses* appears, for Iser, as the text *par exemple*, so Iser's notion of 'the reader' is similarly universalised; yet this model of 'the reader' is inappropriate for Joyce's writing with its focus on the local and specific. Iser makes a distinction between 'participants' and 'observers': the former are 'contemporary readers' and the latter 'subsequent generations of readers'. According to Iser, a text's allusion to social and historical norms allows participants to 'see what they cannot normally see' and observers to 'grasp a reality that was never their own'.[45] As it turns out, however, Iser favours the later observers over the contemporary participants. Just as Iser's idea of 'feedback' between the Homeric allusions and the Dublin city-life means that he over-emphasises the role and extent of Joyce's use of the *Odyssey*, so the 'constantly disoriented' reader in his interpretation becomes a version of the distant 'observer' and not at all a 'participant'. There are political implications here: the 'observer' is akin to Iser's 'open', liberal reader just as a 'participant' can, it seems, be excessively 'committed' ideologically.[46] By distrusting the inevitability of bias, Iser goes back on one of the tenets of his philosophical background, namely Gadamer's insistence that prejudice is a necessary and inevitable condition. For Iser, 'the reader' is defined by the play of literary allusions and shifts of style, and it is instructive that he uses the word 'observer' (not 'participant') when describing the interpretive dilemmas of the chapters' styles. The 'participant' who shares a social context and recognises 'familiar [social] norms' is 'passive' but the 'observer' who 'open[s] himself up to an unfamiliar experience' is the very model of reader-response, a model that replicates the classic, supposedly depoliticised, liberal subject.[47] Iser's notion of 'the reader' thus shares in common with much criticism of modernism a privileging of the later, future audience and a denigration of the 'participant' or roughly contemporaneous (or politically 'inside') reader. Studies of Joyce influenced partly by Iser have similarly tended to ignore reception as a significant *historical* issue in Joyce's writing.[48] One of the implications of the interrogation of reception that is immanent in Joyce's work is a destabilisation of the presuppositions underpinning a politically neutral, self-sufficient, private reader who remains untouched by the text; instead, Joyce's writing focuses on versions of contemporaneous responses as they form part of an inevitably fallible social practice.

Perhaps mindful of the obvious difficulties faced by empirical analysis, reception theory has been notably shy of addressing histories of reception, deriving its impetus instead from the phenomenology of Husserl and Gadamer. Hence reception theorists have focused primarily on aesthetic notions of horizons of expectation and implied or mock-readers, largely textual constructs that offer little to the cultural or political contexts of reading while also tending towards an implicit homogeneity of responses. In contrast, more recent theorists of reception, often including feminist or 'oppositional' strategies of reading, have shown how reading has been constructed as a form of social practice.[49] Notable here are studies influenced by Michel de Certeau's *Practice of Everyday Life*, in which reading is one of many material means by which people construct their own senses of the world, including Tony Bennett's idea of 'reading formations'. Bennett proposes that reading be seen as a dialectical process determined within specific cultural and institutional contexts (including publication, education, etc.) to which it also contributes.[50] This notion – formulated as a theoretical model – may be helpful as a description of how reading is a social practice with particular, local determinants; it also suggests a means to link 'new historical' work with the specific question of reception. However, as Pierre Bourdieu suggests, all reflections on reading at the level of theory risk falling prey to their own critique, further constructing an abstraction that bears little resemblance to the practice of reading.[51] The turn towards social and historical explanations of textual consumption suggests – perhaps with some irony – that reception theory ultimately runs up against the fact that reading is performative or creative and so cannot be 'accounted for' any more accurately than a text can: its 'experience' cannot be recaptured, its 'meaning' as elusive as that of the text it works on.

A number of critics have analysed the *mise-en-abyme* of embedded readers in fiction, that is, those models of interpretation that stand in for the text as a whole.[52] With respect to Joyce, various analyses have, in one way or another, developed the suggestion of a 'mirror in the text'. In *Finnegans Wake*, the letter chapter (I.5) has been seen by Manfred Pütz and others as a microcosm of the whole book, postulating an unstable readerly identity.[53] Critics have also often looked to the characters of *Ulysses* as models for readers: Leopold Bloom has suggested to Patrick A. McCarthy a 'model of the reading experience'. McCarthy equates Dedalus and Bloom with silent reading and modernity, and the citizen with orality and the pre-modern (a fallacy derived from Walter Ong): Joyce is thus seen to endorse those 'modern' readers. In contrast, Molly's 'misreading' has been taken by Brook Thomas as analogous to readers' own endeavours.[54] Other critics rightly emphasise the extent to which all readers must themselves re-create the text.[55] An attempt to place putative readers within a 'given historical moment' has been made by Mark A. Wollaeger, who argues that *Ulysses* constructs a reading subject who 'incorporates without fully assimilating' the role of the Irish colonial subject. However, Wollaeger's analysis still works from the reader-response model in which an implied reader is modelled by the text. His notion that 'Circe' allows this reader to experience a form of liberation implies that readers are always of a particular political disposition.[56]

This book differs from the above studies in two respects. First, its analyses are not so much concerned with the reading practices of Joyce's characters as with the texts' depictions of particular reading practices (including those of individuals). These scenes are not held up as 'mirrors' of a putative reader or presupposed interpretive practice but are taken as engagements with material, political situations of reading and the constraints upon it. Herein lies the second difference: this study differs from studies of *mise-en-abyme* in that it includes analysis of the ways reading practices exist in relation to various social discourses: revivalist ambitions for national audience; Catholic educational 'reading strategies' in *fin-de-siècle* Ireland; notions of an ordinary and time-pressed reader and of readerly competence; the conditions surrounding the formation of the Free State and the interpretation of the Treaty.

Seamus Deane has described Joyce's quest 'to find new relationships between author and audience through language, so that language (and author) could escape from history . . . and yet at the same time be rooted in history'.[57] The peculiar representation of readers in Joyce's work is one of the means through which it is embedded in a particular set of historical conditions. Yet, in his writing, reading appears as a sort of semiconductor of historical forces, which are harnessed into new, textual charges. To borrow Deane's terms, the act of reception partially escapes from history but at the same time is rooted in history. Joyce's representation of readers is part of a cultural and historical concern as well as a textual *mise-en-abyme*. The question, 'What does it mean to read?' has long been recognised as an important one in Joyce studies but the social significance of this question, as Joyce engages it, has rarely been extensively pursued. As such, this study takes the issue of Joyce's reception beyond the personal and into the wider political sphere. All the same, it does accept that reading is also implicated in bodily needs: the conditions of reading described here are not universal but particular states which often resonate with somatic effects.

V

By attaching the terms boredom, surveillance, exhaustion and hypocrisy to the following chapters, I have deliberately signalled an inevitable 'performativity' in my own reading of Joyce and of the conditions of his reception. The following chapters offer readings of Joyce's texts which are both speculative – they are analyses of texts – and historical, in that they seek to illuminate important but neglected contexts for understanding that work. These four conditions do not pretend to compile a comprehensive account of Joyce's reception but offer an interpretation of what seem to me to be some of its more important aspects.

Chapter 1, 'Boredom: reviving an audience in *Dubliners*' places Joyce's stories within the context of revivalist concerns over the relationship between an ideal and an actual audience. Within this frame, even Joyce's earliest work (pre-*Dubliners*) expresses a notable anxiety over its own reception. In reading 'The Dead' – which was written after Joyce had already failed to publish *Dubliners* and whose composition was interrupted by the *Playboy* riots – as a reflection upon the importance of audience response within revivalist theatre, this chapter argues that Gabriel Conroy enacts a range of responsive positions from theatrical reviewer to reader. The story's famous lyrical ending may be seen as Gabriel's attempted appropriation of Gretta's tale from the perspective of a reader (rather than a listener or viewer). The point is that Gabriel, like those Dublin theatre audiences, displays inappropriate cultural and generic expectations when confronted by a tale he cannot understand, or which is initially 'unreadable' to him. Whereas *Dubliners* is a deflation of attempts by the Irish Literary Theatre and the Abbey to educate an audience and to imagine an audience quite different from that in the auditorium, it is not simply a 'realist' counter to a 'romanticised' Revival but a self-conscious staging of the tensions instilled by the particular assumptions of these conventions. Although *Dubliners* does not inscribe versions of actual and specific readers, as in Joyce's other work, it can be seen to develop his concern for the material conditions of reception. One of these conditions – boredom – describes the soporific Dubliners of his stories and seems particularly apt for Gabriel. Such boredom is Joyce's retort to the Revival theatre's misjudgement of its own actual audiences and its attempt to install a different audience.

As a Catholic Dubliner, Joyce might have been co-opted as a writer for a Catholic audience: indeed, despite the obvious obstacles to such an accommodation, many reviewers attempted just that. Chapter 2, 'Surveillance: education, confession and the politics of reception', argues that the educational context of Joyce's early fiction situates him in relation to a Catholic middle-class readership whose intellectual tradition was inscribed in his work but *for* whom he refused to write. This chapter shows how Joyce's fiction from *Stephen Hero* to *Ulysses* makes allusion to some of his actual readers. These readers include not only Stanislaus and friends in Dublin, but also his mother, and – I would suggest – the un-named addressee/subject of *Giacomo Joyce*. All reappear as transformed 'readers' in Joyce's work, friends to whom his work 'confesses'. This confession takes the form of what Derrida calls a 'contretemps', that is, a contrary *address to* and *denial of* that local readership. In addition, the contretemps can be seen as an admission that 'time is out of place'. In this sense, the spectral and allusive 'returns' of Joyce's 'lost' local readers, as well as the proleptic imagination of Stephen Dedalus in the National Library as he looks forward to the composition of that same scene, both suggest that reception is not the sort of simple chronological path assumed by Deasy when he admonishes Stephen with the command, 'I want that to be printed and read' (*U* 2.338). These issues are most fully played out in Stephen's discussion with Eglinton and others – itself a debate over the politics of literary reception – in the Library episode of *Ulysses* (the example of Eglinton is germane as he was one of Joyce's principal critics in Ireland; another early reader represented in the text). In this episode, Stephen Dedalus explicitly lists and compares his various readers and listeners. This is a key moment in Joyce's fiction: the impossibility of an appropriate audience is established and yet at the same time versions of those contemporary readers are recalled, as if to insist upon a 'historical' location of the 'unreadable'.

The Library debate is characterised also by a form of surveillance in which the characters attempt to place one another's 'cultural belonging' by indirect means. In this situation, though, it is not difference but also familiarity which is estranging: in some ways it is the shared aspects of the divergent group that unsettle. The debate over Shakespeare exemplifies this: it is a debate between particular reading strategies (those of Dedalus and Dowden) associated with different religious and educational traditions – strategies which, despite their political diversion, carry significant similarities. Here, the scene is one of surveillance in which proximity is estranging (as with the uncomfortable familiarity of earlier readers): in the National Library this is physical, intellectual and institutional. The claustrophobic conditions of literary reception in 1904 Dublin – shaped in part by educational and religious politics – are brought to the fore by Joyce's careful negotiation of Stephen Dedalus's false opposition between himself and his listeners. The library scene brings out Dedalus's anxiety at the proximity of his listeners, showing how Joyce subtly undercuts his character's attempts to portray them as an audience or homogenous group. The point here is that the discomfort engendered by reception is due to the sense of a continual surveillance within a contested cultural space. By reading this scene of reception as a 'contretemps', chapter 2 shows that Joyce's practice of inscribing his past readers offers an interpretation of his work within a specific context, but one from which, nonetheless, it was already irreparably riven.

The first two chapters establish the deep concern evinced by Joyce's work with some of the important contextual conditions his writing faced in Dublin. In the final two chapters, which deal for the most part with *Finnegans Wake*, the form of that last book plays a crucial role. With this deliberately obscure text, Joyce clearly addressed something 'unreadable' to his readers. Chapter 3 shows that this form contributed to contemporary notions of reception – of the ordinary reader and his/her lack of time – and constructed a form through which Joyce could 'reply' to critics. Having demonstrated how Joyce's final work referred to some of his readers and to broader discourses of reception, the final chapter returns to Ireland and to the reading of Joyce by Yeats in the early years of the Free State. This shift back to a specific context exemplifies an underlying argument of this book: namely that while Joyce's reflections on his own reception may have broader resonance for a notion of reception, they do not necessarily offer a 'universal' or transhistorical theory of reception. Joyce's work enacts many returns to its local scenes of reading.

Chapter 3, 'Exhaustion: *Ulysses*, "Work in Progress" and the ordinary reader', shows first that so-called ordinary readers did read Joyce's later work, and then, more substantially, how the writer contributed to the critical discourse of the ordinary reader. In doing so he incorporated into his final work versions of some readers' responses, in the process creating a sort of generic mode of responsiveness. This chapter establishes that in beginning 'Work in Progress' Joyce collated the critical responses to *Ulysses*, including the responses of non-professional readers, in order to include within that new work a sort of archive of reception. Yet of course this 'anarchive', as I call it, is a construct: one that not only offers a glimpse of 'data' but is also a fictionalisation and transformation of that readership. In 'Work in Progress', Joyce created a form that responded to – and was suited for – his readers' complaints, especially of the lack of time for reading. In the face of his own and his readers' exhaustion, Joyce constructs a form that can be studied infinitely or perused at random. Yet Joyce never fully collapses the distinction between the critic and the ordinary reader and so maintains the need for competence. The form of the work reinvigorates a supposedly worn-out language, and so a principle of exhaustion is established as that which is 'sold out' (like *Ulysses*, reading and language itself) must yet be renewed. The chapter concludes by addressing the apparent tension between the auratic and the mechanical in the technique of *Finnegans Wake* and in doing so returns once more to the responses to *Ulysses* by John Eglinton.

Having shown how *Finnegans Wake* was in part developed to include readers' responses, chapter 4 – 'Hypocrisy: *Finnegans Wake*, *hypocrites lecteurs* and the Treaty' – takes up one particular example of this inclusion. This chapter traces the manifestation and political resonance in Joyce's last work of Yeats's reading of *Ulysses* and his apparent hypocrisy. Yet the idea of hypocrisy in relation to *Finnegans Wake* is peculiarly self-defeating: in many ways Joyce's last work is itself inevitably hypocritical, a text founded on the fragile ground of the *hypocrite lecteur* who signals the dissonance of reception. The context for Yeats's reading of *Ulysses* and his various responses to it, was the immediate post-Treaty, Civil War period from 1922 to 1924. The letter in the *Wake* is also a version of the Treaty (and of *Ulysses*), which, like them, proved capable of contrary interpretations. Yeats here figures as another version of Shaun the Post (often associated with de Valera) attempting to deliver the letter-Treaty-*Ulysses* to Ireland. This process illustrates the internal divisions within a potential audience; divisions which are instituted even by a text that on another level attempts to repair them. Just as a text can be contrary, so can a reader, and so, as brother to Shem the Penman, Yeats is also, to Joyce, a '*hypocrite lecteur, – mon semblable, – mon frère*'. One notable context for the possible address of the Letter-Treaty-*Ulysses* is the transfer of power in the Post Office / *An Post*. The chapter shows that the practice of over-printing stamps in the Civil War period – to which the *Wake* refers (as it does to the 1922 stamp of all Ireland) – is an analogue not just for the contrarieties of readers of the *Wake* (such as Yeats and others) but also for the *Wake*'s own practice in overwriting its sources. Such an 'overwritten' text can have only a divided reception. In this sense, *Finnegans Wake* is an oddly fitting book of the Free State.

Finally, the Afterword examines some of the broader implications of this study and, in particular, returns to Derrida's reading of Joyce by briefly suggesting some of the ways in which Joyce's writing of reception differs from Derrida's implicit 'deconstruction of reception'. This study thus seeks to build upon the 'unreadable' Joyce of Derrida and the Joyce critics he has influenced, by showing some of the cultural ramifications of this unreadability. At the same time, it offers a further resistance to the 'universal' Joyce of another generation, influenced by Ellmann and others, by refusing to universalise the immanent speculation on reception that is found in Joyce's work.

VI

This study does not discuss in detail the censorship that met Joyce's work – a topic that has received thorough attention elsewhere – but it complements the recent argument that his writing provocatively engaged with the various discourses of censorship rather than being merely a passive victim of them.[58] One interesting recent study of Flaubert's negotiation with the law argues that this process authenticated his novel as art: the judge in the *Bovary* case legitimated what other readers had already approved. Having 'appointed his friends as a kind of review committee' Flaubert took steps to seek a justification of his art as a distinct, even professional, exercise – one that, having secured support no longer needs to appeal, like Baudelaire, to a reader or even to a *hypocrite lecteur*.[59] With Joyce, the situation is different. Unlike Flaubert, Joyce does not place authority in the hands of his 'review committee' but instead exposes the process of reception and revision with an ironic detachment. If Flaubert's appeal against censorship secured art its own niche, Joyce's provocation of the censors, coupled with his demystification of the reception of (his own) art, interrogates the social and political presumptions that could inhere in the creation of such a niche. This suggests that the nineteenth-century formation of a professional space for literature was a process that, given the conditions in Ireland at least, was manifestly inappropriate. The act of reception, as Joyce displays and displaces it, could also be its own critique of the formation of Art.

In this respect, Margot Norris has built on Peter Bürger's idea that surrealist and other 'minority' art stages its own critique of art as an institution. She argues that Joyce's work offers 'an ideologically critical metatextuality' which exposes the 'lies' of the art industry. By presenting itself as art, Joyce's work uncovers what art tries to hide, that is, the 'social conditions of artistic production', and, one might add, of its consumption.[60] In particular, I would argue, Joyce's work interrogates the very notion of reception while 'exposing' its cultural conditions in the Ireland in which he grew up. Joyce *rewrites* his reception, which is to say that his writing becomes a distorted record of that reception and its context, alluding to actual responses and situations of his (especially Irish) readers by placing them in a fictional frame which at once invokes and overwrites their specific historical locations, responding to their responses. In this way, Joyce's art is seen to come in part from its reception: if adverse reading conditions and even specific readers are already a part of the 'product' then the secure niche of a Flaubertian art (which some attribute also to modernism) has been shown up as a delusion.

Joyce's writing of reception might be thought of as a sort of archive so long as that term is understood as an incomplete, imagined but material record. Derrida has referred to 'le mal d'archive' which is 'always finite and therefore selective, interpretative, filtering, and filtered, censuring, and repressive, the archive always figures a place and an instance of power' which 'produces the event no less than it records or consigns it'.[61] Like his allusions to actual responses, Joyce's inscribed readers sit on the edge of the archive, fictionally inscribed in his text. His work thus displays a motif of 'local' actual readers and scenes of reading in a manner that captures how reading itself sits on the cusp of the historical, balancing between the textual and the worldly, referring back to those moments, caught up within chains of reception that are 'interpretative', 'repressive' and 'an instance of power'. Joyce's interrogation of the issue of reception is thus, simultaneously, a cultural history of the reading of his work and a sustained reflection on what it means to be a reader.

By playing upon the thin division between fictional character and actual reader, the relationship between the security and the performance of the reading subject is highlighted in Joyce's writing, thus representing a *suggested* contamination between the historical and the textual.[62] One anecdote tells how an elderly Richard Best was apparently forced to exclaim in exasperation to a BBC journalist, 'I am not a character in *Ulysses!*'[63] He was not; but he is. By deliberately exposing the faultline between actual readers and fictional inscribed versions of them, Joyce is able to undermine various assumptions regarding literary reception: to show how reading always inheres in the act of writing and is itself a creative enterprise; how textual transmission is not a simple process starting with writer and ending with reader but is instead a continual loop between composition and reception; how reading is a social as well as a private exercise; how it is embedded in broader political powers and events. This has important cultural implications for a writer whose personal struggles both to find readers and to avoid an audience is symptomatic of the difficulties of reception. If, as some readers have found, Joyce's texts are peculiarly self-obsessed, they also demonstrate an acute concern for the social expectations that conditioned their own reception.

CHAPTER I

Boredom: reviving an audience in Dubliners

It might be said of Joyce, as is said of Jimmy Doyle in 'After the Race', that he 'felt obscurely the lack of an audience' (*D* 41). In writing his early stories, of course, Joyce had few readers to draw upon: what readers he had at this stage were, mostly, a private rather than a public readership, such as those who had received his hand-delivered satirical verse, 'The Holy Office'. This lack of an audience – indeed, its impossibility – is one of the principal preoccupations of Joyce's work. Such a lack would remain with him throughout his career as, paradoxically, one of the constituent characteristics of reception: whereas his work refers to particular readers and scenes of reading, it is unwilling to foresee an audience for itself. Unlike Yeats, for instance, who at various points imagined differing visions of an ideal audience, Joyce refuses the possibility of this prospect. Instead, a dual concern with the need for readers, but also an unwillingness to write for a readership, can be detected in Joyce's work from the earliest stages.

Although Joyce shared many of the concerns and even some of the aims of revivalist writers such as Yeats and Synge especially, his well-known estrangement from both the Abbey and the Gaelic League, as well as from both the Anglo-Irish establishment and the Catholic hierarchy, presented formidable barriers to securing a readership. Having been frustrated in his attempts to publish *Dubliners* in 1905 and 1906, the composition of 'The Dead' in 1907 – the writing of which was 'blocked' by the notorious *Playboy* riots – represents an intensification of Joyce's relationship with the Revival. Joyce's engagement with Abbey Revivalism in particular centres not only on his own relationship with possible readers, and his own part as a viewer of the Revival, but also on the disjunction between the Theatre's expectations of an audience and the expectations actually held in its auditorium. Just as the question of audiences is crucial to the Revival, so too is it an important and neglected aspect of Joyce's developing aesthetic and political sensibility. Joyce formulated an understanding of reception during the composition of *Dubliners*, both in response to his perceived lack of a readership and in response to the writings of, first, Yeats and Lady Gregory and, then, Synge. 'The Dead', it could be said, is Joyce's characteristically ambiguous, distanced and deflating contribution to the idea of a national audience.[1]

'The Dead' has often been associated with a shift in Joyce's cultural politics, whether that shift has been seen as an exilic 'softening' towards Ireland, a commitment to a form of modern nationalism, or a turn to an ambivalent aestheticism.[2] This chapter argues that 'The Dead' results from a fuller and more serious engagement with Revivalism. As such it is part of a concomitant development in Joyce's political views away from his former rather high-handed dismissal of revivalist ambitions and to-wards a more complex understanding of the generic and political ambitions of that movement (which had itself developed in the meantime).[3] Joyce's revival turns out to be a caustic commentary on the estrangement of readers and the impossibility of an appropriate audience.

I

I think the Abbey Theatre is ruined. It is supported by the stalls, that is to say, Stephen Gwynn, Lord X, Lady Gregory etc who are *dying to relieve the monotony* of Dublin life . . . This whole affair [the *Playboy* riots] has upset me. I feel like a man in a house who hears a row in the street and voices he knows shouting but can't get out to see what the hell is going on. It has put me off the story I was 'going to write' – to wit, 'The Dead'.

(*Letters* II, 211–12; my emphasis. Letter dated 11 February 1907)

That is God. [. . .]
    A shout in the street, Stephen answered, shrugging his shoulders.

(*U* 2.383, 386).

As these observations suggest, Joyce perceived, from a safe distance, a close relationship between boredom and rioting. Monotony is occasionally provoked into action; but action, including Acts of God, proceeds at the level of the ordinary. Joyce witnessed, either at first hand or from abroad, the famous controversies of the Literary Revival and, in his short stories, he satirised the distance between actual Dublin theatregoers and the rural Ireland, especially of the West, that was performed on the Revival stage. Certainly, Joyce was conscious of the extent to which 'ordinary Dublin' formed an audience to the protestant-led Revival's construction of 'Ireland', and, of course, he himself became part of an overseas audience to Dublin. Since one of the observations often made in his work is of the extent to which an audience, especially a dramatic one, is a part of the action, it might be suggested that the Dublin with which Joyce was familiar was already a part of the revivalist theatre.

Boredom might be thought of as one of the conditions of Joyce's Dublin and, in this respect, his role as an emigrated 'reader' of his home city may have consolidated that perspective. Seamus Deane has written of 'the immobility . . . imposed on the native culture by the exilic position' and to some extent Joyce is guilty of this, trapped within a memory of colonial, Edwardian Dublin that compels him to recreate the period 1902–4 in *Dubliners*, in the last and longest chapter of *A Portrait*, in *Exiles*, and most famously in *Ulysses*.[4] (Perhaps *Finnegans Wake*, with its renewed interest in the nation state, represents a loosening of that 'immobility'.) At the same time as fixing a boredom onto Dublin, however, Joyce's writing leaves open the possibility of change, even as it shows the repetition of the old: the point about the repetitiveness in Joyce's stories is that they constantly hold out this possibly chimerical instance in the very desire to 'try again'. This pattern also structures Joyce's conception of Irish and even world history: a series of would-be seismic events inscribes a repetitive pattern of failure and redemption in which 'all that has been done has yet to be done and done again' (*FW* 194.10). Joyce's famous attention to verisimilitudinous detail also involves writing into that scenery the possibility of difference. As much as he might seek historical accuracy from his relatives, the newspapers or *Thom's Directory*, he also has Stephen Dedalus lodge an appeal on behalf of those 'infinite possibilities they have ousted' (*U* 2.50–1). The same relationship was expressed also in the well-rehearsed ending of *A Portrait*: Dedalus goes 'to encounter for the millionth time the reality of experience' and yet this monotony might yet lead to the 'forging' of something as yet uncreated. Perhaps Joyce's 'exile' – 'the high cultural form of emigration'[5] – was a particularly apt condition since the exile, by virtue of his having left, knows that at least this singular event is possible. By refusing to return permanently, Joyce kept alive the distinction of his escape – even if millions of others had done so too.

Dubliners registers a modern ennui as the symptom and cause of the conditions it describes: poverty, subservience, confusion.[6] The circularity of boredom is recounted with vicious insight in these stories in which potentially momentous events mingle with the banal to become the regular staple of life. In 'An Encounter', what might be a once-in-a-lifetime experience is but *an* encounter occasioned by the boy-narrator's desire to flee the boredom of school and its 'circulated' adventure stories; yet his round-trip journey ends in another narrative of boredom in the old

josser's 'slowly circling' mind, his phrases 'repeated . . . over and over' in
a 'monotonous voice' (*D* 18). On the brink of escape, Eveline is finely
caught between the desire to flee and the fear of departing, between the
'familiar' home (*D* 29) and the possible event of the new, but this is
represented by another voice that speaks 'over and over again' (*D* 33).
Even the death of Mrs Sinico echoes in the 'laborious drone of the engine
reiterating the syllables of her name' (*D* 113). In each case, a thwarted
journey is associated not just with monotony, but with a language of
monotony, a repetition at once meaningless and all too significant. Joyce's
own stylistic tick, the use of chiasmus, might be considered characteristic
of this still movement. The relationship between monotony and the new
was, then, also a textual one: Joyce's use of repetition and circular
narratives mimics a kind of readerly boredom, and yet his texts also often
carry within them a possibly singular event, from these early stories to
Molly's affair and the *Wake*'s letter-version of the 1921 Treaty.

The refusal to return not only maintained Joyce's vantage point as part
of an audience to the Revival and his home, but also kept his would-be
Irish readership at a distance. In the letter to Stanislaus cited above, it is
not only the relationship between boredom and rioting that is of interest
but also Joyce's inscription of his own peculiar position: he is both part of
and not part of the audience to the event he 'witnesses'. This fundamental
self-division is a crucial aspect of Joyce's understanding of the roles
members of an audience play (for they are no passive onlookers) and is
one reason why an audience as such cannot be described or anticipated.
The image in that letter is somewhat odd: in the house, Joyce hears but
does not see; he has become a version of Eveline (who sees but does not
hear) and of the boy in 'An Encounter', stuck in a port, desperately trying
to envisage the other side.

II

Joyce's writing of his reception was bound up with his long-distance
specular relationship with Ireland. Indeed, the beginnings of Joyce's
invocation of a readership – the fictionalisation of actual readers and their
responses – can be traced back to the verse satire he wrote shortly before
leaving Ireland, in August 1904. Usually seen as a repudiation of his more
established contemporaries (Ellmann understands this episode as the
familiar tale of 'vengeance' on 'betrayers'[7]), 'The Holy Office' can be seen
as Joyce's attempt simultaneously to instil an initial readership among
those contemporaries *and* to deny them as an appropriate audience. The

fact that 'The Holy Office' was reprinted in Pola six months after the first (Dublin) printing was destroyed – that is, long after the moment of supposed 'betrayal' – suggests that Joyce was at least as keen for the text to have a readership as for it to avenge directly any perceived slight. Nonetheless, that initial slight was significant since George Russell's exclusion of Joyce from his anthology, *New Songs: A Lyric Selection*, was a denial of a readership to the aspiring writer. This 'non-reading' of Joyce was in its own way indicative of the act of reception.

Copies of Joyce's satirical sketch implicating about a dozen of the Abbey's leading players (Yeats, Horniman, Gonne, Gregory, Synge, Gogarty, Colum, Magee, Roberts, Starkey, Russell) were hand-delivered to its targets by the hesitant postman Stanislaus.[8] The majority of these were thus both readers of and characters within the poem, a pattern that Joyce repeated, in some form, in all his fiction with the exception of *Dubliners*. College friends such as Byrne, Curran, Elwood, Skeffington, Cosgrave, and others were also given copies: they would have been familiar with Joyce's tactic, having already read about themselves in the early drafts of his novel, *Stephen Hero*.[9] In one respect, 'The Holy Office' differs from the later fiction in that these University College friends were themselves implicated in 'The Holy Office' as the satire's absent but implied audience, one that would be more sympathetic than the 'mumming company'. This poem might therefore be seen less as 'vengeance' and more as an attempt to establish a cultural marker, one in which the question of who would read Joyce is paramount.

'The Holy Office' suggests the importance of reception to Joyce at a time when he was desperate to publish. Its poetic source, Yeats's 'To Ireland in the Coming Times', had apparently declared the public role of art in an address to the nation.

> Know, that I would accounted be
> True brother of a company
> That sang, to sweeten Ireland's wrong.

The poet's implied audience – 'you', Ireland – is directly addressed in the final stanza. However, a second, preferred audience has also been invoked in the second stanza:

> to him who ponders well,
> My rhymes more than their rhyming tell.

In this manner Yeats's work contains a process of carefully singling out a future, ideal but unrealised audience, located here in the figure of a scrupulous reader, or, later, in that 'dream' model of a cultured people, the fisherman. Whereas 'To Ireland in the Coming Times' appears to be publicly directed to 'you' the nation, it is in fact more earnestly addressed to that second-person 'he' who is more prescient:

> Yet he who treads in measured ways
> May surely barter gaze for gaze.[10]

The inscribed 'he' thus stands in for a careful reader, one who is 'measured' in a way that the national audience is not. This recognition of the distance between a careful reader and a projected, imaginary audience is itself a necessary if reluctant political admission of the poet's own estrangement. It anticipates the distinction later made in 'The Fisherman' between the 'reality' of reception – in which the poet is 'In scorn of this audience' – and the solitary imagined reader ('but a dream') for whom the poet *intends* to write, projected as a 'wise and simple' fisherman.[11] Yeats's 'potential audience' and 'ideal of culture', then, is an isolated figure, a model which, it is implied, *might later* translate into an actual reader. As I will suggest, Joyce's writing of his reception bears a reversal of this pattern and a very different cultural inflection. Deane argues that Yeats very early realised the incompatibility of actual audiences with his projected ideal. In response, he incorporated into his poetry symbolic images of the 'projected audience of the future' such as the Fisherman, or allusions to 'the select few who preserved the values of true culture' such as those (usually dead) literary and political friends who populate his writing, so that a 'proper audience' might form in their mould.[12] By contrast, Joyce's later writing refuses to address or identify an appropriate audience, instead developing a model of reception in which versions of actual readers are inscribed within his writing, showing how reception already inheres in composition and denying the possibility of a 'proper audience'. For Yeats, an audience (even if invented) could lend a form of social stability, a lineage of likeness, whereas for Joyce such continuity was unlikely and undesirable. Perhaps Joyce's reception is figured so uncertainly because his writing admits its own historical uncertainty, refusing to read the future.

Although based on 'To Ireland in the Coming Times', 'The Holy Office' reverses its construction of an audience and this suggests their writers' cultural differences. Whereas Yeats's poem was apparently addressed to the national public but actually inscribes a more particular, careful reader, Joyce's supposedly specific, private address had in fact been written for a public reception. The apparent privacy of Joyce's poem is underscored by the nature of its printing and dissemination and by its knowing references to the anonymous satiric targets who are individually, and scornfully, singled out. On the face of it, then, the poem creates a readership among that motley crew of private recipients who find themselves addressed in Joyce's poem. Yet satirical broadsides like 'The Holy Office' imply a double reception: both those directly invoked and others who will recognise the targets and share the writer's sentiments.[13] In fact, Joyce's verse initially had an intended readership that was more public than may appear from its later, private dissemination: it had first been submitted to the University College literary magazine *St Stephen's*, among the readers of which it would surely have found an amused and knowing reception, had it not been rejected by the editor, Con Curran (later a perceptive reader of Joyce's work). That Joyce sent copies to many of these friends, as well as to the poem's targets, suggests that he recognised this dual reception. Hence the satiric mode and attempted publication of Joyce's poem imply that it was written in order to form as well as criticise a potential readership (and so is more than 'vengeance'). As such, then, this early text stands apart from Joyce's later work in that its satire implies a knowing audience who share the joke; whereas both *Ulysses* and the *Wake*, for instance, make allusions that can be 'caught' they also, as I will argue, take care to undercut the presumption of any implied audience. At this early point, the unpublished writer seeks a shared language with his friends; very shortly, however, that language will be invoked only to be undermined as well.

Both poems *appear* to invoke a broader collective audience: Yeats's nation and Joyce's 'mumming company'. The specular process of grouping reception is made apparent.

> So distantly I turn to view
> The shamblings of that motley crew (*CW* 152)

Here Joyce begins a process he would continue throughout his career of inscribing an apparently communal critical readership, a 'motley crew'. By construing his critics as 'other' to his work, Joyce casts them as a single body that has to be overcome, and, by implication, recreated. The specific readers to whom allusion has been made are brought within the text as a means of prevailing over both them personally and the cultural project they imply, a project which is exemplified by the attempted formation of an audience by the Irish Literary Theatre. Joyce's process of 'othering' these readers complements an overt recognition of his own role as part of the new theatre's actual audience. What begins in 'The Holy Office' as a satirical swipe becomes, in his later work, a potent but subtle means of keeping open a social dialogue between past and future readers.

If Yeats and Joyce appear to imply collective audiences, they each also seek to overcome that 'reality' (however forged it may be) in favour of another audience which is more discerning. Despite this similarity, Yeats's 'better audience', is explicitly imaginary: the solitary reader, 'he' who 'ponders well'; Joyce's, on the other hand, is implied by the satiric form and not by a Yeatsian historical desire: there is no idealisation of a model response, just the formal suggestion that another reading is possible. It is the act of writing then that performs the 'better' reception, implicitly correcting that tawdry response of actual and 'unfit' readers: 'I relieve their timid arses,/Perform my office of Katharsis'. Two points can be drawn from this. In the first place, Joyce has created his collective readership for this poem by giving them copies: the 'motley crew' bears some displaced resemblance to a real readership (in Yeats's verse this public reception remains vague). A readership has been created, represented and, at the same time, shown to be, in a crucial sense, lacking. Joyce's renowned 'filthy streams' of realism (as against the 'dreamy dreams' of his contemporaries) thus have their structural counterpart in the inscribed readership. Secondly, Joyce's poem is at pains to establish a literary frame (Dante, Ibsen) and a Catholic intellectual heritage ('Steeled in the school of old Aquinas'; his use of Aristotle) while standing aside from 'Grandmother Church'. That is to say, like Stephen Dedalus in 'Scylla and Charybdis', it implies an interpretive strategy that is specifically Catholic while also disclaiming any sense of 'belonging' (as discussed in the following chapter). In this sense, Joyce's 'Myself unto myself' again contrasts with Yeats's explicit identification with the nation ('I write for you . . ./From our birthday until we die') and this refusal to identify fully with a 'better audience', whether imagined as national or Catholic, remains a crucial aesthetic and political aspect of Joyce's writing, while still invoking the conditions and limitations of other actual reading practices.

Joyce's characteristic political ambivalence is inscribed in this writing of the act of reception: a prosaic refusal to identify with an audience that is also the most eloquent – because elusive – retrieval of the social forms of his generation. That, initially, Joyce worked his fascination with his reception (heightened by the inability to share in a public readership) into satire suggests a portraiture that is more Swiftian than Flaubertian, a characteristic of his first and last works in particular, and which speaks more to his Irish context than his European exile. While his writing becomes less satiric, and takes on instead forms of realism, his work moves towards what this book calls a generic mode of responsiveness in which the act of reception inheres in the writing. While it frustrates classifications as either realist or as a textually self-sufficient modernism, Joyce's writing may be placed in relation to those traditions of Irish writing that looked to varying readerships, from the characteristically nineteenth-century address to an English reception to the Revival's attempted identification of an Irish audience. In the very act of refusing these audiences, Joyce's writing places itself as the capstone to a cultural problem that had impacted on varying traditions of Irish writing – the identification of, and possibly with, an Irish reading public. By emphasising the fictionality of identifying (with) an audience, Joyce's writing is formulated as one in which readers remain immanent: referring to some of its specific readers, his texts could carry with them a sense of the historical significance of the act of reading and of the construction of a reading public. It could thus display and displace the social pressures of reception, unencumbered by the limitations of a false audience.

III

A further comparison can be made between two different expressions of an audience: the manifesto written by the founders of the Irish Literary Theatre (or Celtic Theatre, in its first, shortlived title), which was sent to potential subscribers; the other suggested by Joyce during his early years abroad. The contrast both encapsulates the cultural divergence of Joyce from Revival theatre but also signals the reasons for its intense interest to him – that is, its own problematic relationship with imagined and actual audiences. The existence, and possible formation, of an audience surely went to the root of what a national literature could be.

Yeats, Lady Gregory and Edward Martyn had founded their company in 1897 to produce 'Celtic and Irish plays'.

We hope to find in Ireland an uncorrupted and imaginative audience trained to listen by its passion for oratory . . . We will show that Ireland is not the home of buffoonery and of easy sentiment, as it has been represented, but the home of an ancient idealism. We are confident of the support of all Irish people, who are weary of misrepresentation, in carrying out a work that is outside all the political questions that divide us.[14]

The crucial enabling factor of the Revival's success was its willful historical ignorance of centuries of Irish theatre, which was also the condition for this imagination of an 'uncorrupted' audience. Yeats, however, was less hopeful than this manifesto implies. After all, his distaste for 'commercial ambition' was fundamentally at odds with the business of the box office. As Yeats told readers of *Beltaine*, the journal of the Irish Literary Theatre (which he edited), its real audience was 'that limited public that gives understanding, and not that unlimited one that gives wealth'. As for those with less understanding to give, the Theatre 'will not mind greatly if others are bored'.[15] These confiding comments echo the pattern of 'To Ireland in the Coming Times': the basic structure of reception as Yeats describes it is one of boredom versus understanding. In Yeats's implicit notion of reception, dissent – and even rioting – are subsumed within boredom. Dissent does not feature in the Theatre's manifesto, presumably evaded by its supposedly non-political status and rhetoric. The speciousness of this manifesto's presumption to forge a consensus might be attested by the Theatre's increasing use of the word 'national'. In fact, the Theatre's intimacy with 'constructive Unionism' is itself suggestive of this desire simultaneously to ignore political division and to imagine an ideal audience.[16]

The idealism of the new Theatre's projected audience – what Martyn called a 'people . . . ready to receive' – would inevitably be betrayed in the auditorium (in fact, it already had been: Martyn wrote this after the performance of *Countess Cathleen*).[17] Indeed, Joyce was himself already a part of that public reception of the Irish Literary Theatre – attending Yeats's plays and learning by heart much of his early poetry and some short stories – but he was also of course keen on a range of dramatic productions, from music hall to opera. Joyce's cultural and intellectual differences, allied to his physical absence from Ireland from October 1904, meant that he was in a position to record from afar the Revival's failed attempts to form an audience. It is interesting to compare the Theatre's 'audience trained to listen' with Joyce's refusal of an audience that takes 'dictation'. Bemoaning his personal as well as literary 'struggle against conventions', he wrote to Stanislaus in July 1905:

To be judged properly I should not be judged by 12 burghers taken at haphazard, judging under the dictation of a hidebound bureaucrat, in accordance with the evidence of a policeman but by some jury composed partly of those of my own class and of my own age presided over by a judge who had solemnly forsworn all English legal methods. (*Letters* II, 99–100)

Of course, his primary concern was to find a publisher; readers, even money, would surely follow. Writing this a year after 'The Holy Office', he still had neither. Instead, he had amassed a sheaf of verses (and several publishers' rejection slips), most of *Dubliners* and over twenty chapters of 'my novel' (*Stephen Hero*). On several occasions, Joyce would adapt the format of the mock-trial to accommodate disputes with his critics and he did so here, for the first time, with more at stake than self-mockery.[18] At this stage Joyce can clearly be seen appealing to his own 'class' and 'age' as well as to a mode of judgement that is not English and does not replicate that which is 'handed down'. (The refusal of 'dictation' neatly encapsulates the degree to which Joyce's attempted independence was both linguistic and social, as well as being a self-constraining pose.) As if to emphasise the impossibility of this jury-audience, he had written to Stanislaus just four days earlier, commanding: 'You are to make a copy of it *at once* and return it to me *on the same day* if possible' (*Letters* II, 98, original emphasis) – clearly *some* people were suited to taking dictation. To add to the slight, the story he sent was 'Counterparts', in which a put-upon copyist exemplifies the implicitly colonial shaping of the law. In addition, Joyce also sought critical feedback and reassurance: Stanislaus, then, was cast in the irreconcilable position of both copyist-printer and reader-critic. As Joyce would later discover to his irritation, the printer also effectively occupied this position under British law.

Ellmann characterises Joyce's notional juridic audience as 'ludicrous', mistakenly thinking that Joyce appealed to an audience of 'people who thought exactly as he did'.[19] While his plea shows that Joyce was part of the Catholic-educated lower-middle class, estranged from the colonial state but nonetheless necessarily a part of its attendant institutions, the trial metaphor suggests also something of desperation, born out perhaps by the contradiction of the appeal. For the irony of this image is that it is precisely 'those of my own class' who are criticised in *Dubliners* as 'gratefully oppressed' (*D* 35), downtrodden by spiritual corruption and political collusion. Joyce's petition to a jury of his own cultural background is thus a complicated allusion to a social body that is also critically depicted in his stories as an 'unfit' audience. These are, it seems, the people to whom Joyce *would* want to speak, yet at the same time he would address them in a court that has 'forsworn' English legality, which is to say, under conditions that did not exist. In this sense, the jury, or audience, that Joyce looked to could not have existed either: its impossibility is already written into the idea of an address.

Yet it would be wrong to characterise Joyce as uninterested in the formation of an Irish audience. Like many of his contemporaries, he was intimately concerned with the state of a potential readership in Ireland, and, in a quite different way to Yeats and Gregory, he sought (initially at least) to encourage as well as analyse an Irish reception for his work. Joseph Kelly has recognised that Joyce favoured an Irish publisher for *Dubliners* (it was temporarily taken by Maunsel, which had been founded in 1905 as part of the Revival's rather grandiose 'outreach' programme). Prior to its eventual publication in 1914, Kelly argues, Joyce's readers were primarily 'the Irish'.[20] Despite, at various times, having argued the potential interest of English readers (*Letters* II, 129), 'some fifteen millions' of Irish in America (*Letters* II, 131), and even 'the world' (*Letters* II, 122), credence should still be paid to Joyce's well-known claim in 1906 to his would-be publisher, Grant Richards, that 'you will retard the course of civilisation in Ireland by preventing the Irish people from having one good look at themselves in my nicely polished looking-glass' (*Letters* I, 64). This image not only suggests the primacy of Joyce's Irish reception at this stage but also the importance to that reception of his mode of realism. Kelly's point is that it was precisely this realism that was incongruous with an Irish readership – especially the rural readers of the *Homestead* – and that consequently it is this, rather than any symbolism, that made his stories radical.[21] Yet by mis-characterising *Dubliners* as a 'prose that perfectly reflects reality', Kelly aligns Joyce with the naïve realism that Yeats and others had been trying to escape for years.[22] Instead, Joyce's writing is a part of the revivalist rejection of a realism that they associated with modernising and utilitarian nationalism. It was not their realism so much as their disparagement of traditional pieties that made Joyce's stories unpalatable to H. F. Norman and some among the *Homestead*'s circulation, as Russell's appeal 'not to shock the readers' had anticipated (*Letters* II, 43). Norman received 'numerous letters of complaint from his readers both in the city and in the country' (as Joyce pointed out) but his stories' radical challenge lay in their very *refusal* of a realism that could address 'the people'. Their mix of generic expectations, and inability to be representative, thus formed a political critique that was both legible and uncertain.[23] In doing so, Joyce contributed to the revivalist discourse over audience formation and behaviour. Moreover, the format of *Dubliners* would be radically altered after this period: Joyce's composition and inclusion of 'The Dead' in 1907 signals a reflection on the revivalist theatre's appeal to an audience and his own lack of a readership.

IV

It might be suggested that Joyce developed his understanding of reception initially, at least, through his relationship with theatre audiences, especially in relation to the many controversies that attended the Irish Literary Theatre and the Abbey. Although he had been writing scornfully about the audiences at the Irish Literary Theatre since 1901, he had not always been so dismissive. In May 1899, Joyce was at the Antient Concert Rooms to see the first performance of *The Countess Cathleen*. One eye-witness remembered that

at the fall of the curtain a storm of booing and hissing broke out . . . But close to me, at the time unknown to me, was a lad who vigorously contributed his share to the applause. It was James Joyce.[24]

When, about a decade later, it came to *A Portrait*, Joyce seemed to have forgotten his own enthusiastic response to Yeats's play. On the steps of the National Library, Stephen Dedalus is reminded of the Countess's farewell speech, but this time he has affected boredom.

He was alone at the side of the balcony, looking out of jaded eyes at the culture of Dublin in the stalls and at the tawdry scene-cloths and human dolls framed by the garish lamps of the stage. A burly policeman . . . seemed at every moment about to act. The catcalls and hisses and mocking cries ran in rude gusts round the hall . . . (*P* 245)

Replacing his initial eagerness with Stephen's 'jaded' viewpoint, Joyce focuses on the controversial reception of the new theatre movement which was accused of both replicating the stock images of colonial rule and being anti-Catholic.[25] Boredom and rioting are once more seen to go hand-in-hand. This scene further suggests one of the principles of reception in Joyce: that the audience is very much a part of the performance. A policeman, 'about to act', seems unsure whether he is in the crowd or on the stage – he might even be seen as a mock-figure of the melodrama that Yeats so detested. However, the scenes at the Antient Concert Rooms for the opening of the Irish Literary Theatre hardly required the action of the police.[26] Joyce's ready policeman seems to have been drawn from composite theatrical controversies, including those around Synge's *In the Shadow of the Glen* and the *Playboy* riots, reports of which Joyce read in the *Freeman's Journal* and in which he was intensely interested just before writing 'The Dead'. Clearly, in *A Portrait* Joyce was rewriting actual audience responses in order to represent a particular image of the Revival theatre's misjudged politics and idealised reception. This is reinforced by Stephen Dedalus's position as a viewer of the audience. This theatre audience was, for Joyce, the 'cultivated rabblement', a Catholic middle-brow Dublin audience, pious and conservative, 'enthroned in boxes and galleries amid a hum of approval' (*CW* 70), whose taste had begun to dictate policy at the Irish Literary Theatre.[27] Stephen's studied indifference indicates Joyce's favoured attitude, an indifference affected as a form of boredom which Joyce, in his first review of the theatrical scene, had described as endemic to Dublin. 'Life indeed nowadays is often a sad bore' he had told his listeners in 'Drama and Life' (January 1900) and yet 'out of the dreary sameness of existence, a measure of dramatic life may be drawn' (*CW* 44–5).

Dubliners shows that city as 'the world capital of boredom' and does so by reference to the theatre and reception.[28] Boredom could be described as the condition that Joyce's Dubliners experienced, and which was to be distinguished from the falsely rapturous or rioting responses he found in theatrical audiences. In this way, the ordinary people of *Dubliners* appear as a bored audience to life. They are, in effect, Joyce's version of the specific audiences whom the Revival ignored or misjudged. In this respect, the stories have both a social realism and, at the same time, a self-consciously staged symbolic value. Through their generic uncertainty, these stories frustrate any identification among their readership, effectively denying an 'imagined audience'. The frustration of given generic expectations is encoded into them in part by the insertion of figures who dramatise reception, from the boy in 'The Sisters' who 'puzzled [his] head to extract meaning from [Cotter's] unfinished sentences' (*D* 3; sentence added after *Homestead* publication) to Gabriel Conroy and Molly Ivors in 'The Dead', through whom Joyce explores the social character of theatrical audiences. Joyce's mixture of genres in *Dubliners* is important: not only is the 'realism' of the stories self-reflexive but also their 'symbolism' (as the boy's puzzled head implies) is notoriously indefinite. While depicting the causes of Eveline's inertia, for example, the story also cuts against its apparent realism by inscribing her as a muddled reader or viewer of her own misfortune. Repeatedly, she is a figure of the actual audience confronted by the boredom of Dublin life, from the scenery of the famous first paragraph ('watching the evening invade the avenue . . . She was tired' (*D* 29)) to the home ('reviewing all its familiar objects' (*D* 29)) to the port where, 'among the swaying crowd' she knows Frank is speaking 'over and over again' (*D* 33). The swaying crowd with uncertain sympathies is itself a theatrical performance as is Eveline's 'elated' attendance at the *Bohemian Girl*. Whichever way she sways, her 'choice' is between two traditional narratives, the 'tales' and 'stories' of Frank or the fireside 'ghost story' of her father (*D* 32). Eveline is confronted with the treacherous prospect of her own potential revival *within* the boredom of colonial modernity. It is, of course, a 'revival' that would merely reconfirm her position as part of the audience to life rather than a full participant (an ennui that is typical of Joyce's estranged Dubliners), and this is the root of her sickness, 'the nausea in her body' (*D* 34) that these lived narratives inflict. In this sense, the boredom of Joyce's Dublin is a modern but ordinary condition of physical and intellectual alienation in which characters are displaced from the narratives that house them, even to the extent that, like Gabriel Conroy in 'The Dead', they are an audience to the events in which they participate. This condition is dramatised as a comment upon the Revival's own misjudged performance which, Joyce implies, had failed to comprehend the capital's modernity.

If Joyce 'felt obscurely the lack of an audience' (*D* 41) for *Dubliners* – as surely he did when repeatedly failing to secure its publication – he could atone for that lack by inscribing figures such as Eveline who act self-consciously as symbols of an internally divided and oppressed audience to Dublin's boredom. In *Dubliners*, a deflating series of specular dramas plays out before these inscribed internal figures of the audience. The emphasis is on the material conditions from which audiences respond (however unpalatable some of them may be) as opposed to the doomed attempts of the Irish Literary Theatre to sidestep that issue by 'educating' their audience into an 'ancient idealism'. Joyce's subsequent inclusion in his work of actual readers' responses – and their all too frequent banality – can thus be seen as a rewriting, and undercutting, of an earlier revivalist ambition. If the latter misjudged its reception either by addressing itself to an imaginary audience, or by over-compensating and playing to the pious middle class, Joyce's writing sidesteps the question of reception by refusing any such address.

V

In *Dubliners* and *Ulysses*, the combination of economic and theatrical metaphors suggests Joyce's well-known scorn of the Abbey's decision to co-operate with the Gaelic League as well as his suspicion of the ultimate interests not only of Yeats and Lady Gregory but also of their English backer, Annie Horniman. (In 1905, Horniman used the term 'Home Rule' to stipulate her increased – and anti-nationalist – control over the Irish National Theatre Society and eventually withdrew support when the Abbey failed to close as a mark of respect on the death of Edward VII.)[29] The entwinement of the fiscal and dramatic is perhaps most clearly evident in 'A Mother', which is set 'when the Irish Revival began to be *appreciable*' (*D* 135; added emphasis), but it can also be seen in 'After the Race', written in the autumn of 1904 just after Joyce left Ireland. It appears that the participants in the Gordon Bennett cup are continental and the spectators Irish, yet Jimmy Doyle's attempted transgression of this border brings confusion both to himself and to the distinction between actor and audience. Having performed for the crowds, Jimmy is pleased 'to return to the profane world of spectators amid nudges and significant looks' (*D* 37). The day passes to the constant accompaniment of music and banter, the friends acting for one another and for the 'people [who] raised the cheer of the gratefully oppressed' and who 'pay homage' (*D* 35, 38). Jimmy is clearly one of these people, although one whose hypocritically gained wealth has enabled him to find his way onto the stage. 'He had been seen by many of his friends that day in the company of these Continentals' (*D* 37). This 'company' continue to act when alone, square dancing, singing and playing music; mistaking the act for 'seeing life', Jimmy 'took his part with a will' (*D* 40). Jimmy, the crowds, and even the whole city – which 'wore the mask of a capital' (*D* 39) – are subsumed by theatricality. Jimmy's speech, not unlike Gabriel Conroy's in 'The Dead', must have gone well because there was 'a great clapping of hands when he sat down' (*D* 41), perhaps because he sat down. Unlike the distanced narrative irony, Jimmy remains confused under the 'globes of light' (*D* 38) that illumes them, such that during the card game he finds only 'excitement' in his loss and the Englishman's win. It is at this point, when the game is serious, that Jimmy 'felt obscurely the lack of an audience' (*D* 41). He is (literally) at sea, performing a part beyond his range; the distinction between stage and audience has been crossed but not erased. The story recounts the exploitation of native 'poverty and inaction' by overseas 'industry' and of the subsequent ways in which the 'mite [not 'might'] of Irish money' mimics foreign power (*D* 35–7).[30] The dramatic scenario fills perfectly the picture of economic exploitation, suggesting the hegemonic relationship between 'gratefully oppressed' Irish audiences, hypocritical play-acting, and conniving foreign actors and producers. Joyce's Dubliners thus form an audience willing to pay to watch its own demise.

Later, in writing the first episode of *Ulysses*, Joyce once more staged the politics of cultural production as a drama riven by misjudged generic expectations and economic corruption. In the opening episodes, realism is not only slowly unravelled, as in *Dubliners*, but is also shown to be collusive with the ethnographic project of which Haines is a part.[31] This stage-Englishman is more successful as a colonialist than as an ethnographer, however: his first action of the day is to awake firing his gun. His particular style of folklore collection might be contrasted with Yeats's myth of Synge, that 'when he [Synge] lived in some peasant's house, he tried to make those about him forget that he was there, and it is certain that he was silent in any crowded room'.[32] The presumption of the ethnographer, like that of the realist and naturalist writer (to present the scene as it is), is of course riven by contradiction. Such a form of realist description, argues Luke Gibbons, 'was appropriated by a colonial ideology in its attempts to make Ireland "intelligible",' informing not just ethnography but tourism, journalism and literature.[33] Of course, realism is not to be reduced to a colonial function. One of the interesting aspects of Joyce's use of the form is the trail of false expectations that it maps, so that it can intersect with ethnography and, as we will see, with the playful demystification of Revival theatre in 'The Dead'.

'Telemachus' is a particularly staged episode in which Haines's money (like that of Annie Horniman) lies behind the misperceptions that structure the drama. Emer Nolan has suggested that the milkwoman represents 'an uncomprehending Irish audience' and Haines stands for a 'metropolitan readership'.[34] In addition, both the milkwoman and Haines, along with Mulligan, are character-types (the stage Englishman, the betraying mimic-man, the 'cuckqueen' (*U* 1.405)) who perform before Stephen Dedalus. Crucially, the narrative is modulated through Stephen, whose affected boredom in front of this cast of characters complicates the depiction of a complicit audience. The scene is a self-conscious dramatisation of mock-Revival tropes in which Joyce's own role as part of the audience to Revivalism is being played out.

When Haines announces his intention to collect a volume of Stephen's sayings, it is the 'deuced good' phrase that the symbol of Irish art is the cracked looking glass of a servant that is mentioned in particular. Haines was 'just thinking' of the phrase, he says, 'when that poor old creature came in' (*U* 1.484, 488–9). The milkwoman, then, is explicitly rendered as a convention by Haines's ethnography: his use of the term 'poor old creature' signals both his presumed superiority and his misuse of another 'phrase', the *Sean Bhean Bhocht* or 'poor old woman' of *Cathleen Ní Houlihan*. Haines has thus learnt to read the scenery in figurative terms derived from an aestheticised political discourse: his 'ethnographic realism' is inevitably distorted in this way. While the contradiction between Haines's ethnographic and aesthetic representations is highlighted here, Stephen's role is also significant. His role has, for the most part, been that of an audience to this encounter, listening in 'scornful silence' as the 'poor old woman' – as he self-consciously calls her – is addressed too loudly by Mulligan, yet he cannot help but respond to the others as conventional types. On the one hand, he is a weary and jaded internal audience to a dramatic scene of 'characters'; on the other hand, he is another of Joyce's audience-figures facing the prospect of possibly leaving a situation in which he is all too engaged. This pattern of boredom and dissent bespeaks the troubled past that Stephen cannot relinquish (or that will not relinquish him). If Yeats shows tranquillity to be built upon violent foundations, Joyce suggests that the nightmare recurs. Once more the reception of a quasi-revivalist theatrical scene is represented in Joyce's prose as cultural disaffection that expresses itself in the relationship between boredom and rioting. As such, it is a self-reflexive emblem of a modernity that the Revival had itself recognised. As Joyce was an active part of an audience to the Revival, so with Stephen: his perception of the scene around him is structured by the same contradiction apparent in Haines between ethnography and aesthetic convention. However much Stephen might wish to be apart from the scene which he surveys, he is instead a 'part' in it. This is how Joyce writes the Revival into his work, transforming its project by incorporating a figure of the audience as a performative character, self-consciously exposing the narratives and types on view, and undercutting an imagined audience with a version of the actual audience.

Joyce's engagement with the new theatre movement, in both fiction and essays, can be seen not so much as defining *its* audience as setting out the conditions of what *might* come to be his own. By initially por-traying the Revival theatre as pandering to 'the rabblement', Joyce found another convenient collective label for an audience who could then be overcome. However, as Joyce must have been aware, since he was so regular and varied a theatregoer, Dublin audiences were far from homo-genous, consisting instead of various class, religious and political factions (in fact, rather like the theatre's writers, producers and actors). Moreover, as Synge recognised in 1904, 'Dublin audiences' were 'hardly blessedly unripe' since contemporary European, ancient Greek and modern Irish drama all played in the capital's theatres at this time.[35] Joyce typically depicts this varied audience as performers, implying also that Revivalism was itself an act or pose. Any creation of a 'national audience' for a national theatre would therefore be an 'imagined community' and itself a performative gesture. Joyce's rewriting of revivalist theatre and its audiences suggests that an audience could not be fashioned as an ideal projection and nor could it be 'educated' into being: the 'looking glass' of realism would not be enough. Instead, Joyce sets about depicting the conditions of reception that he encountered without writing *for* any readership – this would always involve generic modes that allowed for inscribed versions of particular audiences and readers. He would thus avoid the pitfalls of the theatre initially with a mode, the short story, that had no need for the apparent successes of live drama and could instead reflect upon the supposed proximity of stage to auditorium while at the same time casting the formative role of the reader. Joyce's ongoing refusal to identify an audience finds expression later in the development of generic forms that would allow the question of reception to become part of the productive process. A staging of the relationship between generic expectations and social audiences is worked through extensively for the first time in 'The Dead'.

VI

A number of critics have called attention to the contemporaneity of the composition of 'The Dead' with the lecture, 'Ireland, Island of Saints and Sages', delivered in Trieste in April 1907; others have remarked on the interest Joyce took in the *Playboy* riots (January 1907) as he started work on that story.[36] All three might be read together. 'Ireland, Island of Saints and Sages' rebuts D. P. Moran's *Philosophy of Irish Ireland* (1905) by asserting a hybrid racial and cultural 'fabric' (*tessitura*) without any single pure 'thread' (*filo*). It goes on to liken current political action to a 'show' or 'play' (*spettacolo*) (*OCPW* 118, 126). The combination of these metaphors reveals the extent to which Joyce saw cultural and political identities as constituted by and within their reception. Just as no national or racial thread is 'uninfluenced by other threads nearby' so too every political stage implies and requires audiences whose responses help constitute the significance of the show.

The rhetorical flourish of 'Ireland, Island of Saints and Sages' sees Joyce placing himself within an audience to the stage of Ireland's political history – that is, one awaiting emancipation – and this allows Joyce subtly to align himself with his Triestine 'modernist, anti-clerical and agnostic' listeners while nonetheless asserting the validity of Ireland's lost grandeur.[37] Joyce acts, then, as both part of the audience to Ireland's 'resurgence' (*risorgimento*) and as a guide for his host culture; yet his use of the theatrical metaphor also distances himself from the Ireland which he describes. Joyce's trope for the political drama of Ireland is one of death, arguing that if Ireland 'is truly capable of resurgence, then let it do so, or let it . . . decently descend into the grave forever'. The lecture closes in anticipation of his own death before Ireland's rebirth: 'If it wants finally to put on the show [*spettacolo*] for which we have waited so long, this time let it be complete, full and definitive. But telling these Irish actors [*impresari*] to hurry up . . . is useless. I, for one, am certain not to see the curtain rise, as I shall have already taken the last tram home' (*OCPW* 125–6).[38] Joyce's perception that the curtain will rise on a new Ireland only after his death indicates his profound scepticism towards seemingly dramatic historical shifts (a view reinforced by his reading of Guglielmo Ferrero).[39] Once more, rioting and boredom seem to be interconnected in both revivalist theatre and Irish politics: indeed, the 'ordinary' is already a 'dissonant' discourse. In a sense, all of Joyce's work, from 'The Dead' to *Finnegans Wake* is about waiting for something that always both promises and yet fails to happen: such is Beckett's great debt to Joyce. Indeed, this denial of the dramatic historical shift turns out to be evocative of precisely the sort of gradual piecemeal change at the level of the 'everyday' that Joyce found in Ferrero: the historical is happening even as it appears not to be; like a shout in the street; like an 'ordinary reader' reading.

In Joyce's lecture, as in his fiction, a possible national rejuvenation is cloaked in theatrical metaphor, sceptically invoking and deflating the heady optimism of *Cathleen Ní Houlihan*, the price of whose reclamation of her 'four green fields' is the death of the young. While Lady Gregory's and Yeats's play had been generally 'received with rapturous applause' on its production in 1902, Joyce's response had been 'exactly the contrary of the rest of the audience'.[40] (In *Ulysses*, the 'poor old woman' returns as Old Gummy Granny promising Stephen, who is about to be 'done' by Private Carr, 'At 8.35 a.m. you will be in heaven and Ireland will be free' (*U* 15.4737–8).) Although Joyce continued to see the play as populist and naive, his lecture had anticipated the eventual resurgence of a 'rival, bilingual, republican, self-centred and enterprising island next to England', whose 'materialist civilization' he referred to in a very revivalist phrase (*OCPW* 125). Joyce's theatrical metaphor clearly ties his analysis of national '*risorgimento*' to analysis of the cultural stage: it is a cautious endorsement of *Sinn Féin* and a challenge to the Abbey either to transform its practices or to admit defeat. Defeat for the Abbey, in this case, would mean to lose out to the rival Catholic Theatre of Edward Martyn, which Joyce evidently favoured (*Letters* II, 208). The self-conscious metaphors of this lecture are an acknowledgement that political as well as theatrical and literary acts operate in tandem with an actual audience and that reception is consequently constitutive of any performance. The theatre and its politicians, it is implied, must recognise the presumptuousness of speaking to and for an audience. Joyce's own refusal to address an audience in his fiction is a refusal of a representative responsibility that could only ever be a form of misrepresentation. That did not mean, however, that he was insensible to the social conditions of these audiences.

Joyce's combination of theatrical and deathly metaphors at the close of his lecture was inspired not only by *Cathleen Ní Houlihan* but also by Synge's *Playboy*. His interest (noted in the letter cited at the beginning of this chapter) was sparked by accounts in one of those English newspapers he had warned Triestines not to trust. It was there that he read how the opening night (29 January) – and subsequent nights – were disrupted by the Abbey audience.[41] From Rome, Joyce wrote to Stanislaus giving a very full account based on the *Daily Mail*'s report under the heading 'Riot in a Dublin Theatre'. A week or so later he acquired copies of the coverage of the incident by the *Freeman's Journal*, and sent them on to Stanislaus as well. It appears, then, that Joyce was blocked in writing 'The Dead' because he was fascinated with the *Playboy* riots; indeed, he was so taken by the event that *he sent clippings to Dublin*, a reversal of the usual pattern whereby he received clippings. (His aunt, Josephine Murray, then sent Joyce a copy of the play, published by Maunsel.)

The Playboy thus played to a wider audience than those packed into the Abbey Theatre, for it created stories in international newspapers as well, securing an interest in the play and providing a basic plot structure not only of the text (complete with offensive phrases) but also of the wider drama of the evening. If newspapers could create a further 'imagined community' that was beyond the borders of the state (as a nation may be), then a case such as the *Playboy* surely also confirmed the fractures within that wider audience. Joyce's position regarding the *Playboy* riots, as 'a man in a house who hears a row in the street and voices he knows shouting but can't get out to see what the hell is going on', might be considered in these terms, suggestive as they are of a broader audience beyond the 'actual' event. That he sent clippings to Dublin underlines the peculiarly specular structure which near-global communications facilitated. At the same time, however, Joyce's language in this letter also betrays an ignorance in his position among a sort of 'secondary' audience, one reliant upon reportage, a distantiation that is further underlined by the generic presumption of a live performance for theatrical drama. The fallacy is that had he been in Dublin he may very well have simply read the same reports (but heard more from word of mouth). His relationship to the *Playboy* riots would have confirmed for him not only the social and performative character of audiences but also the dispersed character of a textual audience. The whole effect of the extended *Playboy* performance is to imply the impossibility of an audience at all, that is to say, the impossibility of an informed, 'live' and appropriate audience, and of a unified one, not just for the theatrical performance but also in general. For however well-informed Joyce was of the events, he surely saw that the audience, in the theatre and at large, was 'in the dark', recognising voices but essentially blind to the action. One reason for this ignorance is that the 'action' of Dublin was in fact 'inaction' (*D* 35); that God is a 'shout in the street' (*U* 2.386). The audience, like the producers, are merely 'dying to relieve the monotony of Dublin life', performing their own revival, their ennui both symptom and cause, a circular entrapment – a version, perhaps, of 'theatre in the round'.

It is possible to suggest, then, that Joyce's voluntary exile provided one of the key facets to his analysis of the conditions for the lack of an audience to his work, for it is via his physical distance – a distance already accomplished intellectually while in Dublin – that he is able most fully to cast himself as part of an audience to the Ireland he has left, an Ireland which nonetheless continues obliquely to offer potential readers for his own work (and some actual readers, as discussed in the following chapters). Joyce's inscriptions of audience-figures such as Eveline often include a voyeuristic sense of double-perspective as if they were watching their own indecisive lack of action. This gives that viewed audience a somewhat 'staged' air, lending a seemingly inevitable circularity to the process that is foretold in the very seeking of readers and in the very structure of writing.

VII

The interruption to the composition of 'The Dead' caused by the *Playboy* riots, and furthered by the composition of Joyce's Trieste lecture, may suggest a kind of textual pause in which the question of reception, and its relationship to genre, came to prominence. Joyce had already learnt much from Revival theatre about audience construction and behaviour, as well as about the vagaries of reception; the events of early 1907 perhaps enabled him to reflect on the self-conscious staging of these questions within his own writing. Joyce surely recognised that the *Playboy* riots resulted from a clash of generic expectations, and this represented not only an aesthetic but also a very material difference. As Christopher Morash has shown, in

1904 the new Abbey changed the setting for Irish theatre audiences by removing the cheap seats from the gallery, where audiences were traditionally most volatile. At other theatres such as the Gaiety, the gallery traditionally had the cheapest seats in the theatre, furthest from the stage and at considerable height. Instead, the Abbey created a smaller space, or pit, for fewer cheap seats much closer to the stage. In addition, the Abbey had high ticket prices. Indeed, Joyce was well accustomed to conventional audience behaviour at a wide range of theatrical spectacles, and would have known that Dublin audiences had become familiar with the theatre as a space of public protest. Since, moreover, the Abbey had been designed by Joseph Holloway (when he was not writing his diary) as a 'fairly traditional auditorium' rather than the 'modern performance space' that the theatre directors had desired, it could be said that the material infrastructure itself embodied different horizons of expectation – in terms of cultural etiquette and theatrical genre – between producers and consumers.[42]

In 'The Dead', Joyce restages a clash of generic and political expectations within the context of Dublin theatrical audiences. The narrative of the story is a peculiarly performative one, from the register of Dublin's declining operatic culture, against which Gretta's tale stands out, to the dramatic metaphors and meticulous choreography of characters. The Epiphany party resembles a play put on (again) for the amusement of the actors: 'It was always a great affair' that 'Never once had . . . fallen flat' (*D* 175). Not only is the conversation at dinner about the 'old days' of opera and 'galleries packed night after night' (*D* 200) at the Royal and the Gaiety (a period of successful productions of high opera in Dublin that had ended around 1880), but Gabriel is presented in explicitly theatrical terms. Aunt Kate summons him with the words, 'there's everyone waiting in there, stage to let' (*D* 197); he is accompanied by 'a chorus of voices' (*D* 199); he begins his speech by announcing that it is 'my lot this evening . . . to perform' to a 'row of upturned faces', his imagined audience even including some 'people, perhaps . . . standing in the snow . . . outside, gazing up at the lighted windows' (*D* 203).

However, Gabriel's role in this domestic drama is, like him, confused. The free indirect narrative and conditional tense reinforce the implication that he is both an actor in his domestic drama and an out-of-touch spectator to it at the same time. This combination of roles casts him as a participating reviewer of that drama: Gabriel behaves 'as if' not quite himself, which perhaps explains his awkward and self-conscious performance. He 'saw himself . . . acting as a penny boy for his aunts' (*D* 221);

'it hardly pained him now to think how poor a part he . . . had played' (*D* 223). In this respect he is akin to James Duffy of 'A Painful Case', whose self-referential existence includes 'regarding his own acts'. Given that Duffy 'had an odd autobiographical habit which led him to compose in his mind from time to time a short sentence about himself containing a subject in the third person and predicate in the past tense' (*D* 104), he is both writer and reader of his story – and Gabriel's role is not dissimilar. Gabriel's fault, again like Duffy, is to think he is the star of the show. He pretends his speech is successful – 'The table burst into applause and laughter at this sally' (*D* 205) – but such 'success' is the judgement of his own review of the occasion: the clichéd 'burst' and the pretentious 'sally' suggest that Gabriel is, literally, self-regarding. As the party winds down, Gabriel increasingly adopts the role of spectator: 'In the gloom of the hall . . . gazing up at his wife' as she herself listens to 'The Lass of Aughrim' (*D* 211), and of course he finally adopts the role of inscribed audience to Gretta's story.

The figure of Gabriel, then, represents part of the Dublin theatre audience, Catholic, 'well-to-do' and respectable, tied to an older (dying) generation. His personal boredom is later disturbed by Gretta's mock-revivalist narrative, producing a 'riot of emotions' (*D* 224) followed by an ambiguously renewed torpidity. The cultured, complacent passivity of Gabriel is another version of the torpor that afflicts the city. His boredom is self-consciously modern, but it lacks the romantic ennui, or disaffection, found in Molly Ivors. She can be seen to play out another pole of the Dublin audience, a middle-class nationalism which celebrates its idea of 'the West' as the site of cultural belonging. Enthusiastic as she is for the Gaelic League and Maud Gonne's *Inghinidhe na hÉireann*, her role is to offset Gabriel's response to Gretta's tale.[43]

The clash of genres in 'The Dead' might be described as a realist narrative (the party at which Gabriel is the principal actor) which is confronted by its gothic or perhaps romantic other (in Gretta's tale). The latter, it is implied, is the hidden correlative of the former: Gretta's repression is already embedded within Gabriel's apparent liberalism. John Wilson Foster has claimed that in learning to accommodate his 'romantic anti-self' Gabriel 'becomes a transcendent realist' and this represents 'a visionary rather than a nationalist or romantic orientation'.[44] In these terms, an enlightened, liberal realism accommodates its other. This process of cultural identification of the self sees Gabriel respond to 'his wife' by testing the rational and realistic limits of her tale with a 'cold interrogation'. In Foster's reading, his liberalism encompasses her romantic enthusiasm: while the 'gathering forces' of 'vague terror' rise within him, an 'effort of reason' quells them. The narrative, though, first has Gretta enact the revivalist trope of a Cathleen Ní Houlihan figure, that Michael Furey 'died for me' (*D* 221–2). Gabriel's final 'transcendence' would, then, be the evolved triumph of his enlightened ego, itself enlarged by recognition of the cultural unconscious that ties Gabriel to the West.

Yet this sketch of the clash of genres in the story is reductive; it leaves the universalism of the ending intact and once more relegates the uneasy elements of the story to a comfortable recess, just as Gabriel himself tries to walk away from every awkward situation. Although the mode of Gretta's tale is a shock to Gabriel, as if he had stumbled across the wrong stage, his haughty reasoning has at least modified the trope, eliciting the detail that Furey was an urban boy from the gasworks. Gretta's narrative is thus revealed to be mock-revivalist, just as the story's apparent realism cannot be completely distinguished from Gabriel's voice: 'the failure of his irony' (*D* 221) may also be that of the narrative. His 'interrogation' of her backfires, exposing his desire to be 'master of her strange mood,' a desire, that is, to overwrite 'the quaintness of her phrase' with his own 'brutal language' (*D* 218–19). So 'The Dead' plays out a clash of generic forms and expectations while also undermining the differences between them: Gretta's 'quaintness' and the apparent 'terror' of her tale turn out to provide a sensible and controlled narrative about a long-dead urban boy; likewise, Gabriel's rational questioning leads to his later conventionalised vision of the revived Furey-like figure in the final section.

Gretta's position and narrative, as well as Gabriel's response, resonate with the controversies that characterised the reception of revivalist theatre. A not dissimilar controversy to the *Playboy* riots had previously occurred in October 1903 over Synge's *The Shadow of the Glen* (it is possible that Joyce associated the two). Joyce had seen this play and Stanislaus records in his *Dublin Diary* that, along with *Riders to the Sea*, it is 'the best thing the Irish National Theatre Society has produced'. The debate centred on the realism or otherwise of the story, not only in the depiction of Nora (and her lover, Michael), but also in the conventional defence mounted by Yeats in 1905, when the play was re-staged, that Synge had heard the story on the Aran Islands. It met the 'moral' objections of Griffith and others because they assumed, in Stanislaus's words, that its characters were 'typical Irish peasants'.[45] According to Joep Leerssen, the controversy arose because 'Synge failed to make the peasantry's oral narrative sufficiently palatable to the Dublin theatregoers and their metropolitan, middle-brow demands of *vraisemblance* and *bienséance*'.[46] What 'the Dublin audience' – especially the pole represented by Molly Ivors – demanded was not so much *vraisemblance* as characters who accorded to the pious and noble peasantry of their imagination. 'The Dead' underscores the discrepancy between 'the West' as an imaginary space, as it is in Revivalism generally, and its topographical reality. Setting his story in Dublin, Joyce could depict his real point of interest in Synge: the reactions of his audiences.

In 'The Dead', the suggestion that Gretta's tale is not necessarily the impulsive outpouring of tragic grief but instead a shaped and carefully told story, marked by literary convention, further underlines the theatricality of the narrative. She pauses 'to get her voice under control' and the narrative position is carefully ambiguous when it announces 'Perhaps she had not told him all the story' (*D* 222–3), a phrase which is not necessarily to be associated with Gabriel's thought. Joyce's story thus encompasses differing literary modes and expectations: the point is not the realism or otherwise of a tale but the conventional form that it adopts and the reactions they imply and induce. Gabriel's responses to this tale could be said to embody the social contestation over the public space of the theatre in Irish Revivalism. He has been caught between, first, a 'riot of emotions' and second, 'generous tears' (*D* 224). Gabriel thus displays all the paralysed anxiety of an educated Catholic and staunchly middle-class audience to cultural nationalism, torn between distanced propriety and a recognition of belonging. The faded gentility typified by his family finds it difficult to embrace the western roots of Gretta let alone the *arriviste* enthusiasm of Molly Ivors; at the same time, of course he *is* married to Gretta and he appears to have some awareness of his disabling boredom. In the course of events, Gabriel is taken through the whole spectrum of audience responses, culminating with an exhausted shock at the late dramatic entrance of the Furey-like figure, when he is finally lulled into torpidity. This shift of response is indicative of a broader cultural tension in revivalist theatre audiences, one which goes to the heart of Gabriel's own class-anxiety. His torn loyalties encapsulate the same division that was found at the *Playboy* riots between the sixpenny seats in the pit and the three shilling stalls, that is, between a Catholic, mainly nationalist audience and an upper middle class, predominantly unionist one.[47] The desire 'to say that literature was above politics' (*D* 188) is forcefully shown to be no longer tenable in this contested generic and social space.

In her reading of 'The Dead', Nolan refers to Walter Benjamin's essay 'The Storyteller' to suggest that Joyce's short story represents the modern condition of the nation, as an imagined community-in-anonymity, as it encroaches upon the traditional folktale.[48] By briefly returning to Benjamin's essay, it is further possible to position Gabriel's role as an audience-figure, especially in relation to the generic significance of Joyce's story. In turn, this leads to Joyce's engagement with the early revivalist ambition of a possible national audience, an ambition that was crushed by its theatrical controversies.

Benjamin describes the communal audience of the story as necessarily relaxed, even naïve, one whose self-forgetting is necessary to the successful retention of the story in memory. On the other hand, the novel reader is an isolated individual whose self-interest leads to an eager consumption of the text.[49] It can be suggested that Joyce uses the form of the short story to display a fundamental discordance between Gabriel as audience and the genre that he reviews. Gabriel offers two responses, separated by a textual break, an indeterminate blank space on the page before the paragraph 'She was fast asleep' (D 223).[50] On first encountering Gretta's mock-revival, oral tale, he comprehends it only in terms of his own life, like the over-eager novel reader, reconfirming his selfhood. Later, as the story works upon his memory, overwhelming and destabilising his ego, Gabriel is returned to a listless boredom that allows his mind to rehearse the narrative he has heard, like the audience to the story as Benjamin describes it. He is said to be 'listening' only *after* the textual space, that is, once she has fallen asleep (D 223). In each case, Gabriel's position is inappropriate: first, his response to Gretta's *tale* is that of a *reader*; second, in the privacy of his own space, he apparently melts into a broader, anonymous role among an *audience*. So whereas the dramatic content and tropes of the narrative have set up an apparent discussion of the revivalist stage, Joyce uses the very textuality of his own story to articulate the rather different nature of his own revival, a '*risorgimento*' that is acted out across an indefinable blank space.

On either side of this space, which occupies an 'empty' time, like an interminable boredom, Gabriel is in the classic pose of the jaded waiting audience, first at the window and then 'leaning on his elbow' (D 223). The reception of Gretta's story occupies these two moments. It is only after the space that the textual voice of free indirect narrative can imply that Gabriel's superior self-confidence has been troubled. Gabriel's *mémoire involuntaire* has been jogged, causing him to re-tell the story to himself. At first his re-telling of the story appears to confirm his readerly distance, enforcing the distinction of his world from that of her tale, anticipating Julia's death and maintaining his social superiority (especially towards Gretta, 'she who lay beside him' – *D* 224). Appropriately enough it is the image of Furey's eyes – returning his gaze – that triggers an irruption within the liberal and rational self of an almost gothic repression (possibly, as the name suggests, a violent, furious one). In order to attribute this transformative power to the story, Gabriel has had to invest it with the auratic quality of an art that has 'the ability to look at us in return'.[51] This occurs through his *mémoire involontaire*, while gazing blankly at the sleeping Gretta (whose aversion of her sobbing eyes had previously shielded the return of his gaze). The crucial points about this form of remembrance are that it plays upon the subject and that it is a form of inventing the past and not a 'pure' recollection: as such, it comprises a fiction that grips its teller. In similar fashion, Gabriel's 'evocation of a figure from the dead' (*D* 221) is an uncertain and stylised affair, as if indeed a trope or figure from 'The Dead' has been evoked: 'he imagined he saw the form of a young man standing under a dripping tree' (*D* 224). Further, this construction gives way to more classic gothic tropes: a mass of similar dead 'beings'; the 'light taps upon the pane'; bad weather closing in; sleepiness; a dream or trance-like state. It appears, then, that Gabriel's re-telling of the tale has aestheticised Furey into a nameless, spectral character and in so doing he has once again appropriated Gretta's voice. The shift of narrative away from Gabriel's self-destructive gothic version is like a call of reason, a willful shaking-off of inner torment, that is effected by a deliberate recall of the newspapers ('Yes, the newspapers were right. . .') and of the cold fact that 'Michael Furey lay buried' (*D* 225). Having induced disruption in a narrative that has spiralled beyond control, Gabriel strives to displace those demons onto the world without. Even in the closing paragraphs, then, Gabriel does not 'transcend' his selfhood or attain a 'mutual' humanity but remains a displaced misreader, an inappropriate audience.

'The Dead' plays out in its narrative, metaphor and form the very generic disruptions that the theatre of Yeats and Synge (in particular) had created. By presenting an image of 'the West' as a community divided by deceit, Synge's *Playboy* had challenged its Dublin audience to respond to an imaginary picture of its other self. In effect, Gabriel has faced the same challenge. He has had to accommodate to a new mode and then to adjust his rationalism to a haunting interruption. Like the Dublin audiences, he is ill-equipped for the shock. Moreover, as a newspaper man, he is most comfortable as a reader, continually seeking privacy and favouring a realist narrative mode that confirms his own social and ontological security: the final paragraphs record his battle to assert a set of generic borders and expectations on a story that seems capable of taking on a life of its own. The notable shift at the end of 'The Dead' can then be understood as part of an emerging self-critique in which Joyce responds to and provokes the difficulties of addressing an audience in his stories. The Abbey's encounter with actual audiences in the form of riots only underlined the disparities between text and audience and within audiences. It also, it could be said, showed the disparities within Synge's own text, being at once 'romantic' and 'realist'. 'The Dead' underscores its distance from that scene in its very textuality: Gabriel's role is thus to perform as various audiences, from the self-divided Dublin middle-class theatre-goer to the rational reader and the listener to the tale. In no role, however, is he ever comfortable. Joyce's generic games, which centre on his story's textuality (with its use of blank space), illustrate that reception is inevitably a discomforting experience.

IX

There is a sense in which Synge anticipates Joyce in that his revivals also fail to usher in a new dawn: the older characters retain their power over the younger, the comic mode never quite wins through.[52] A caustic deflation also characterises the reception Synge's plays received: no ideal audience could be located either in them or for them, their actual audiences proving themselves, in Yeats's terms, a 'mob' and not a 'people'. Perhaps this is why Joyce found Synge 'better' than Yeats (*Letters* II, 211), when he was comparing, most likely, *Riders* with *Cathleen Ní Houlihan*: the 'return of the dead' in Synge suggesting a more ironic, less optimistic social revival as well as exposing nationalist pieties. Yet there is a crucial difference between Joyce's and Synge's revivals for all their shared scepticism: Joyce's revivals are always self-consciously borrowed theatrical costumes that are tried in order to show that they don't fit and that the audience is not paying attention. In addition to Furey, consider 'A Mother', which stages the false revival of 'the poor lady', Madam Glynn, who 'looked as if she had been resurrected' (*D* 145) ('I wonder where did they dig her up?' (*D* 141)). Her performance is an ironic version of Maud Gonne playing the lead in *Cathleen Ní Houlihan* on its opening at St Teresa's Hall in 1902. Dressed as the Poor Old Woman, she arrived ten minutes before curtain rise, marching from the street through the audience in full stage dress and ghoulish make-up (dark around the eyes to accentuate her paleness). Joseph Holloway recorded in his diary that 'the tall and willowy' Gonne, who played the part with 'creepy realism', 'chanted her lines with rare musical effect, and crooned fascinatingly, if somewhat indistinctly'.[53] In 'A Mother', Madam Glynn sang in a 'bodiless gasping voice' and 'looked as of she had been resurrected from an old stage wardrobe' (*D* 145). All the other artistes are gathered in the Antient Concert Rooms when 'an unknown solitary woman with a pale face walked through the room. The women followed with keen eyes the faded blue dress which was stretched upon a meagre body' (*D* 141). She plays to a disruptive, unappreciative, even 'bored' crowd (*D* 143). In this manner, mock-Revival tropes and characters crop up in disorientating settings in Joyce's work, their self-conscious appearance as conventional figures emphasising the continuities and disjunctions of their generic and cultural world with Joyce's. These tropes and characters do not, then, simply represent an opposition between Joyce and his contemporaries but a textual mode of enquiry into the conditions of cultural production and reception in Ireland, conditions in which Joyce's own work was implicated.

Like Synge's inglorious rebirths, Furey's appearance is also a sombre twist on the revivalist manoeuvre, but he is muted in Joyce's story as against the charismatic verbosity of Synge's characters. (In *The Shadow of the Glen* Nora leaves with the tramp: 'you've a fine bit of talk, stranger, and it's with yourself I'll go' – a line that Stanislaus found hilarious.[54]) While the characters of Yeats and Synge were associated with an eloquence that revitalised English, the mock-revivalist Furey is notably silent. Joyce's text has intervened, its blank space a silence that precedes and juxtaposes the famous lyricism of the ending which is then all the more notable in the context of the silences of Joyce's text: Gretta pauses several times; Gabriel asks only brief questions of Gretta but does not speak any response; the blank space says nothing; and Furey himself is given no dialogue. Eloquence was, after all, a conventionalised quality of which Joyce was sceptical, especially in his condemnation of Synge's 'long overweighted sentences' as a 'misuse of the stage'.[55] The fickle Mulligan is Joyce's most eloquent character (even adopting Syngean brogue in 'Scylla and Charybdis') and Joyce argues at the end of his Triestine lecture that 'though the Irish are eloquent, a revolution is not made of human breath' (*CW* 126). The implication, then, is that one should read with scepticism the apparent lyrical eloquence of the ending of 'The Dead' as a textual exercise, a form of stylistic *bravado* that hovers somewhere between Gabriel and the narrator. Indeed, Joyce might be thought of as the conduit that made possible the silences of Beckett.

As Margot Norris has recognised, 'through the painful experience of rejection and censorship', Joyce learned that 'it was his aesthetic effects, his lyricism, his romanticism, but not his social critique, that would earn him publication and acclaim'. If he 'polishes these effects to a commercially marketable gloss', he does so while 'covertly ironizing his lyrical language'.[56] Seamus Deane also sees Joyce's predilection for concluding passages of 'fine writing', from the ending of 'The Dead' onwards, as a rhetorical aestheticism at the expense of social critique.[57] This regrets a lost moment of potential radicalism in which Joyce *had* challenged the colonial and modern conditions of alienation, poverty and disempowerment. Instead, his famous endings have opted for the universal and the humanistic while retaining the image of a spectral liberation. Yet aestheticism and social critique come together in Joyce's engagement with the reception of revivalist theatre. His writing implies an estrangement of any audience or readership just as his 'social critique' interrogated the constitution of Revival audiences and the material conditions they faced. In the final section of 'The Dead' the lyrical seduction offers the opportunity to read 'against the grain'. There is an invitation to such resistance elsewhere in Joyce's work: Stephen Dedalus appears to mimic the closing lines of 'The Dead' in the diary section of *A Portrait* ('Faintly . . . Not so faintly now'; 'to what journey's end – what heart?'). The following day he writes 'Read what I wrote last night. Vague words for a vague emotion. Would she like it? I think so' (*P* 274). So Joyce's later, more autobiographical fiction could be taken to signal the self-consciousness of the ending of 'The Dead' as a piece about the social forms that literary reception takes: the context is revealing, for Stephen imagines the seductive power of his 'vague words' and his own disenchantment with such 'success'. To the extent that 'The Dead' is about the politics of form and reception, it is not merely an annulling aestheticization of political critique, for it is Joyce's first serious engagement with the revivalist social and ideological formation of a national audience. It can be admitted, though, that this engagement with Revivalism (as well as with the Catholic and colonial state) may well have brought home the futility of such 'engagement' more generally since it only reinforces the impossibility of directly addressing an audience.

X

The form of reception that Joyce inscribes into 'The Dead' is not merely a textual *mise en abyme* but also a specific, local act, in which his difference from a revivalist imagination crystallised over the question of an audience. As 'G.C.' betrays his 'own people' (*D* 190) by writing for the *Express*, so Joyce had similarly betrayed Lady Gregory in the same newspaper when reviewing her *Poets and Dreamers* in 1903. Although Joyce did not quite 'slate her drivel to Jaysus' as Mulligan says of Stephen (*U* 9.1160) – some passages he disliked less than others – he was still, as he admitted, 'very severe' (*Letters* II, 38). Both Gabriel and Joyce have been betrayed by their initials. Joyce's initials were (uniquely) printed by the paper's editor, E. V. Longworth, beneath his review (*OCPW* 76). However, at the precise moment of enticing a biographical comparison it is undone: unlike Gabriel, Joyce-the-reviewer hardly valued the books more than the cheque.[58] These details are well known, but the wider debate surrounding Lady Gregory's book is apposite.

In 1903 Joyce was probably not going to be immediately receptive to Lady Gregory's compilation of stories and 'translations': having just read Synge's *Riders* – and having found it insufficiently Aristotelian – Lady Gregory's volume was hardly going to satisfy the classical taxonomy. In the Library episode of *Ulysses*, Mulligan asks Stephen, 'Couldn't you do the Yeats touch?' (*U* 9.1160–1). The 'Yeats touch' was not just his review of Gregory's *Cuchulain of Muirthemne*, which Mulligan parodies, but also, presumably, Yeats's own review of *Poets and Dreamers*, which had called it 'beautiful' in the first line. Mulligan echoes this judgement and possibly also Yeats's Preface to *The Well of the Saints* when he adds 'One thinks of Homer' (*U* 9.1165).[59] Joyce's principal criticism of Lady Gregory's book is its naïve presentation as art of a disordered storytelling tradition 'in the fullness of its senility' (the Aristotelian in him evidently came through). The contrast with Yeats's reading could hardly be clearer. *Poets and Dreamers* provoked in Yeats an optimistic and rhapsodic invocation of a united community as the audience that the Revival might inspire.

There is still in truth upon these great level plains a people, a community bound together by imaginative possessions, by stories and poems which have grown out of its own life, and by a past of great passions which can still waken the heart to imaginative action. One could still, if one had the genius, and had been born to Irish, write for these people plays and poems like those of Greece. Does not the greatest poetry always require a people to listen to it? England or any other country which takes its tunes from the great cities and gets its taste from old custom may have a mob, but it cannot have a people. In England there are a few groups of men and women who have good taste, whether in cookery or in books; and the great multitudes but copy them or their copiers. The poet must always prefer the community where the perfected minds express the people, to a community that is vainly seeking to copy the perfected minds. To have even perfectly the thoughts that can be weighed, the knowledge that can be got from books, the precision that can be learned at school, to belong to any aristocracy, is to be a little pool that will soon dry up. A people alone are a great river; and that is why I am persuaded that where a people has died, a nation is about to die.[60]

Similarly, to 'write for these people' was the advice famously given by Yeats to Synge (even if he did not quite follow it) when he advised him to return from Paris and live on the Aran Islands 'as if' he were 'one of the people'.[61] Joyce, however, has taken this imaginative Revival, with the advice to return to and write for 'the people', and built a collection of stories around its impossibility. Benjamin's suggestion that 'a great story-teller will always be rooted in the people' may sound Yeatsian but his inflection on that tradition as shaped by, among others, 'the urban elements in the many stages of their economic and technical development', is distinctly Joycean.[62]

As suggested earlier, Yeats's poetry, while sometimes apparently addressing a national people is more clearly directed towards particular figures who embody a great heritage or represent ideal emblems of a culture not yet achieved. Like Joyce, Synge too was unable or unwilling to address 'the people': the *Playboy* depicted an unruly West just as it performed to an unruly Dublin audience. It was here, among the inappropriate audience – in that 'crowd' – that Joyce located his stories. Yet this was not in order to 'write for' them (such would be the false hope of an exilic view: a further paralysis, a boredom). Rather than an idealisation of a communal audience, or a realistic account of particular theatrical audiences, Joyce's response was to dramatise revivalist aesthetics and audiences, and, in his other fiction, to transform his own readers. As he had said in 'Drama and Life', 'the deadest among the living, may play a part in a great drama' (*CW* 45). Boredom, the underpinning condition of Dublin's would-be readers, is no stranger to great drama. In the figures of Gabriel Conroy, Molly Ivors and others, 'The Dead' portrays a fractured Irish audience, which Joyce remembered, and which the *Playboy* riots brought back home to him. It also inscribes into the collection a reminder of the writer's distance from his would-be readership, a distance not only embodied by physically staying away but also better suited to fiction than to lyric or theatre with their knowingly false implications of sincerity and immediacy. If Synge, at least in Yeats's crude version, had returned home in order to revive among 'the people' his writing and a national literature, then compared to this myth, 'The Dead' seems like the wisdom of hindsight, for the bored know they have no one to talk to.

At its close, then, *Dubliners* is unable to address an audience or even to anticipate a readership. Written when the collection lacked a publisher, 'The Dead' reads like a rumination on the impossibility of an audience, a feature that Joyce may have wryly noted in theatres in Dublin. It can only inscribe the presumptuousness and futility of such an address and identify an underlying malaise as the ongoing condition of the society from which any audience would have to be formed. This is the state of reception that Joyce postulates: it is not an address to an audience, nor is it even laying the foundations for an audience; it is an analysis of the generic and cultural clashes that colour reception. For Joyce an Irish audience would be conceived only through asserting the contradictory importance of a potential readership and, at the same time, a refusal to bow to a direct delivery, even to inscribe the impossibility of that delivery. The denial of an audience was therefore not necessarily a political evasion. If, like Jimmy Doyle, Joyce 'felt obscurely the lack of an audience' this was no willful ignorance of his 'people' but a culturally and conceptually thorough engagement with what, in his context, an Irish reception might mean.

CHAPTER 2

Surveillance: education, confession and the politics of reception

In any consideration of Joyce's representation of reception, indeed, of his construction of a literary politics in general, 'Scylla and Charybdis' must be a key document. In the middle of that episode of *Ulysses*, Stephen Dedalus lists to himself the characters who have been significant readers of or listeners to his work and ideas. 'Where is your brother? . . . My whetstone. Him, then Cranly, Mulligan: now these' (*U* 9.977–8). The list casts an identity, or role, onto the assembled group, that of audience to Stephen; but it is also a reflection on some of Joyce's actual readers and the transformation which his work has cast on their responses. The earliest extant draft version of this chapter gives a fuller list including Davin and Lynch, and specifies that the brother was the first reader.[1] This earlier draft assembles the fictional versions of Stanislaus and those college friends who had read and appeared in *Stephen Hero* (Clancy, Byrne, Cosgrave) and brings them up to date via Gogarty and now 'these' figures in the National Library (Lyster, Best, Magee and Russell). The list is a characteristic grouping of readers as both collective and other (Joyce would do the same with critics in *Finnegans Wake*), but it is also a list that has been carefully compiled and ordered. Like any archive, it has form. Divided into two, it broadly distinguishes different cultural groups: the earlier named readers plus Gogarty and the current audience, 'these'. While Stephen constructs 'these' as 'other', Joyce carefully shows the ways in which such a construction is itself a kind of false 'reading' by Stephen. Further, the list's chronology gives the illusion of completion when, in fact, Stephen has neglected to mention his mother, who had earlier been his first familial audience. This chapter discusses both aspects of the list: the incomplete first half and then its apparent 'othering' of readers into distinct sets.

In showing how Joyce arranges Stephen's construction of his readers and listeners, I argue that Joyce both encourages and challenges attempts to read his own work within a religious (and therefore political) frame. The representation of reception is intimately linked to Joyce's religious

and educational contexts, which have provided interpretive strategies for
Stephen Dedalus in the library. Yet Stephen's 'othering' of 'these' implies
a simple oppositional politics that Joyce also undermines. This paradoxical stance is traced, at the beginning of the chapter, to Joyce's early
disclosures of his work to family and friends. These disclosures were a
sort of confession, but one in which the relationship between confessor
and penitent has been overturned.[2] Through such confessions, Joyce can
be seen to address while simultaneously erasing a 'local' reception. While
his relationship with those 'local' readers, comprising family and friends,
as well as with the various inscribed literary figures has traditionally been
seen as oppositional, my analysis brings out Joyce's imaginative echoing of
others' responses, and the provision of his own response in turn, creating
a form of reciprocation and an acknowledgement of social proximity.
Everyday forces of cultural appropriation are shown to be silently at work
through the very sense of claustrophobia among 'local', familiar readers
that is evident in both *Stephen Hero* and the later library scene. In the
conditions Joyce experienced, reception, it is suggested, acted as a form
of covert social surveillance: not official monitoring, but a process of
mutual implication.[3] By tracing these 'local' responses and Joyce's rewriting of them, it becomes possible to construct a political reading of his
work within the context from which, nonetheless, it has been irreparably
riven. It is this sense of being both part of a time and place, while escaping
and transforming it, that these scenes of reception achieve.

I

In Ireland in the nineteenth century, education was one of the key areas
of reform in the gradual extension of opportunity to Catholics and, in
Joyce's time, the 'university question' (as Molly Ivors calls it in 'The
Dead') – a set of debates that led to the creation of the National University of Ireland – was a 'question' precisely because of religious dispute.
As a Jesuit-educated student from University College and 'schooled in old
Aquinas', Joyce could not help but be bracketed under a certain label no
matter how much his first publications had railed against the Catholic
'rabblement'. At the same time, there could be no presumption of his
finding a 'natural readership' among his Catholic peers: Joyce's work is
careful simultaneously to invoke the image of this potential readership
but not necessarily to write *for* it.

Joyce's complex cultural 'belonging' could be a point of confusion for
his readers, particularly across the murky waters of the Irish Sea. Writing

in *The Nation* in 1917 H. G. Wells found *A Portrait* to be the 'most living and convincing picture of an Irish Catholic upbringing', but he also went on to underline the difference between an Irish and an English reader's perspective since those same 'conditions' had 'passed almost altogether out of English life', to the point where they were alien to a 'modern' (i.e. English) environment. Wells went further, claiming that the value of the novel lay in the 'convincing revelation' it made of the conditions of a 'great mass of Irishmen' to the 'intelligent reader' who, presumably, could not be part of that Irish 'mass'. No other book, he said, had spelt out so clearly how different were 'the liberal English' (the intelligent readers, perhaps?) from the 'bright-green' Irish, and this was due to 'training and tradition'.[4] Wells's response, while seen by Ellmann as 'highly appreciative', exemplifies the colonialist nature of this liberalism by which a recalcitrant Irish Catholicism has yet to attain 'modern' English secularism.[5] Notably, Wells links educational 'training' to this 'civilising' process. His is one among many accounts that reveal an interesting paradox: as *Everyman* put it, Joyce's portrait was 'true to life' while simultaneously 'too allusive to be readily understood by the English reader'.[6] If Joyce's early work was notable for its use of realism, then sometimes the people who most noticed this were the least qualified to say so. These reviewers thus underscored a disjunction between different reading communities even as they sought to overcome it.

Reviewers in Ireland could be more subtle in their allusions, conveying information in codified manner, as in Thomas Kettle's knowing reference to having read Joyce in *St Stephen's* (the University College journal).[7] It was only a short step for W. K. Magee (henceforth referred to under his pseudonym John Eglinton) – in his review of *Ulysses* for *The Dial* – to make the point that Joyce's readers would also be from University College: 'The newly emancipated youth of the national university turn to the pure diabolism of Mr Joyce' (the 'national university' was also, of course, 'a Jesuit house').[8] In 1929, with literary opinion across Europe asserting Joyce's importance, Eglinton argued that with him, 'perhaps for the first time in an Irish writer, there is no faintest trace of Protestantism: that is, of the English spirit'. Foreign critics were disadvantaged by their ignorance of 'Joyce's race and upbringing', i.e. his 'peculiar origins'.[9] In their 'letters' to a British and American potential readership, Eglinton and Joseph Hone presented Joyce as the first decolonised Irish writer, a by-product of what Hone called 'Catholic democracy in Ireland' and its 'opportunities for an inexpensive university education'.[10] An implicit religious and national correlation is an unfortunate side effect of these reviews. One of the points made by Stephen in the National Library is that England, as well as Ireland, is a site of religious disputation.

The responses of Joyce's contemporary critics make clear that educational practice constitutes more than a piece of contextual background. It was also one of the means through which Joyce was read, a shorthand or code for categorising and explaining him and his work. So education – entwined with religion – figures as a feature of the cultural politics of reception not only within Joyce's depiction of particular reading strategies but also as part of the framework for others' reading of his work. Education provided a structure of reception that was both enabling and limiting: it offered a potential readership but also could restrict a writer to a sole identification with that readership. Throughout his fiction, Joyce anticipates and responds to this structure of reception by linking institutions of learning to the reception accorded to his own work. He does this by means of a double manoeuvre: in the first place, such sites produce a readership and a politics of reading, and this allows for the expression, through Stephen Dedalus, of a Catholic and Irish intellectual tradition that is directed at a particular audience. Yet, as will presently be discussed, Stephen has already abnegated responsibility towards that audience through his inverted confessions. Secondly, and simultaneously, by self-consciously staging its own reception amid debates over literary politics, Joyce's work displaces the religious and cultural 'oppositions' which it displays. The significance of 'Scylla and Charybdis' is that it brings together examples of educational reading strategies from Catholic and Protestant traditions (in the form of Stephen Dedalus and Edward Dowden) in a manner that shows their proximity as well as their distance. The surveillance that is implied in this scene is a mutual one which is suggestive of the nature of reception as an ongoing 'responsiveness' between self and other, even as those distinctions are questioned. While showing an alignment between educational traditions and reception, then, Joyce is careful not to force an identification between writer and readership. Instead, his work maintains the relationship between the two as one in which surveillance – and hence a form of social proximity – is crucial.

II

The educational institutions of turn-of-the-century Ireland constitute a material context for an understanding of Joyce's *potential* but ultimately repudiated readership among the Catholic middle class. Joyce's work acknowledges the significance of this context: in *Stephen Hero* and

A Portrait, educational debate is a self-conscious spectacle in which Stephen Dedalus performs before an audience of an emergent class. Schools such as Belvedere and Clongowes were, in general, consciously training a new strata of middle-class Catholics: educated and professional, supporters of Home Rule and defenders of the Church yet at the same time 'a little bit English', trained to play English games and, often, taught from an English syllabus.[11] As we will see, although Joyce's training in English literature was very much English (and protestant) in conception, his exposure to the teaching of Fr Darlington in particular offered the promise of alternative interpretative strategies based on a Catholic intellectual tradition. The very institutional make-up of University College at this time was itself an uneasy fusion of distinct political and religious concerns.

Formed in 1882, the year of Joyce's birth, University College was a reconstitution of Cardinal Newman's Catholic University (formed in 1854). As he later reminded others, Joyce took his degree under the auspices of the Royal University, a non-denominational institution created by Disraeli in 1879 to combine the Catholic University with the Queen's Colleges, which although also non-denominational had been shunned by the Catholic hierarchy.[12] In Joyce's time, University College suffered from the unfortunate combination of an undemanding curriculum and a talented student body.[13] University College was later incorporated into the National University of Ireland – officially non-denominational but in practice designed for Catholics – which was established by the Irish Universities Act 1908 and also included the Queen's Colleges at Cork and Galway.[14] However, the formation of a new independent national university had been seriously mooted long before Joyce attended college; indeed, it provided a necessary institutional context to the elucidation of a Catholic intellectual tradition. R. D. Anderson has argued that the growth of Catholic higher education, amid the milieu of political and religious division at the turn of the century, 'undoubtedly contributed to the . . . creation of a professional and intellectual elite alienated from British values'.[15] Joyce was a part of this small but growing, university-educated Catholic middle class. John Hutchinson has given figures: 'in 1911 only 30,000 Catholics out of a total school-going population of 705,000 went into secondary education, and at . . . University College, Dublin, no more than 100 graduated in any year during the 1890s'.[16] This resulted in a 'blocked mobility', which may explain the popularity of the Revival among the men and women educated at elite schools and university. Mobility was more blocked for women, whose participation at University College was restricted to a number of 'feeder' colleges.[17] Molly Ivors, it is implied, is a part of this frustrated Dublin audience awaiting a revival of the (imagined) West and equality for women.

Joyce's temporary desire to study medicine was entirely conventional. Judging by student numbers at University College, medicine and law were the favoured careers of young Catholics trying to get on.[18] The problem for these students was that the number of professional positions remained static between 1871 and 1911. In addition, access to the restricted higher ranks of the civil service, a traditional route for the educated colonised, was by direct appointment rather than open competition. The study of English had long been seen as preparatory to a colonial career in the India Civil Service and some followed this path from Trinity College and the Queen's Colleges but access was more difficult for Catholics. Indeed, articles in Joyce's school journal *The Clongownian* at the end of the nineteenth century warned of the need for 'a very large and influential connection' for students entering professions.[19] Joyce may well have seen this article and in any case he was surely aware of the situation it described. This 'blocked mobility' for educated Catholics was epitomised by overcrowding in the already inadequate facilities used by University College on Earlsfort Terrace.[20] The physical conditions may have been poor but the growing numbers and examination successes (the Queen's Colleges were markedly out-performed) would have helped create the sense of a new class beginning to thrive amid hopes and, increasingly, expectations of Home Rule. At the same time as they were 'blocked', then, these students were also the 'coming men and women' of a rising generation.

The emergence of an apparent community of readers amongst this class would have been further underlined by the creation of the student magazine, *St Stephen's*, in 1901 and by the revival of the Literary & Historical debating society (known as the L&H) which had originally been established under Newman and was later rekindled under President Delany during Joyce's time at University College. This potential audience was one with professional, middle-class expectations: the L&H 'trains young men . . . for the bar and political platform' (*SH* 83). Yet this was a pious, socially conservative class: it was *St Stephen's*, under the control of the Jesuit authorities, that declined to publish both Joyce's essay 'The Day of the Rabblement' and Francis Sheehy Skeffington's 'A Forgotten Aspect of the University Question', which the two then had printed privately. Skeffington's essay was of course a powerful argument in favour of the foundation of a new co-educational university. That one of Joyce's first publications should appear alongside an analysis of the university issue calls attention, albeit coincidentally, to the importance of the educational context for his early work. At the same time that Joyce was rejecting one potential readership in 'The Day of the Rabblement' – the pious, middle-class Catholic audience of Dublin theatre – he was being rejected by a closely related one at the university. His work then appeared in a private edition, which also drew attention to a different potential readership – educated women – whom Joyce had not directly sought to attract (and to whom this chapter will return).

The appearance and erasure of a potential audience among the educated middle class can be sketched with reference to two passages from *A Portrait*. Joyce's autobiographical fictions foreground educational debates as powerful images or set-piece spectacles in which a local readership and potential audience are displayed. In the famous 'pandying' scene in *A Portrait* – when Stephen is punished for 'not writing like the others' (*P* 50) – the action is clearly set up for a voyeuristic audience and an actor who returns their gaze: Stephen 'saw . . . that all the fellows were looking after him' and even the walls carry 'portraits of the saints and great men of the order who were looking down on him silently' (*P* 55–6).[21] After the interview with Fr Conmee, Stephen steps into daylight and recounts the scene to his classmates, who then hoist him up for applause. Here is the real drama, as he 'told them what he had said and what the rector had said' and the fellows 'closed round him in a ring, pushing against one another to hear' (*P* 60). Stephen's performance may have been rehearsed before the backdrop of a longer, specifically Catholic, tradition (exemplified by the portraits) but his audience is the more local and palpable one of contemporary schoolfellows, that is, the potential constituents of an emerging class of Catholic professionals. Yet the would-be writer is not attracted to the crowd: Stephen 'escaped' from the self-satisfied audience. As with the play-scene that shortly follows this, in which Stephen acts the part of a 'farcical pedagogue' (*P* 77), its significance lies in the recording, imagining and observation of the play's reception. In this second example, the audience is at first identified as a cultural class, 'Old Belvedereans' (*P* 76) and family visitors; next it is more narrowly projected as a specific recipient ('he saw her . . . eyes watching him'); and then finally it is observed during the play as an indefinite collective – 'the innumerable faces of the void' (*P* 90). Joyce here offers a reflection on his own reception. This pattern in notation of the audience is indicative of the reception of the text: a potential readership among peers is narrowed to a few specific readers (who are recorded in *Stephen Hero*) and then, as their roles are erased or transformed, the final published text implies not so much an audience as reception among a 'void'. There is a historical echo here although the patterning also illustrates Joyce's continuing transformation of that middle-class readership. While *The Belvederian* would help populate *Ulysses* (providing names for characters and establishments), it is not clear that *Ulysses* would help populate Belvedere.[22]

To those who knew Joyce in the first years of the twentieth century, it was his 'novel' in progress – *Stephen Hero* – rather than his stories, his criticism or even his poetry that was considered to be his primary work. When, in the 1904 of *Ulysses*, Mulligan makes the snide comment that Stephen might write something in ten years, it not only anticipates the beginning of *Ulysses* a decade after its setting; it is also a backward glance, on Joyce's part, to another work and a lost readership, a small agglomeration of family, friends and acquaintances who read *Stephen Hero*, or at least had it read to them. It has been suggested that *Stephen Hero* presupposes a readership just as parochial and censorious as the college president, whereas *A Portrait* appeals to more worldly, knowing readers for whom such censorship was – as for Joyce – not to be feared.[23] This might be borne out by the private circle of friends who appreciated, in the first version, those satirical moments at the expense of people they knew, but who, when the satiric gaze fell on them, were distracted by the petty squabble of memory. Cosgrave's reaction is typical: both 'greatly pleased' at the caricature of others and upset at suggestions that he would not stand a round (*Letters* II, 103–4). Similarly, J. F. Byrne retorted, 'I wonder why you have satirized your friends; was it because they had no money?'[24] C. P. Curran, who read both versions of the novel with more perspicacity than many others, wrote to Joyce that the 'friendly readers' of *A Portrait* felt they had been assembled as a homogenous group simply to act as foil to Stephen ('the only character you were really interested in').[25]

The first readers of *Stephen Hero* had been Joyce's mother, sister and brother, and his college friends; when, ten years later, he rewrote it as *A Portrait*, among the first readers were Dora Marsden and Ezra Pound. This passage from the familiar to the foreign partially describes the trajectory of Joyce's reception. At the same time, however, he continually responded to his 'local' readership, to its cultural implications and to the notion of a local or private audience (he went on in later life giving small-group readings of 'Work in Progress'). Dedalus's characterisation of the English language might be considered in this light, for the point about reception is that it too is both 'familiar' and 'foreign' (*P* 205). Indeed, Joyce's inscriptions of a familiar and local audience show that it can often be precisely the 'otherness' within the supposedly familiar with which it is most difficult to come to terms.

III

While Joyce's education offered one possible source of readers (and a means of reading) it also constituted an institution in which writing could be monitored. In this respect, the form of Joyce's novel is revealing (and concealing), for it may be taken as a kind of confession. Indeed, much of Joyce's early writing shows a notable engagement with the confessional mode, which allows him to inscribe while distancing a 'local' readership of family and friends. In Joyce's version of this form – for instance, the well-known reversal of roles between boy-narrator and Fr Flynn in 'The Sisters' – the confessor (or priest) and the penitent are mutually impli- cated. This confusion of roles is suggestive of two related and powerful aspects of Joyce's work: a refusal to submit to forms of censorship and the essentially undecidable nature of confession. The reader cannot assume the role of the priest since the capacity to 'forgive' or to judge is consist- ently sidestepped. As with the moral dilemmas that keep priests in work, Joyce's readers, it is intimated, would require 'books as thick as the *Post Office Directory* and as closely printed as the law notices in the newspaper, elucidating all these intricate questions' (*D* 5). The result is a displacement of confessional roles, that is, a relinquishment of the metaphysics of guilt that would inhere in the act of judging.

In Trieste in 1905, Joyce became interested in the question of confes- sional writing and its reception when his 'novel' – including 'ardent wayward confessions' (*P* 252) – was passed among family and friends back in Dublin. Indeed, it was sometimes accompanied by letters outlin- ing the author's latest scrapes (*Letters* I, 55). Writing to Stanislaus, Joyce referred to Lermontov's remark on Rousseau's posthumous *Confessions*, that 'they were vitiated by the fact that Rousseau read them to his friends' (*Letters* II, 106), which is to say that the point of confessing is corrupted or delegitimised by being shared among interested parties. In sharing his confessions with friends before his death, then, Rousseau was open to the charge of ingratiating himself. It is instructive to follow some of the threads in this citation. Rousseau's 'Preamble' to his *Confessions* is itself a reworking of Montaigne's address 'Au Lecteur' in his *Essais*.[26] There Montaigne purports to lay himself open (like the volume itself) before the reader who has been invited into the author's private inner circle since the book is 'dedicated to the private convenience of my relatives and friends'.[27] It was precisely Montaigne's patriarchic sense of security and social superiority that allowed this gesture to be recorded positively as a way of entrusting the safe dissemination of his life's work to a familiar reader.[28] By contrast, Rousseau – a social and religious outsider in Catholic France, and a victim of censorship – asserts his difference from his peers and, consequently, the strangeness of the autobiographical subject matter. Not unlike Stephen Dedalus, he insists 'Simply myself . . . I am different' ['Moi seul . . . je suis autre']. For Rousseau, the apparent trust in a smooth textual transmission ('a portrait in every way true to nature') is all the while ironically undercut by his failing memory, which has required 'immaterial embellishment' to 'fill a void'.[29] The textual insecurity of Rousseau's *Confessions* bespeaks his political insecurity. Joyce's position is similar to the extent that he too was an 'outsider', and no doubt the parallels with Rousseau's situation were partly responsible for Joyce's interest in Lermontov's remark just as *Stephen Hero* was undergoing revision and dissemination. Indeed, one reviewer of *A Portrait* would perceptively note that 'Whether it is self-portraiture we do not know, but it has the intimate veracity, or appearance of veracity, of the great writers of confessions.'[30] In the critical assessment of Joyce's first novel, much attention has been paid to the ironic narrative voice; it is worth noting that its form implies also a distantiation of its readership.

It seems to have been a rendering of the text as impure or illegitimate, by virtue of its being read to an 'inner circle', that stirred Joyce. A short time later, he complained to his brother that 'the MS of my novel' has 'circulated from hand to hand' in Dublin (*Letters* II, 114): he had heard that Thomas Kettle, his University College acquaintance, was now reading it, and feared that it might be passed on to others (Stanislaus dutifully retrieved it). This episode suggests that Joyce may already have been thinking of how culpability resides on both sides of the confessional screen, and of the form's inherently undecidable character.[31] Unlike Rousseau, Joyce makes no appeal to an audience or address to his readers and holds up no model for judgement. This non-address is politically charged: it admits its difference and hints at oppression or exclusion. When he alludes to material scenes of reception and the acts of particular readers, Joyce suggests their vitiation, that is, the incompletion, corruption (of the already corrupt reader) and invalidation that attends those scenes of reading.

If Joyce feared the charge levelled at Rousseau, he might have been reassured by an entry in his brother's diary from 1903. Stanislaus had commented that, whereas Joyce could 'become the Rousseau of Ireland': Rousseau, indeed, might be accused of cherishing the secret hope of turning away the anger of disapproving readers by confessing unto them, but Jim cannot be suspected of this. His great passion is a fierce scorn of what he calls the "rabblement".'[32] 'Jim' cannot be accused of surreptitiously ingratiating himself with the 'rabblement', who were not really his readers at all, although this comment does imply the closeness of Joyce to that detested 'rabblement'. It also implies that in some respects they might have been assumed to form an audience for Joyce, being also Catholic and middle class. In the first instance, Joyce's readers had been family and friends, including, of course, Stanislaus himself. Joyce's 'confessions' might be seen as an attempt to record and transfigure these initial readers but not to write for them.

Autobiographical confession is a peculiarly specular form in which the younger subject is recreated, displayed and viewed by the later self. The structure of Catholic confession even anticipates this later redemptive self and so has a transcendent double temporality built into it. Joyce obliquely transmutes the sacrament into a kind of writing (Stanislaus noted that his brother 'confesses in a foreign language'[33]) so that, in his fiction, there is only an opaque specularity between the author and the 'artist as a young man'. Such a backward glance introduces a double-time to the narrative (which we will see replayed as a forward look in 'Scylla and Charybdis'). The paradoxical 'double-time' within a phrase is what Derrida calls a 'contretemps', a term which he assigns to Montaigne's repetition of a saying attributed to Aristotle, 'O my friends, there is no friend.'[34] It is just such a contradictory notion of friendship (or self – other relations) that structures Joyce's reception among his 'local' readership. The appeal cancels itself in the writing. Moreover, at the fold in this structure in Joyce's more autobiographical work, between *A Portrait* and *Ulysses*, is a personal confession: Stephen's refusal to kneel at the deathbed of his mother (admitted at the beginning of the latter book) – itself recalling the refusal to have confession at the end of the former book. As the rupture from the mother is the primary example, and sometimes cause (with Cranly and Mulligan especially), of Stephen's lost friendships, another sense of 'contretemps' is suggested, that is, a disagreement or dispute. The contretemps, here, then is the dispute in the fold of the reflective narrative that conditions Joyce's reception among his familiar and local readership.

The contretemps thus signals a double-time, a disagreement and a paradoxical address. Joyce's inscription of his reception carries these meanings but it also situates that reception as a form of confessional in which a past response among local readers is replayed and transformed. In doing so, these scenes establish a notion of reception as a form of ongoing responsiveness between specific reader and the author but also between later readers and the historical moment.

IV

In a number of cases, forms of confession are made by Stephen Dedalus to women: May Daedalus, E–C– and the unnamed woman in *Giacomo Joyce*. For these different characters reading allows complex forms of assumed custody: a combination of surveillance and guardianship. Their associations with institutions such as the family, the Church, and education, show that reading – particularly women's reading – could enact a form of social surveillance. It seems that their inscribed responses are based on particular episodes in Joyce's life, but in each case Joyce either erased the character from his writing or diluted her presence. The traces of their responses that the writing still carries are indicative of Joyce's transformation of their surveillance into a parodic and self-defeating discourse, while at the same time continuing to allow Stephen Dedalus to construct literary reception as male.

The scene in *Stephen Hero* in which May Daedalus is depicted as a reader/listener begins with a summary which again confuses the roles between penitent and confessor as between writer and reader.

Stephen regarded his loans of manuscripts as elaborate flag-practices with phrases.[35] He did not consider his mother a dullard but the result of his second disappointment in the search for appreciation was that he was enabled to place the blame on the shoulders of others: he had enough responsibilities thereon already, inherited and acquired. (*SH* 78)

Through this staged spectacle of false opposites by which 'he was enabled to place the blame' on others, Stephen positions the reader (in this case his mother) as confessor or judge, but also absolves the penitent writer-self *in advance.* The double-time of Catholic confession hints at this heretical strategy since if anything can be forgiven, so anything can be committed. Stephen has already taken on something of the guile of Hamlet who, having killed Polonius, beseeched his mother to 'Forgive me this my virtue.' In turn, the claim to innocence suggests its own inducement of guilt if 'Virtue itself of vice must pardon beg.'[36] Although Stephen attempts to shift responsibility onto his readers and listeners, it is apparent from Joyce's undoing of the confessional form, and in his distance from Stephen, that responsibility consists not in taking or placing blame but in a movement of responsiveness between the roles of penitent and confessor.

Looking ahead to the publication of *A Portrait* in 1916, Joyce's sister Mary ('May') recalled that he had read from its early drafts (i.e. *Stephen Hero*) to their mother: 'The stir Dubliners made will be nothing to this,' she wrote. 'You have rewritten it since we lived in St Peters Terrace when we used to be all put out of the room when you were reading each new chapter for Mother. I used to hide under the sofa to hear it, until you said I might stay. I am looking forward to reading it now' (*Letters* II, 383). A similar scene is depicted in those early drafts when Stephen twice reads his infamous paper for the L&H to his mother as she irons and folds handkerchiefs, shortly after Stephen's apparent abnegation of responsibility. She is sufficiently alarmed by his paper to read Ibsen. Having accepted the Church's interpellation of her role as responsible guardian (an anticipation of the censorship that her son would soon encounter from his Jesuit teachers), May Daedalus is caught between interested pride and parental concern: her judgement on the circulation of such 'dangerous authors' is that it would only do harm to the ill or the 'uneducated'. (Although the extent to which she herself is 'educated' remains unclear, that Mrs Daedalus used to read 'a great deal' before her marriage suggests a certain aspiration to cultured gentility.[37]) Yet this 'proper' response – to take custody – has been preceded by two crucial factors. First, her son's construction of her 'uneducated' ignorance ('the mind of such a woman') implies her own susceptibility to the 'dangers' of Ibsen and, by extension, her own son's work. Second, her own hesitancy ('she said . . . she couldn't follow'): it is this lack of surety in her initial reaction that suggests May Daedalus might be a fit reader (*SH* 78–9). As we will see, it is the complacency of some groups that inhibits their reading. By diverting the reception of Stephen's paper through these channels, Joyce's presentation of the scene challenges the rights of the Church and education to prescribe a readership, indeed it questions what exactly an 'educated' reader would be like.

By omitting May Dedalus from his list of readers and listeners in 'Scylla and Charybdis', Stephen constructs a solely male reception (like his schooling and the Royal University, both the newspaper offices and the National Library appear to be all-male preserves). Emma Clery, for instance, had wanted to hear Stephen's paper – but the L&H was male-only.[38] The exclusion of Stephen's mother from this list echoes the abbreviation of Emma Clery to E–C– and the removal of Maurice (based on Stanislaus) between *Stephen Hero* and *A Portrait*. The scene in which Stephen anticipates his villanelle being read by Emma's family signals a further claustrophobic repression in which the woman-as-reader is elbowed out of the scene by her male counterparts.

If he sent her the verses? They would be read out at breakfast amid the tapping of eggshells. Folly indeed! The brothers would laugh and try to wrest the page from each other with their strong hard fingers. The suave priest, her uncle, seated in his armchair, would hold the page at arm's length, read it smiling and approve of the literary form. (*P* 241)

This passage is also subject to a double time frame, since it begins with the admission that 'he had written verses for her again after ten years'. It thus calls to mind both the current act of writing and a previous scene of composition and imagined reception, not only giving a depth to Stephen's history but also recalling Joyce's own earlier composition of the same villanelle that he had written as a schoolboy. As Joyce now finds a place for his old verse, the specific reader has been overwritten by the fictional transformation of the poem and the near-anonymity of E–C– echoes this loss of identity in the process of reception.[39]

The composition of verses to Emma is also a symbolic redress by Stephen to his mother. Going back to the scene ten years previously, in the second chapter, his poem 'To E–C–' had, from 'force of habit', been couched in the form of an educational exercise (with A.M.D.G. and L.D.S. written at the head and foot as in a schoolbook). Once completed, this exercise allowed him immediately to enter 'into his mother's bedroom' where he 'gazed at his face for a long time in the mirror of her dressingtable' (*P* 73–4). Writing verses to E–C– was another means of reverting to his mother with the possibility of seeing himself through her perspective (in her mirror).[40] The omission of May Dedalus as a reader between *Stephen Hero* and *A Portrait* is hence symbolically alluded to in Stephen's poem, which has both reduced Emma to a typographical cypher and reinscribed the mother as symbolic reader. A further comparison may be drawn between May's custodial interest in Stephen's paper and Emma's handing over of his poem to her uncle and brothers, each suggesting an impending censorship provoked by a female audience that is subservient to Church control.[41] In the reconstruction of a would-be readership from *Stephen Hero* to *Ulysses*, Joyce shows that

Stephen's imagined public reception is a male one, although a private female, and especially motherly, audience cannot be expunged so readily as a name from a list. The implications of this manoeuvre can be followed more fully through the use to which Joyce put another confessional text with an educational setting, *Giacomo Joyce*. Here, too, a specific response is reinscribed anonymously and then feeds into Joyce's later writing, illustrating some of the key points of his scenes of reception.

V

To the extent that, as with *Stephen Hero*, *Giacomo Joyce* was reserved from publication and so perhaps had no expected public audience, it must solicit a different order of response from later readers. The publication of a 'private' text presents ambiguities for any notion of reception, especially if that text has an intended reader. *Giacomo Joyce* is a special case among Joyce's work in that it apparently inscribes in its final line a direct addressee, a specific reader to whom the text is dedicated. At the same time, the text is clearly a fiction: if its addressee is 'an inscription of the reader within the poem as crucial to it', as Eide says, then a certain ontological uncertainty must be attributed to 'her'.[42] This addressee is also obscure, 'Envoy: Love me, love my umbrella' (*GJ* 16). Moreover, the fact that Joyce kept the manuscript, retrieving it in later life, could suggest that he was aware of its public (scholarly and material) as well as personal value, and therefore that it would be read by others.[43] In any case, his redeployment of some of its fragments in *A Portrait* and *Ulysses* also implies a scattering of its singular address.

Un-named, the text explicitly objectifies 'She' (*GJ* 15), the principal model for whom was most probably Amalia Popper, a seventeen-year-old pupil of Joyce's in 1908–9.[44] In addition to the weight of historical evidence which suggests that Popper is the inscribed reader-character, this apparently private text appears to invite an identification of its addressee, who may be recognised in the frequent close conjunction of the letters a and p throughout the text. If its first word seems like a tease to later readers, it is also self-answering: 'Who? A pale face' (*GJ* 1): 'Who' is 'A p'.[45] If Popper was the immediate addressee of this text she was also, in most interpretations, its victim.[46] The object of a patriarchal gaze, she is consistently seen as through a veil, associated with a liminal physique: quizzing glasses, beating eyelids, a mask of false smiles, laced boots, a black veil and an orange shift, the 'lace edging' of underskirt, a furled umbrella. Her Jewishness, and so her 'otherness' to the narrator, is emphasised, as is her perceived intellectual immaturity (although Popper was apparently an excellent student).

The writer has less shyness about naming himself as 'Jim' and 'Jamesy' (*GJ* 15, 6): the eye and 'I' of the text are that of the author of '*The Portrait of the Artist*'. At times Joyce himself used the Italian 'Giacomo' or the Triestino 'Jacamo'.[47] In this regard, the text bears some of the hallmarks of a confession: a private declaration; with apparently one direct addressee; it recounts an incident of potential shame to the writer who explicitly identifies himself. This reading would imply that the text protects 'the victim' by not naming her. Whereas the Jim of the text hardly confesses, the writing of the text can be seen as itself a partial redress especially in so far as it explicitly identifies the social relations of its participants and offers a reflective time frame. As with the inscribed fictionalisation of Popper's own reading, later readers are confronted with an apparently private sexual and autobiographical confession. Readers are thus placed in an analogous position, one in which simply to read is to be implicated in a sexually voyeuristic process. The roles of confessor and penitent are again confused.

At the time of writing, Joyce was known in the Triestine press as an English-language teacher rather than a writer and as 'Prof. James Joyce' for his lectures on Shakespeare (which are referred to in *Giacomo Joyce*).[48] This teacher evidently gave his unfinished autobiographical novel, *A Portrait*, to his students to read. A humble letter from Ettore Schmitz (Italo Svevo) dated February 1909 contains his assigned 'review' of the first three chapters (*Letters* II, 226–7). Popper may well have been given a similar task; certainly She has.

She says that, had *The Portrait of the Artist* been frank only for frankness' sake, she would have asked why I had given it to her to read. O you would, would you? A lady of letters. (*GJ* 12)

The response to *Portrait* is astute, for it sceptically anticipates the casual censorship that John Quinn alluded to when he declared it 'pas pour la jeune fille'.[49] In doing so, She reveals the narrator's sexual design: it is, in effect, a challenge to her teacher, a coded recognition of the scene – her reading of his confessional text – as an attempted seduction. Joseph Valente remarks how 'Joyce' and his object have entered an asymmetrical reversal: that in giving his autobiographical novel to her, he becomes an exhibitionist while remaining the narrating voyeur; in turn, She becomes the voyeur by reading it yet remains the narrated exhibition on show in his later text. For Valente, the scene is primarily narcissistic: 'Amalia' (as he calls her) becomes 'his symbolic double and ideal reader, an enlarging mirror for his ego'.[50] Yet Joyce's act of giving his book to his students to read was more than the textual self-aggrandisement of a self-dramatising autobiographical narrating voice. Popper was not an 'ideal reader' but, like Schmitz, an actual student and reader of Joyce, one whose voice has been ventriloquised – somewhat violently – into a more or less fictional image of itself. By setting his own novel as a reading assignment to his students, Joyce was not only exhibiting himself but also surveying their reactions. The response he has (re)created, rather than exemplifying her unambiguous victimhood, implicates the act of reading as a necessary surveillance in which she detects the ulterior motive of his confessional *Portrait*. As we have seen, however, such 'surveillance' is not that of a distant spectator but a mutual reading. While Joyce further erodes her voice through the use of reported speech rather than dialogue, her readerly reactions continue to echo in the text as it is reread.

In two significant and related ways this scene echoes in Joyce's later work and contributes to that work's implicit conceptualisation of reception. First, it shows how literary reception is a 'responsive' cultural dialogic, a question, in part, of a mutual social surveillance in which such markers as racial appearance, age and position inflect the scene. Second, it begins a suggestion – made explicit in Joyce's later writing – that the act of reading, because so socially embedded, is itself sexual. Across all of Joyce's writing there is a proximity of watching and reading, as if either to write or to read is inevitably to be complicit in an illicit voyeurism.

On Sandymount Strand in 'Proteus', Stephen Dedalus has just 'scribbled words' – his poem that readers will not see until 'Aeolus' – and immediately a scene of imagined reception follows. He asks himself, 'Who watches me here? Who ever anywhere will read these written words. Signs on a white field' (*U* 3.414–15). This well-known line is usually taken to anticipate Bloom in 'Nausicaa' and to signify the self-reflexivity of Joyce's presentation of Dedalus, the signs in question being those of the white pages of *Ulysses* itself. A continual to-and-fro of reception plays out in Dedalus's mind. After asking 'Who?', his next line is, 'Somewhere to someone in your flutiest voice' (*U* 3.415–16): an invocation of the inevitably indeterminable future audience, but also, perhaps, a recollection. This can be supported by the direct address to an imagined or remembered lover that shortly follows: 'Someone' becomes 'You' as if a specific respondent is brought to mind. By the time his 'monologue' (but actually more of an imaginary dialogue) reaches the following paragraph, a particular, anticipated scene of reception seems to have formed. That paragraph is, I would suggest, an allusion to 'her' reading of *A Portrait* as presented in *Giacomo Joyce*.

> She trusts me, her hand gentle, the longlashed eyes. Now where the blue hell am I bringing her beyond the veil? Into the ineluctable modality of the ineluctable visuality. She, she, she. What she? The virgin at Hodges Figgis' window on Monday looking in for one of the alphabet books you were going to write. Keen glance you gave her. Wrist through the braided jesse of her sunshade. She lives in Leeson park, with a grief and kickshaws, a lady of letters. Talk that to someone else, Stevie: a pickmeup. Bet she wears those curse of God stays suspenders and yellow stockings, darned with lumpy wool. Talk about apple dumplings, *piuttosto*. Where are your wits?
>   Touch me. Soft eyes. (*U* 3.424–36)

Though more complexly interwoven – and ultimately more ironically distanced – than the direct gaze found in *Giacomo Joyce*, this is still a voyeuristic act addressed to a voyeuristic reader, with clear overtones of She from that earlier, private text. In each case the phrase 'a lady of letters' condescendingly describes the character, though there are also other features that recall *Giacomo Joyce*.[51] 'What she?' recalls both Stephen's 'Who?' and the 'Who?' that opens *Giacomo*. Stephen's 'veil' of sight recalls the veils, actual and symbolic, associated with *Giacomo*'s 'her'; this woman carries a sunshade rather than an umbrella; the underwear of each is imagined, albeit in different tones; the phrase 'touch me' (which Molly also uses) is thought by both Stephen and the Jim of *Giacomo*; and 'her' eyes and hands are the focal point of his gaze, as they are for Stephen's image of this woman reader in *Ulysses*. Not least, each is a 'virgin' (*GJ* 9). If the woman reader in 'Proteus' is a distorted version of *Giacomo*'s representation of Popper, she has been given an almost de-sexualised innocence and (a harsh punishment this) lumpy woollen stockings. All the same, the phrase 'apple dumplings, *piuttosto*' with its 'ap' sign, Italian speech, and anticipation of the young 'apple harlottes' (*FW* 113.16) in the *Finnegans Wake* letter, reinforces the suspicion that a transformed, spectral Popper lingers in the Dublin of *Ulysses*. Joyce's pupil, has, then, gone from being an actual reader of *A Portrait*, to a textual She, harassed in the eyes of her professor, to a 'virgin reader' of Stephen's imaginary juvenilia in *Ulysses*. As one of those reading figures who populate Joyce's texts, this 'virgin at the window' inscribes a personal history of Joyce's reception, which is also a narrative of the sexuality of reading.

The sexual complicity of reading is spelt out in *Giacomo* in the narrator's recollection that her 'quiet cold fingers have touched the pages, foul and fair, on which my shame shall glow forever'. Both the repressed,

erotic fingers ('Have they never erred?' – *GJ* 13) and the 'immortal' text are
kept in view. (In *A Portrait*, the 'strong hard fingers' (*P* 241) of E–C–'s
brothers holding Stephen's verses similarly imply the somatic nature of
reading though here they appear more violating than erotic.) The knowledge acquired from her teacher, voyeur and author means that She is
'vitiated' in the inscription of her reading. The particular care taken by the
author in copying out the short fragments of *Giacomo Joyce* is pertinent
here: most of its pages are dominated by blank spaces, almost as if the
text were but a screen for his projection. The white field, then, is itself a
sign, perhaps of the narcissistic fetishism that dominates the page.

By contrast, *Finnegans Wake* is visually dominated by print and, not
by chance, the sexual roles have altered. The pupil–teacher relationship
is again one where reading is sexualised by rendering the book as body
and where specular appropriation attempts but fails to control its object,
but here the pupil-reader gives as good as she gets. In the 'nightlessons'
chapter (II.2), a lengthy footnote in the voice of Issy (in the guise of her
twin Maggy) refers to Popper:

I remembered all your pupil–teacher erringnesses in perfection class. You
shouldn't write you can't if you w'udn't pass for undevelopmented. This is the
propper way to say that, Sr. (*FW* 279 F1)

Signorina Popper – or possibly her father, Signor Popper, who is referred
to in *Giacomo* – is coyly alluded to, just as those imperfect 'erring' classes
recall 'her' unerring fingers. In the earlier text, the book She held was
symbolically Joyce's body and life; however here Issy is the book – 'I lie on
my back spine' – handled by the teacher-figure as they 'conjugate together' (to get her). Issy also refers to 'my. Impending marriage' – an
allusion to Popper's engagement in 1913 which broke off Joyce's interest
(when she did the 'propper' thing). In the *Wake*, however, the reader
writes back: Issy-as-Popper replies to her teacher, and does so in part
through the title of a teaching guide used by Joyce, *Errors in the Use of
English.*[52]

While Joyce presents reading and learning as somatic and sexual he
also situates reception within an educational context in which power attempts (but fails) to control a knowledge which in turn corrupts. The
scene of reception in *Giacomo Joyce* intimates a physical surveillance
which is mutually corrupting; the confused confessional roles suggested
in Joyce's previous work make this once more an appropriate mode. In
May Dedalus, Emma Clery and She, Joyce has overwritten some of his
notable women readers just as Stephen Dedalus omits them from his list

in the library. If this is 'placing the blame onto others', as *Stephen Hero* had it, then it is not only an abnegation but also a deferral of responsibility, for it enacts a series of responses between writer, reader, text and other readers. The revision of 'her' response to *A Portrait* into *Ulysses* is an implicit admission of Joyce's inability to control his reception: the private text spirals into a series of indeterminable signs. It is as if these responses or judgements could only be 'atoned' by rewriting them, and this act in itself sets up a dissonant echo: not only are later readers inadvertently reading within the terms of their predecessors but so too the 'contretemps' of the negative response reverberates through the writing.

VI

At roughly the mid-point of *Ulysses*, Stephen brings together (some of) those early readers, registering their chronological order of response. It is a key moment in both Joyce's fiction and his scrutiny of reception. 'Where is your brother? Apothecaries' hall. My whetstone. Him, then Cranly, Mulligan: now these' (*U* 9.977–8). In addition to the omission of the women respondents from Stephen's library list, other interesting aspects of his conceptualisation of an audience emerge here. Notably, 'your brother' – not 'my brother' – features in this self-interrogation. Of course, Stanislaus was a key figure in Joyce's initial reception. Having been very often the first reader of his early material, Stanislaus must have wondered at the question Stephen poses to himself: 'Where is your brother?' The 'whetstone' (a device used by 'Kinch, the knifeblade' (*U* 1.55) for sharpening) is peculiarly absent from every other page of *Ulysses*, as well as *A Portrait*, 'Maurice' famously having been silenced with the stewing manuscript of *Stephen Hero*. Perhaps after all 'a brother is as easily forgotten as an umbrella' (*U* 9.975). Like 'She' in *Giacomo Joyce*, the brother is now 'Him'. This brief nod of recognition is one of admission; it is even perhaps confessional. It places 'Him' as the first in a series and in doing so helps create a template for Joyce's reception in which Stanislaus is the primary reader. Indeed, the brother's invaluable but partial testimony has been a bedrock of Joyce criticism for decades, having had a powerful influence on Ellmann in particular.

The distinctly male lineage of reception spelt out by Stephen has contributed to a sense of Joyce's relationship with his readers as antagonistic and even oppositional: male rivals to be overcome. It is Joyce's portrayal of how Stephen constructs reception that is important. Stanislaus, J. F. Byrne, Gogarty. . . as if these readers of the early fiction and verse could be dismissed as versions of the same, and, having been dismissed, replaced by a different cultural set, an overtly literary and learned one, 'these'.[53] Stephen 'now' posits a collective set of responses and no longer only a list of singular names. The deictic 'these' is the first explicitly collective grouping of Joyce's critics to appear in his work. Since the characters grouped under 'these' bear the actual names of some of Joyce's contemporaries and literary figures whom he knew, they differ from Him, Cranly and Mulligan. Joyce thus registers in this list a sense of cultural shift and a movement from one kind of representation to another. The introduction of 'Best', 'Eglinton', 'Lyster' and 'AE '– not to mention all those others, including 'WB', 'Martyn' and 'Dowden' – heightens the self-conscious fictionality of the episode. By alluding to these figures under their actual names or accepted pseudonyms, Joyce draws attention to the relationship between his writing and the particular people and episodes to which it refers. The effect is both to allude to a particular historical moment and to question the veracity of the scene. In addition, the apparent consignment of past readers to history is, however, also a reminder of them and a crucial context for different, later respondents. 'These', then, establishes a relationship with 'those' that have gone; just as decades of Joyce's later readers read through the readers portrayed here. A further implication of the list, then, is of rivalry between different reading groups, and this is precisely the political issue at stake in the episode.

As is widely recognised, the temporal disjunction between the setting of this scene in 1904 and the writing of it over a decade later is written into the text. Stephen tells himself, 'See this. Remember . . . Listen' (*U* 9.294, 9.300): a form of mental note-taking for future writing and thus a proleptic contretemps in which 'time is out of joint'. The combination of this disjunction with the close-quartered proximity of characters and linguistic registers produces not so much an opposition between apparent rivals (viewer and object; Stephen and Eglinton; Stephen's Shakespeare and Dowden's Shakespeare; Catholic nationalism and Anglo-Irish paternalism; fact and fiction; quotation and invention) as an uncomfortably close mutual surveillance. In this respect, the episode presents a physically uneasy, claustrophobic scene which Stephen alludes to when departing 'the vaulted cell into a shattering daylight of no thought' (*U* 9.1111–12). Set in the librarian's inner sanctum (just off the reading room), a judgemental audience receives Stephen Dedalus with respectful scepticism. Eglinton's body language is read at several points by Stephen, notably 'leaning back to judge' (*U* 9.152); as it turns out,

Eglinton is also the jury in this mock-trial. Every purring voice or creaking step seems to be noticed. Even the occasional frame-breaking thoughts of Stephen – 'in the future, the sister of the past, I may see myself as I sit here now but by reflection from that which then I shall be' (*U* 9.383–5) – tend to reinforce the sense that the whole episode is about the disturbing physical, cultural and intellectual proximity of different forms of reading, including, of course, the reception of *Ulysses* itself.

Recent critical readings of this episode have concentrated on its political contexts, given its apparent placement within a specific situation, and have generally concluded that it shows Joyce's opposition to Revivalism and the Anglo-Irish.[54] However, these terms are not adequate to encompass the array of characters in the scene. As Clare Hutton has pointed out, none of the company accurately fits the label 'Anglo-Irish'. Russell is the only character generally known as a revivalist and Lyster is more aligned with an older literary culture represented by Edward Dowden than with the Revival.[55] The most prominent among 'these' is Eglinton, whose alliance with Dowden and role as co-editor of *Dana* places him as a mediating figure between different generations and cultural movements. Stephen's construction of his audience in the library as a single treacherous group, one which is other to himself, is indicative of the scene's mutual surveillance while in fact being at odds with the historical record. Crucially, it is also at odds with Joyce's careful but subtle marking of the differences within the group, with Lyster depicted as a Quaker, Eglinton as 'a merry puritan' (*U* 9.873) from a poor country background, Best as effeminate but of no determinate background and Russell as an aloof theosophist. By incorporating these ambivalently hostile figures, *Ulysses* suggests not a straightforward opposition with Joyce but a displacement, as well as a critique, of their readings. It is precisely the uneasy proximity of people and positions – the surveillance that inheres in the conditions of reception in Joyce's Ireland – that structures their relations. A distinction must therefore be made between Stephen's category 'these' and Joyce's subtle undermining of that implied collective. At the same time, it is necessary to recognise the important differences – of age, religion, power – between Stephen and his interlocutors.

As a young man, Joyce would 'seek out' an audience for his stories or ideas. Having exhausted Byrne and college friends he moved onto others at the National Library. The tale of Joyce offering his earliest draft of *A Portrait* to Eglinton for publication in *Dana*, in the National Library in 1904, is suggestive: 'he observed me silently as I read, and when

I handed it back to him with the timid observation that I did not care to publish what was to myself incomprehensible, he replaced it silently in his pocket'. If the picture of an unfit reception is embodied here, it indicates also that Joyce carefully observed these responses. Indeed, he caught dialogue so well, Eglinton surmised, that he 'even then was "taking notes"'.[56] Eglinton's review of *Ulysses* in *The Dial* in October 1922 certainly picked up the echo of that moment (a handwritten copy was sent to Joyce): he noted somewhat self-consciously that the book portrayed 'that company of real imaginary personalities whom we know better than our nearest acquaintances, perhaps better than ourselves'.[57] The formulation *real imaginary* might be awkward but it gets at the crux of Joyce's formal development of a mode in which the fictional and the historical entwine – and this is precisely the point of the library episode with its staged 'debate' that underlines the performativity of knowledge. Recollecting a discussion at the National Library, Eglinton later twinged at recalling 'things actually said'.[58] While it can be tempting to read 'Scylla and Charybdis' as a restaging of that private moment in the Library – as Eglinton himself clearly did – it should be recalled that there is also a broader cultural and literary dynamic at work here. Eglinton's odd position as a privileged reader of Joyce – yet one who to a significant extent could not read him – plays out in this episode in the form of a political contestation over reading strategies that maintains the difference of any reader, including the closest.

By having Stephen construct his audience into a falsely homogenous group, *Ulysses* implies that reception is always in a sense a misrepresentation – not just a partial (in both senses) reading but also a means of categorisation. The text thus reflects upon the necessarily political character of reception, further suggesting that writing (or performance) is often already moulded to a particular form of institutional appropriation. In 'Scylla and Charybdis' Joyce stages a political dispute over the reading of Shakespeare in order to effect a splintering of deterministic habits of reception.

VII

The cultural politics of reception can be further traced through an examination of the reading strategies within Irish education that inform the library episode. 'Scylla and Charybdis' enacts a dispute over the politics of literary reception, explicitly that of Shakespeare but implicitly that of Joyce as well. By setting Stephen's reading of Shakespeare against the interpretations of Eglinton and others, Joyce sets up a political opposition between Stephen and Edward Dowden, then Chair of English at Trinity College, a well-known Shakespearean scholar and Unionist agitator, who, although not physically in attendance, is an important presence in the scene. In this argument, Joyce lends to Stephen a strategy and a set of terms from his own education.

At University College, Joyce was familiar with Fr George O'Neill's support for the Bacon theory since he scoffed at it in a meeting of the L&H, possibly even enlisting the arguments of Dowden, a strong opponent of the idea.[59] It was instead the teaching of Fr Joseph Darlington – the model for the dean of studies in *Portrait* (and Fr Butt in *Stephen Hero*) – which influenced Joyce and left its mark on *Ulysses*. Darlington had introduced another reading (and spelling) of Shakespeare that was different from both Dowden's and his colleague's. His argument had been published as 'The Catholicity of Shakspere's Plays: A Lecture', in two parts in *New Ireland Review* less than a year before Joyce entered university; in addition he spoke often in College societies such as the L&H and lectured on Shakespeare. In class he taught *Hamlet* through a reading of Aristotle and Aquinas to students 'bored with the solemnities of Dowden and Bradley', as Curran recalled.[60] This interpretation lies behind Eglinton's pejorative jibe that 'Your dean of studies holds he [Shakespeare] was a holy Roman' (*U* 9.763–4). Darlington's argument chimes with Stephen's on some key points, yet Stephen's is far less earnest and makes general and implicit claims to a Catholic tradition rather than Darlington's more specific and overt assertions.

Darlington's essay is particularly pertinent here for its sensitivity to the educational context invoked in *Hamlet*. He argues that the Prince was 'the product of' the new University of Wittenberg (established at the beginning of the sixteenth century, while Laertes goes to the ancient University of Paris) and that he 'embodied' its Platonic teaching. Darlington characterises the 'morbid excess' of this Platonism as the notion that 'ideas alone have real being', resulting in a 'paralysis of the will' and consequent inability to act. He argues that, by contrast, 'Catholicism accepted the teaching of Aristotle' (but, like Stephen, he also points out that Aristotle had been 'one of Plato's own disciples'). Shakespeare is then seen to follow Aristotle, Aquinas, Dante and Thomas à Kempis as 'the last legacy of Catholicism to England'. Against this, an inappropriate Platonic education brings 'carnage and disaster' upon 'Hamlet's country – on his parents, relations and friends'.[61] In *Ulysses*, the violent excessiveness identified by Darlington is aligned with Eglinton in his remark that 'it makes my blood boil to hear anyone compare Aristotle with Plato'

(*U* 9.80–1). As with Eglinton, Russell is also associated with a Platonic essentialism that is opposed by Stephen's historicism.

While there is a certain lack of subtlety in Darlington's argument, his essay may have suggested to Joyce that historical anachronism – or, perhaps, contretemps – could be a useful literary and political device. Darlington notes that the University of Wittenberg was a 'decided anachronism' of Shakespeare's, having been founded 'long after the period of Hamlet'. Wittenberg's teaching, he contends, was ultimately responsible for embroiling 'the whole of Europe' in a war of 'frenzy and bloodshed'.[62] The overtone of Joyce's language in 'Nestor' is similarly anachronistic in its allusions to the First World War, and Stephen explicitly takes up the point in his reading of *Hamlet* in light of the Boer War.

Joyce adapted Darlington's practice of asserting a Catholic context in reading English literary history. Curran recalls 'our Aristotelian and scholastic lecturers' and remarks that Thomist thought was 'part of the general atmosphere of college discussions and entered into basic criticism in the literature classes'.[63] However, the teaching of English at University College showed little sense of place in its syllabus design, which found no room for Irish writing.[64] The syllabus, then, may not have encouraged a particularly Catholic ethos in its study of English but it is apparent that such an ethos did permeate the institution and some of the teaching. It certainly did in philosophy, or metaphysics, which was designed to allow for a Catholic training: this was particularly the case with the National University where the subject was dominated by seminarians until the middle of the twentieth century (since the University could not, under the terms of its constitution, teach religion *per se*).[65] Stephen's argument, although hardly pious, is partially a reading of Shakespeare from the viewpoint of an imagined, alternative literature syllabus. Read in these terms, his theory can be seen as a comment upon 'the university question', not only in its assertion of an alternative tradition to that of Dowden and Eglinton, but also in its display of wit and learning, which surpassed the generally feeble lectures Joyce actually attended.

Within this context, as Len Platt has argued, Stephen Dedalus appears resolutely Catholic in his learning, at least until the moment when he declares that he does not 'believe' his theory.[66] Throughout the debate, Stephen's argument has relied upon a particular intellectual tradition and education that is culturally specific, one that is alien to his audience but which also enables him to construct that audience. He deploys a language, a methodology and a history that are not fully shared with his interlocutors (it might be said that they are not even fully shared by

himself). Beginning with a silent allusion to Loyola's *Spiritual Exercises* –
'Composition of place. Ignatius Loyola, make haste to help me!'
(*U* 9.163) – the argument is regularly punctuated by the lessons of
Stephen's education: '*Amplius. Adhuc. Iterum. Posted* (*U* 9.848) are terms
of scholastic rhetoric that Stephen would have been taught by the Jesuits.
'*Amplius*' he thinks, before launching into ' – Saint Thomas, Stephen
began . . . Saint Thomas, Stephen, smiling, said, whose gorbellied works
I enjoy reading in the original' (*U* 9.770, 772, 778–9).

While Joyce adapts Darlington's practice of asserting a Catholic intellectual context for understanding Shakespeare, they also shared a pressing
political concern. Darlington's essay, like Joyce's chapter, is only superfi-
cially about Shakespeare; it is also, despite its protestations, influenced by
the current political conditions of learning and education. Having
appeared in a journal that was thoroughly embedded in 'the university
question', Darlington's argument enters a debate that ran through the
second half of the nineteenth century. The recent controversy of the late
1890s and early 1900s reiterated a discussion that had arisen many times
since the initial argument about the establishment of Newman's Catholic
University. Darlington's essay should therefore be read in the context
of both 'the university question' and Newman's more subtle, influential
and provocative advancement of Catholicism through his *Idea of the
University*. Both men point out that Catholic means 'universal'. Their
arguments for the establishment of a new University are a direct means
of promoting an alternative to a Protestant and capitalist economy of
'advancement'. As such, they also (explicitly in Newman's case; implicitly
in Darlington's) challenge the 'great' Protestant universities, especially Oxford (Newman's *alma mater*) and, in the Irish context, Trinity
College.[67] Seen in this light, Joyce's explicit signal towards Darlington's
essay only underlines the significance of the educational and sectarian
context for a reading of 'Scylla and Charybdis', with Stephen and the
Royal University caught between the current lack of a National University
in 1904 and Dowden's Trinity.

VIII

Dowden held the Professorship of English at Trinity College, from its
inception in 1867 (as one of the first Chairs in English Literature in
Britain or Ireland) until his death in 1914. Described by Eglinton, whom
he much influenced, as anti-provincial (Eglinton credits him with introducing Ibsen to Ireland), he was in fact staunchly Unionist, a man who

campaigned for less Irish representation in the House of Commons.[68] Eglinton's remark that, around 1904, 'the older culture was still represented with dignity by Dowden, Mahaffy and others' suggests his continued but waning influence.[69] Essentially English and Victorian in outlook, Dowden famously quarrelled with Yeats over Shakespeare (having been friendly with the poet's father, who *did* think of him as provincial), and was dismissive of Russell. On the other hand, the librarian, Thomas Lyster, was described by one contemporary as an 'echo' of 'Dowden's views' and his 'most ardent disciple'.[70] Similarly, Eglinton himself had been a Trinity College student and defender of Dowden, and Joyce depicts him in this position in *Ulysses*, where he has retained his 'sizar's laugh of Trinity' (*U* 9.31). The admiration was mutual: 'he [Eglinton] is the only writer of the Revival of whom Dowden regretted not having written a study'.[71] When Dowden is first mentioned in 'Scylla and Charybdis' his renown is assumed by Stephen: 'William Shakespeare and company, limited. The people's William. For terms apply: E. Dowden, Highfield house. . .' (*U* 9.729–30). Dowden's popularisation of Shakespeare is thus mocked, with Joyce alluding also to Sylvia Beach's Paris bookshop and possibly to Dowden's 'at home' gatherings on Sunday afternoons.[72] There may be some bitterness and self-irony in the phrase 'The people's William', as Joyce compares his own dearth of readers with Dowden's populist and influential pedagogy.

The terms on which Stephen takes issue with Dowden are strongly influenced by his education; Joyce's implicit criticisms of Dowden set up a political debate over literary reception that is mediated through religious, and so educational, traditions. (In 1929 Eglinton noted that Joyce had come to represent the 'ascendancy of the National University over the expiring tradition of Trinity College in Irish culture'.[73]) Yet, despite their opposed political positions, in *Ulysses* Dowden and Dedalus share a critical method: each reads Shakespeare as a comment upon his own period. As Andrew Gibson puts it, 'what separates off Dowden and Stephen from the other Shakespeareans and most opposes them to each other is their insistence on thinking politics and culture together'.[74] The assumption made by Dowden was that Elizabethan England was an integrated society whereas Ireland exemplified a fissured one. Dowden's reading of what used to be called 'the Elizabethan world picture' projected it onto an Ireland that he wished to inhabit.

Shakespere was for all time by virtue of certain powers and perceptions, but he also belonged especially to an age, his own age . . . a Protestant age, a monarchical age, an age eminently positive and practical.[75]

Dowden could only long for what he saw as the 'imperial authority' of Elizabethan poetry.[76] 'The creator of *Hamlet*', he says, 'evidently lived in no dream-world but had a vigorous grasp of positive fact.'[77] He found in Shakespeare the 'Protestant', 'monarchical', 'positive and practical' culture that he wished Ireland to be. In turn, the reality of Dowden's own position contrasts unfavourably with that age of apparent organicism, achievement and assurance. His implicit complaint that modern Irish writers were not 'patient, exact, just, enlightened' seems, again, to distinguish them from the 'positive and practical' qualities of Shakespearean England.[78] The error of this position is of course its assumption of a unified English culture against which Ireland appears split and weak; the terms are typically colonial and implicitly gendered. Dowden's interpretation is hence resolutely historicist in that he assumes the difference of his own position from the Elizabethan period and figures Ireland as a less developed, or debased, version of (English) society. Dowden's error has been repeated in readings of Joyce and Shakespeare.[79] Notably, when Eglinton came to review *Ulysses*, he did so in terms reminiscent of Dowden, bemoaning its lack of 'practical purpose' and 'serious intention'.[80] Indeed, there is a sense in which more recent accounts of the 'unrealistic' Irish novel and the playfulness of *Ulysses* have inherited the terms of this critical approach.

It is only a short step from the implied opposition between Shakespearean England and Joycean Ireland to Dowden's reading of Shakespeare as the king – which is curiously repeated by Stephen. Prince Hamlet's tragedy, Dowden contends, is that he is immature since he cannot grasp the qualities that made early sixteenth-century England a model of cultural greatness: 'in the wide-spreading waste of corruption which lies around him, he is tempted to understand and detest things, rather than accomplish some limited practical service'. Out of step with the political maturity of Shakespeare's age, Hamlet does not exhibit 'the practical tendencies of manhood' and is 'incapable of certitude'. Shakespeare, by contrast, 'had entered upon the full maturity of his manhood' when writing *Hamlet*.[81] The mature writer could not then be identified with the immature prince but he could be with the king. In addition, Dowden notes that, 'According to Rowe [Shakespeare's first biographer], the top of his performance was the Ghost in his own *Hamlet*.'[82] Stephen's understanding of Shakespeare as King Hamlet is thus strangely attuned to Dowden's theory, at least in outline.

Stephen draws upon a similar methodology in his very different exposition of the politics of Shakespeare's reception. Although Dowden does not witness Stephen's performance, the latter's argument touches upon the former's work in some notable aspects. In particular, Stephen (correctly) reads the Elizabethan period as itself riven by religious and cultural divisions. It is 'an age of exhausted whoredom' (*U* 9.810); Shylock 'chimes with the jewbaiting' that followed the execution of the doctor to Elizabeth I ('carrotty Bess, the gross virgin' – *U* 9.758); *Hamlet* and *Macbeth* pander to James I, 'a Scotch philosophaster with a turn for witchroasting' (*U* 9.751–2). This period was also, of course, the time when the English undertook the plantation of Ireland and so massively strengthened and regimented their colonial domination.

Both Dowden and Dedalus comment upon the formative influence of Shakespeare on contemporary England. Writing in the 1890s, Dowden argued that 'Now more than at any previous period, our greatest master of Life has a conspicuous part in forming the mind of England'.[83] As a reader of Brandes and Lee, Stephen is, of course, aware of the Victorian and Edwardian bardolatry that turned Shakespeare into the symbol of 'England's genius'. Accordingly, he is critical of the English nationalistic jingoism that characterises both bardolatry and contemporary imperial ventures.[84] In the earliest extant draft of this episode, Joyce had equated Shakespeare directly with English national sentiment and he had even named the British prime minister as responsible for the 'don't hesitate to shoot' policy (*U* 9.133), which, it is implied, operated in Ireland.[85] As recent critics have observed, the allusion to the Boer War illustrates an anti-imperial strategy in Stephen's reading.[86] Yet it would have been a slightly passé remark by 1904: the Boer War had ended two years earlier and Irish national feeling in respect of the war – evidenced in the formation of the Transvaal Committee (including Connolly, Gonne, Griffith and Yeats) – had been at its height at the start of the war in 1899. Indeed, George Moore (whose soirée Stephen, apparently uninvited, does not attend) had been a leading campaigner against the war, leaving England because of it.[87] Stephen's comment, then, hardly sets him radically apart from his setting and underscores the complex tangle of this collective space in which reading Shakespeare cannot but comment upon contemporary conditions.

IX

In the construction of this argument, Joyce clearly aligns Stephen with a Catholic and broadly nationalist tradition against Dowden's protestant and monarchical interpretation. Yet the position of Stephen's interlocutors, his immediate audience, is pivotal. Since Dowden is a significant off-stage presence for Lyster and Eglinton, and since Stephen explicitly links his listeners as 'these' (and joins their names), readers are invited to see the debate as an oppositional one between different political, religious and educational positions. However, situating this microcosm of the Dublin cultural establishment at the centre of *Ulysses*, pushing Stephen and Eglinton, along with Lyster, Best and AE (plus Mulligan, Bloom and an attendant) into the cramped space of the librarian's office, brings their similarities as well as differences to light.

Moreover, the very space of the National Library was a shared but contested one. It was, according to one contemporary, 'a centre for the whole Catholic student population (Trinity having its own much less accessible library)' and Joyce's friend Curran recalled that 'in effect the National Library was the [University] College Library' (he also remembered Lyster's 'paternal guidance').[88] The Library thus accommodated a sometimes uneasy spectrum of readers and opinions, including Dowden's 'old culture', revivalist scholars and University College students. Although for Stephen Gwynn it was 'the most hospitable library that I have ever known' (where Bloom, for instance, is treated with respectful, if perfunctory, solicitude upon arrival), that is not the overriding impression given by Joyce, who as a student was often thrown out.[89] Indeed, Eglinton told Ellmann that, in late summer 1903, Joyce had sought Dowden's support for a post at the National Library only to be told that he was 'quite unsuitable'.[90] As *the* place of literary and intellectual exchange, the National Library provided an alternative to the enclave of Trinity College and more impoverished environment of University College. It was, then, entirely suitable that this national institution, embodying the transition from an old Ireland to the new (it had been formed from the stock of the Royal Dublin Society), should house the debate with its distinct political differences and uncomfortable proximities.[91]

In juxtaposing and complementing Dedalus and Dowden, Joyce shows how a contemporary anti-imperial and traditionally Catholic tradition, based on Aquinas and scholasticism, clashes with an understanding of Shakespeare as scion of a Protestant and monarchic age; however, both demonstrate an understanding of literary reception that comments proleptically and politically on their own time. The significance of Stephen's late disavowal of his theory is that, though he has invoked a Catholic tradition as one legitimate discourse among others, he has not relied upon faith. It had been feared by some who objected to the National University that the strictures of the Catholic Church would interfere with academic freedom. Having already exposed attempted Church censorship in his earlier writing, Joyce here both distances his work from that same tradition (and his 'familiar' readers) while asserting its contemporary political necessity. By staging Stephen's reading of Shakespeare as a debate with the absent Dowden, Joyce has shown how educational and religious institutions inevitably shaped literary reception in his Ireland. Dowden is the ghostly 'father figure' to the librarians but their critical tenets appear to be comfortably liberal: couched in the guise of 'disinterestedness' they make no mention of Shakespeare's political complications and do not rise to the bait. Eglinton assumes the role of 'judge' (*U* 9.152) despite his initial hostility to Stephen's theory. The chapter leaves little doubt that such covertly judgemental liberalism plays a subtle and oppressive role in the context of the cultural divisions Joyce has exposed.

The name-dropping among the librarians – of Moore and Martyn, of Yeats and Dowden – suggests a small and inward-looking society, one of squabbles, gossip and fragile reputations. Key to the mode of reception envisaged here is a form of surveillance in which privacy is dispersed amid known political, religious and social formations. Even Stephen's mock-Shakespearean language, for all its youthful inventiveness, contributes to this sense of an inescapably shared, 'nookshotten' space (*U* 9.315). Stephen's construction of his listeners as 'these' reads increasingly like his own projection of an identity which Joyce's text implicitly dismantles, as if even here – with the appropriation of Joyce's own work at stake – there could only be mis-readers and not a public audience. While the historical figures referred to in this episode are specifically linked for their difference from, and sometimes antagonism towards, Joyce and his work (and even his background), it is also worth recalling their confessed inability to read Joyce, typified by Eglinton's appraisal of an early sketch for *Portrait*. What the chapter establishes, then, is a means by which reception is necessarily politicised but is at the same time a form of misreading.

If Joyce exacts his revenge on 'these' he does so by self-consciously signalling their cocksure confidence when faced by the difficulties of reception. Stephen is sceptical of the complacency of others in acts of reception. In taking Deasy's letter for delivery, he encounters three inner offices and each time runs up against a sureness that alienates him. In the headmaster's study, Deasy hands him the letter with the words 'I want that to be printed and read' (*U* 2.338). In the editor's office at the *Freeman's Journal* and *Evening Telegraph*, Myles Crawford accepts the letter unread but can still proclaim 'That'll be alright . . . I'll read the rest after. That'll be alright' (*U* 7.586). In the librarian's office, the letter is again handed to Russell to be passed onto H. F. Norman, editor of the *Homestead*. In each instance, with the same text linking these culturally disparate figures, the clear expectation is that reception follows an un-problematic line from writing to printing to reading. 'Are we going to be read? I feel we are' (*U* 9.322) is Eglinton's contribution, a pompous and self-aggrandising assertion of the centrality of *Dana*: 'We are becoming important it seems' (*U* 9.312–13). (Eglinton himself later struck the same tone, arguing that *Dana* exemplified the 'fruitfulness of the moment'.[92]) In a similar manner, Haines feels confident enough to refuse the invita-tion to the Library discussion, preferring to buy Hyde's *Love Songs of Connacht*. Having more or less plagiarised from Hyde, Stephen's hastily scribbled poem will, by contrast, go unread on Sandymount Strand just as he will not publish his theory 'for the enlightenment of the public' (*U* 9.438–9). However, versions of both texts are of course read by the later readers *of Ulysses*, but on the condition that the act of reception by a local readership has first been rewritten.

The self-assured certainty of those readers and listeners whom Stephen encounters is emblematic of the political difficulties faced by Joyce, for it suggests an institutionalised comfort within set traditions. Even a pattern of future reception seems at times to have been presumed. The point is still pertinent: although some critics have assumed that *Ulysses* is 'our national epic' the point is that such a work 'has yet to be written' (*U* 9.309).[93] A 'national epic' would presume not only a text but an audience, a culture into which and from which that epic speaks: the point of 'Scylla and Charybdis' is that such a unified culture could not exist in colonial conditions. If *Ulysses* was indeed to be, as Joyce claimed to Linati, 'the epic of two races (Israel – Ireland)' (*SL* 271n), it would necessarily imply a fracture in the shape of the nation. Hence Joyce's work becomes a writing towards a state of division – a state that in some sense was already there – and which can be indexed through his rewriting of his reception. (This issue is taken up in chapter 4.)

X

To return briefly to Joyce's allusions to his earliest 'local' readership of family and friends: these, it was suggested, might be seen as displaced confessions, in which the roles of priest and penitent are confused. If, as in *Stephen Hero*, May Daedalus's apparent incomprehension had 'enabled

[Stephen] to place the blame on the shoulders of others' (*SH* 78), then 'Scylla and Charybdis' recognises moments of dispute and difference: those originary wounds that divide the writer from the readership, the confessor from the penitent, even as they imply the vitiation of both roles. This displacement is, however, the mark of a tension in Joyce's work between the attempt to redress a particular context and the necessity to escape it. In two particulars, 'Scylla and Charybdis' underlines this tension which might be rephrased as that between the concern for a readership and the evasion of an address. One is the role of May Dedalus; the other is Mulligan's appearance with the telegram. These instances effectively frame the discussion of literary reception: the contretemps of the lost but resurgent reader intervenes to dislocate the Shakespeare/political controversy and to complicate the relationship between Stephen Dedalus and his gathered audience.

Linking his mother's passing with that of Ann Hathaway, Stephen remembers 'Mother's deathbed. Candle. The sheeted mirror' (*U* 9.221). The final phrase may be read as a pun, recalling both the traditionally covered mirror in the presence of the recently deceased and the sheets or pages of the book in hand. These pages themselves comprise an autobiographical but distorted mirror on Joyce's life, a 'reflection from that which then I shall be' (*U* 9.384–5). She may not be listed among Stephen's succession of readers/listeners, but his mother's ghostly presence echoes in the way that readers do in Joyce's inscription of acts of reception: she exists in a parallel world as an ontological obfuscation which occasionally and ambiguously breaks into Stephen's own. (The point of repression, it seems, is to allow for a deferred resurfacing.[94]) The dialectical Stephen has constructed a series of oppositions between himself and his lost readers and interlocutors based around the idea of betrayal, be it of friendship, family, love or sexuality. Yet it is the occlusion of May Dedalus that signals his continual dependence. When her name is re-inserted into this list of 'readers', as the missing term in the equation, it becomes clear that the betrayal in question is also Stephen's. When he thinks, immediately after that list, 'Act. Be acted on' (*U* 9.979), a responsiveness and mutuality of influence is belatedly implied (this line was a notable later addition to the manuscript).[95] The scene thus emphasises the continuing interaction between performer and audience in the library, and shows, through the careful omission of May Dedalus and her return, that a 'lost' response can continue to be heard.

Joyce's insistence on continually writing-in versions of his readership might be thought of as a gesture towards an impossible return, but the allusion to a particular lost response instils in the text a new and continual responsiveness. The spectral return of May Dedalus, like the unnamed reappearance of She from *Giacomo Joyce*, is a trace or 'revenant' of a lost, but historically specific act of reception whose apparent rejuvenation transforms a suppressed reader into an encounter with later readers. As Margot Norris puts it, noting that May Dedalus returns also in Shem's chapter of *Finnegans Wake*, the point is 'to stage the suppression of the voices that art silences, that modernism derided or despised', and which, in the *Wake*, 'make themselves heard once more in their discredited vernacular forms'.[96] And they do so without nostalgia or sentiment: these readers remain as part of a fissured textual memory that continues to challenge attempted appropriations of it.

The entrance of Mulligan with Stephen's telegram is also a complex denial of sentimentality for the loss of a readership. The telegram, though itself a quotation – it cites Meredith's definition of the sentimentalist as '*he who would enjoy without incurring the immense debtorship for a thing done*' (*U* 9.550–1) – is the only circulated piece of Stephen's writing to be received and read by another.[97] Of course, the telegram refers to both Haines and Mulligan as those who would irresponsibly 'enjoy' while ignoring their political debts: for Haines 'history is to blame' while for Mulligan there is no blame.[98] This telegram appears in the context of a discussion of Wilde, previously described by Joyce as a 'court jester to the English' in a long tradition of Irish comic playwrights (*CW* 202). The witty aphorism or epigram – the collected 'saying' such as Haines would procure – is an inappropriate eloquence that panders to a 'sentimental' English audience and to the 'Brood of mockers' in Ireland (*U* 9.492). The telegram, which the suspiciously eloquent Mulligan calls a 'papal bull' (*U* 9.548) soon leads to his mockery of Syngean brogue, although it is perhaps more like an 'Irish bull' in that it indirectly addresses the question of the reception of Irish writing in England. The telegram, then, hints at the refusal of responsibility by an English audience. By situating forms of Irish literary tradition in relation to their reception, *Ulysses* attempts to sidestep that anxiety of audience to which so much Irish writing has been 'indebted'.

The telegram is also part of another set of specific responses to Joyce, and his replies, which had also sounded in *Giacomo Joyce*. That text contains an apparent late addition, a long paragraph which inserts into its Triestine context one 'Gogarty' and direct mention of *Ulysses* (this insertion thus establishes another contretemps in that text). 'Gogarty came yesterday to be introduced. *Ulysses* is the reason. Symbol of the

intellectual conscience . . . Ireland then?' (*GJ* 15). Gogarty did not visit
Joyce in this period; they last met in the tumultuous summer of 1909
when Joyce returned to Ireland. Gogarty had, inadvertently, been at
the harbour when Joyce disembarked; that Joyce ignored him may have
influenced the 'silent ship' (*U* 3.505) that closes 'Proteus', which is also
the silent Ship (the pub), the non-meeting at which is the need for
Stephen's telegram in the first place. When they did meet, Gogarty was
anxious about Joyce's representation of him but finally conceded, 'I don't
care a damn what you say of me so long as it is literature' (*Letters* II, 231).
Back in Trieste, Joyce kept an Alphabetical Notebook, into which he
would write: 'He fears the lancet of my art as I fear that of his.'[99] This
phrase is reused in the first chapter of *Ulysses*, begun in earnest in Trieste
in the summer of 1914, where it forms Stephen's judgement on Mulligan.
The insertion into *Giacomo* – quite possibly at this time – signals an
obvious concern for the reception of *Ulysses*, ripping that confessional text
from its Triestine context and resituating it within Joyce's concern for
his reception in 'Ireland then' (*GJ* 15).[100]

In *Giacomo Joyce* the phrase 'Symbol of the intellectual conscience' (an
apparent paraphrase of Gogarty) is then reworked in a more ironic mode
as 'Intellectual symbol of my race' (*GJ* 15). These similar but divergent
phrases are indicative of the political tension in Joyce's inscription of
readers. They echo in the portentous ending of *A Portrait* (Stephen's
desire 'to forge . . . the uncreated conscience of my race' (*P* 276)); and
in the broken mirror of *Ulysses* ('a symbol of Irish art. The cracked
lookingglass of a servant' (*U* 1.146)). Joyce's reworking of the drafts of
three texts (*Portrait*, *Giacomo* and *Ulysses*) moves increasingly towards a
denial of any imaginative identification with, or address to, a public
audience. The role of the Gogarty paragraph in *Giacomo Joyce* is to chart
a recognition of the naiveté of the desire to represent a readership; but,
at the same time, of course, this recognition is displayed, as if to show
that the conditions of Joyce's reception still mattered. This little drama
would have its denouement in 'Scylla and Charybdis'. The telegram that
is read out 'joyfully' is a form of non-address to a local reader, one that
echoes within a series of responses. It both accuses Mulligan (and by
implication Gogarty and his class) of being two-faced and admits its
own willingness to pay a debt. The price to be paid, by Joyce, is precisely
the inability of his texts to make a direct address to an Irish reception,
to speak to and for a particular audience. It is just this tension that
the confession and the contretemps imply, saying, with the telegram,
'O my friends, there is no friend.' Instead, the political work of the text

must be achieved indirectly, through an exposition of the conditions of reception for Joyce in Ireland.

Hence the Shakespeare debate – one over the politics of reading in contemporary Ireland – is interrupted by two different returning readers, one 'familiar', one 'foreign': May Dedalus and Mulligan. Each is associated with a distorted mirror just as each contributes to the contretemps of the scene, allowing lost, perhaps illegible, historical moments to flicker evanescently on the page. The sounding of these, and other, readerly echoes is a particular form of the underside of modernity reasserting itself in Joyce's text. Unlike those lingering memories of the historical past that interrupt Joyce's present,[101] these scenes of reception echo Joyce's contemporaries and interrupt future reading: later readers are already mired, and sometimes oddly mirrored, in these engraved responses. Those 'lost' readings reappear as if spectrally, often not easily tied to a historical event but nonetheless reverberating with the cultural contexts of reception. Thus the past of Joyce's writing recurs, disrupting the present and presence of readers. It is thus not possible to escape fully those contemporary readers, or conditions of reading, and to imagine a future audience since any such audiences will also, the texts suggest, be still a part of their pasts. The chronology of reception is awkwardly shaped. Later readers of Joyce, decades after his death, are still haunted by the readers he knew: the contretemps disrupts us as well. If 'Scylla and Charybdis' confirms that reception is a two-way process – 'Act. Be acted on' – then so too this surveillance is historical, between one set of readers and another. As Joyce would later put it in *Finnegans Wake*, reception involves 'watching the watched watching' (*FW* 509.02–3). So our appropriations and commodifications of Joyce remain disrupted by the inability to read – an inability that is not only ours but previous readers' as well, and one that is structured into the text, via its non-address, as part of its historical and political significance. In 'Work in Progress' Joyce would test the conceptual and cultural implications of an 'unreadable' writing.

CHAPTER 3

Exhaustion: Ulysses, 'Work in Progress' and the ordinary reader

Adorno claimed that 'with Schoenberg affability ceases'. Benjamin said of Proust's 'invectives against friendship' that 'he cannot touch his reader either'.[1] Joyce's texts are just as unfriendly, though perhaps less aloof than Proust, since they display their scepticism with an open face, staring back at the readers looking in, acknowledging the difference. One point of this refusal of affability is to guard against the transformation of writing into Culture, to prevent the *biens culturels* from appropriating the 'fahroots hof cullchaw' (*FW* 303.20), and Joyce succeeded in this more than most by showing that the 'fruits of culture' had far-off roots and spoke in many voices. By resisting the critical appropriation of his writing into Culture, Joyce both refused the affable handshake of the *biens culturels* and remained aloof from ordinary readers. The well-meaning individual who wrote to Joyce in 1926 to express his sense of 'a real friendship between reader and author' may not have received the reply he requested.[2]

We have become used to thinking of modernism as a collective movement distinguished in part by its expulsion of mass culture and so-called ordinary readers. The critical invention of an 'ordinary reader', which was concomitant with modernism, belied a nostalgic but misleading appeal to a false sense of shared cultural values and representation. While Joyce may be regarded as something of a special case in the general account of modernist politics, the question of who exactly might read him was much debated in his own lifetime as well as now. The debate also has a recent inflection. On the one hand, an anti-intellectual denigration of the 'excesses' of modernist writing in defence of the ordinary reader would have it that 'people like Bloom' cannot read *Ulysses*.[3] (A strange defence of the ordinary reader!) On the other hand, a celebration of those same excesses would claim that 'there is no model for *Joycean* competence', that there can be no 'bad readings' of *Finnegans Wake*.[4] Yet this too is troublesome. In fact, Joyce did have what might be called ordinary readers (even for that prized collectible, the first-edition *Ulysses*) but of course his work demands as well as questions varieties of competence. In the following pages, I show that Joyce was deeply engaged with contemporary discourses of reception such as the very notion of an 'ordinary reader' and the formation of specialist readers. This engagement continued Joyce's established concern with actual readers and their conditions of reading (especially the time for reading), allowing these conditions to inflect the production of his new work.

Although modernism might be characterised in part by the supposed 'great divide' fracturing it from mass culture, the stratification of readers that this implies was hardly new to the period. Whereas Andreas Huyssen influentially valorised modernism as an exclusive, self-referential enterprise in contrast to the doomed political challenge of the avant-garde, more recently Laurence Rainey has catalogued the forms of selling and buying of modernist work that formed new institutions for the reception of art as it was produced in the 1910s and 20s, thereby allowing us to see some of the ways in which writers like Joyce interacted with the social formation of their work into art.[5] For both critics, modernism is depicted as a discrete collection of movements that conspired to exclude mass culture and ostracise ordinary readers. However, it is particularly the case with Joyce that his work should be seen not only in the context of European modernism and its institutions but also in the terms of its own engagement with the conditions of reception, notably (but not exclusively) in Ireland. In addition to the record of purchasers / readers, we need to read Joyce's revisions to his texts for they too constitute part of the 'social dialogic' that surrounds Joyce's reception. Accordingly, this chapter moves from the question of some of the actual readers of *Ulysses* into the relationship between responses to it and the composition of 'Work in Progress'.

A motif of exhaustion can be traced through this chapter: initially in the sales of *Ulysses*; then in the responses of readers who complained of the lack of time to read; in the worn-out materials of Joyce's writing; and in the somatic exhaustion of the writer himself. In responding to the particular accusation that people lacked time to read his work, Joyce engages contemporary discourses of reception and rewrites their responses in the figures of inscribed readers in 'Work in Progress'. In doing so, his work raises the question of readers' competence. Finally, this chapter returns to one specific reader, John Eglinton. Joyce's writing of reception is therefore continued in its articulation of the local and historical responses to his work and of the material situations in which those responses were formulated.

I

Rainey suggests that modernism sought to produce an art that would be collected; one that would carry the illusion of its own unique aura: many modernist works, including *Ulysses*, were directed, initially at least, at investors rather than readers; as such, these collectors and subscribers were effectively also patrons. Owing to an increased dependence upon forms of patronage, from the individual dealer to the museum and university, modernism can be seen to have negotiated a new institutional space for the reception of art. Rainey's argument is thus a provocative recasting of modernism as a formation of new institutions for the dissemination of literary culture. However, Sylvia Beach's records of the initial sales of *Ulysses* suggest that it was purchased and read by more than just specialists: it seems that ordinary readers also were buying and reading *Ulysses*. In addition, the terms of this debate need to be widened. While the question of who bought the *Ulysses* first edition can, in part, be settled, their motives and their readings are not so easily retrieved.

According to Rainey, the purchasers of Beach's edition of one thousand copies (in three distinct categories of price and production value) bought it 'to be able to sell it again'. Rainey extrapolates from this the wider 'paradox' that 'the effect of modernism was not so much to encourage reading as to render it superfluous'.[6] Based on the large orders placed by well-known book dealers, Rainey argues that 'individual readers played a limited role in shaping the success that greeted the first edition of *Ulysses*' compared to the 'dealers and speculators in the rare book trade who bought the overwhelming majority of copies of the first edition'.[7] He estimates that *Ulysses* 'entered the public sphere' only after Sisley Huddleston's review in the *Observer* (5 March 1922) but this is to discount its pre-publication history in the *Little Review*.[8] However, even focusing solely on the first edition, more than half of the 150 francs copies had already been sent to their purchasers before Huddleston's review appeared (which then added a further level of interest from English readers).[9] Given that Beach lost out heavily on exchange rates by demanding payment in francs, it is not unreasonable to suggest that among the subscribers to the cheaper run of the first edition were a number of individual readers – and the Beach Papers bear this out. Edward Bishop has shown that among trade orders for the first edition, many came from small or ordinary booksellers rather than specialist rare-book dealers and collectors (sixty-eight stores or agencies in total, including twelve in Paris and four in Dublin); Bishop also points to the range of individual purchasers in his emphasis on the ordinary readers of the first edition. Among these were several who applied on the headed notepaper of their firms, mainly from England. In addition, Bishop speculates that further pockets of the first edition readership existed in gay communities and among acquaintances of T. E. Lawrence, whose copy was passed around.[10] Beach also recalled that Robert McAlmon would collect subscribers' signatures among the 'Paris night-life'.[11]

Analysis of the Sylvia Beach papers shows that the subscribers to the first edition did indeed include many ordinary readers who were neither investors nor dealers but individuals seeking to secure a copy for their own reading. Yet what they thought they would be reading – and how they would read it – are different matters entirely. These papers contain letters from individuals from many parts of the world (but primarily Europe and the United States) seeking to secure or reserve a copy of *Ulysses*, as well as other letters from readers of the book. Some copies were purchased through Beach's innovative mail order subscription service, others were collected from Shakespeare & Co. on Rue Dupuytren in the sixth arrondissement. A number of actual and potential subscribers were individuals in Ireland, such as one Miss Whitfield of Cabra Park, Dublin, who successfully purchased a copy. In the early months of 1922, four bookshops a short walk from each other in south central Dublin received about twenty-five copies, although they sought more, suggesting that there were individuals ready and willing to purchase the book in Ireland as elsewhere.[12] The order slips show many shops returning for more and more copies, especially from late February onwards. In addition, other Dubliners purchased the first edition independently of bookshops, and still others were disappointed. These included Mr Keane, editor of the *Kilkenny People*, Charles H. Rowe of Trinity College and one E. M. Clery (presumably not Emma Clery!) of the Secretary's Department of the National Bank, College Green, Dublin, who requested 'P. S. Please mark envelope "Private" when replying. EC' – as did several other correspondents.[13] Presumably, the notoriety of the book led to surreptitious reading. Some enquiries – from England and the United States – apparently thought *Ulysses* was pornography and sent accompanying notes stating that they required it for psychological or medical research, even including 'my prior qualifications, as proofs of my bona fides'.[14] There were also many requests with military addresses – in Sylvia Beach's words, 'retired Colonels' – who presumably sought out the alluring combination of 'high art' with 'sex' that Sisley Huddleston in the *Observer* had called 'the very obscenity [which] is somehow beautiful'.[15]

However, any history of reception must recognise its limitations. Records of the purchasers of the first edition are incomplete. Furthermore, as soon as one is no longer limited to discussing the first edition, the range of ordinary individuals buying and/or reading the book increases dramatically. Significantly, the readers of *Ulysses* were not restricted to its purchasers. It is safe to assume that many more borrowed the book than bought it, if only to satisfy their curiosity or confirm their suspicions; Joyce's letters suggest as much in at least two places (*Letters* I, 193 and *Letters* III, 74) and some later correspondents with Beach refer to their attempts to borrow it.[16] One such reader from Chester, England wrote to Beach in 1926 to say that, 'after years of impatience', she had at last borrowed the book, read it, and now sought a cheap edition. First editions were also passed around: in addition to T. E. Lawrence's, whose copy came complete with annotations on Dublin, was another owned by Virginia Woolf. Her diary recalls, 'Shanks borrowed it; saying it must be hidden from Bowen Hawkesford' (Edward Shanks, the poet, was in a relationship with the daughter of the Rodmell rector). Katherine Mansfield would later find the same copy, once more hidden, this time in a drawer at Hogarth House. Woolf recalled this event having just heard of Joyce's death: 'She began to read, ridiculing: then suddenly said, But theres something in this.'[17] A similar trajectory of reception may well be common, just as a first edition can have an interesting afterlife.

To characterise the reception of *Ulysses* as divided between collectors and ordinary reader-purchasers is to engage in the further construction of putative types of reader. One of the most interesting aspects of the various readers and dealers who bought or attempted to buy *Ulysses* is the extent to which different groups overlapped. What emerges from an analysis of Beach's subscriber lists is the difficulty of the kinds of classification of readers made by Rainey. As Bishop acknowledges, there is often a thin line between ordinary reader and patron-investor. Some individuals were also keen to own a valuable object: one of the 'medical men' specifically sought an early number (he fortunately received no. 11). Others sought autographs for their first editions, so *Ulysses* potentially crossed the line between investment and book. After receiving no reply to his first request for an autograph, Harold Kamp wrote again to express his wish 'to feel that the author is interested in those who collect his first editions'.[18] This time he received a signed photograph. Joyce also seems to have taken the view that the book was both a reading experience and an investment. Towards the end of 1922, writing to his aunt Josephine Murray regarding her presentation copy, he pressed upon her its growing 'market value' and a critical commentary to aid reading (*Letters* I, 193). From the start, *Ulysses* had both readers and investors, sometimes within the same person. This problem of classification has implications for how we characterise readers and readings of the book, especially as so many reviews (critical and supportive) referred to the type of reader it might attract or dispel. Valéry Larbaud, for one, famously distinguished between 'the unculti-vated or half-cultivated reader who will throw *Ulysses* aside after a few pages' and 'the cultivated reader'.[19] Of course, the question of *who* (again, this means what type, that is, what construct or notion of who) might read *Ulysses* would have an important bearing on the trial that eventually saw its public release in 1934. Although readers (or buyers, or browsers) clearly crossed the boundaries of classification, it is notable that such borders were operative at least in critical discourse. Huddleston, for instance, had disingenuously offered the pretence of bridging the gulf between writer and reader by claiming that *Ulysses* was eagerly awaited by the 'little inner circle of book-lovers and littérateurs'.[20] It was just this sort of critical creation of reading types that Joyce's work engaged with in its allusions to actual readers and in its depictions of the act of reading.

II

The meticulous particularity of *Ulysses* notoriously attracted the ire of Wyndham Lewis in *Time and Western Man*. As part of one of the most famous critical retaliations in 'Work in Progress', Joyce dubbed Lewis's book '*Spice and Westend Woman*' adding in parenthesis '(utterly exhausted before publication, indiapepper edition shortly)' (*FW* 292.6–7). Not only does this imply that the English artist-author had 'sold out' his principles but Lewis's book also merges with *Ulysses*, the 'foist edition' (*FW* 291.27) of which had sold out ('utterly exhausted before publication') thanks to the subscription service established by Sylvia Beach. When the English second edition was announced by John Rodker and Harriet Shaw Weaver in the middle of 1922, Rodker issued a slip saying that Beach's first edition was 'already exhausted'.[21] In April 1922, having packaged off the last of the 150 francs copies, Beach was forced to alter a printed sign announcing '*ULYSSES* by JAMES JOYCE' by adding beneath, in pen, 'IS SOLD OUT'. A few months after that, she sheepishly advertised the controversial English 'new edition' by stating once more that the first edition was 'already exhausted'.[22]

A principle of exhaustion can be seen in this narrative: exhaustion is productive. As one edition runs out another begins. A version of this will be found in Joyce's writing and in his responses to readers' responses. Both Weaver and Beach amassed long lists of potential subscribers: their clients from *The Egoist* and Shakespeare & Company would seamlessly merge into prospective readers of *Ulysses*. Both women set about drumming up interest for their respective editions, which fed into demand for later editions as well; Joyce himself contributed a list of potential buyers for the Egoist Press. A marker of the difference between the two women who did so much for *Ulysses* is the disorganisation of the Beach archive – with its duplicate and contradictory entries – compared to the careful annotations on Weaver's promotional list, which include parenthetical remarks such as 'very wealthy. . .' and 'Australian: keen feminist: has money'.[23] Most of Weaver's addresses are in London; by contrast, Beach kept many address books arranged by nation. While these publishers could create a readership they could not, however, define it. A concentration on the first edition purchasers (*pace* Rainey and Bishop) – while offering a fascinating glimpse of a particular moment of cultural consumption – allows for only a partial reading of Joyce's complex relationship with his readership. Not only should other editions and stages in the publication of *Ulysses* be considered, but so too should the unlucky would-be purchasers and potential readers (who may never have later read the book), as well as the composition of 'Work in Progress'. The concomitant beginning of the new work with the distribution and reception of *Ulysses* is a point usually ignored in debates over the sales of *Ulysses*. The English second edition of *Ulysses* was published in the middle of October 1922; before the end of that month Joyce had already proof-read half of the third edition, and these typographical corrections can be found in Notebook VI.B.10, which became the workpad for Joyce's next project. The exhaustion of *Ulysses* turned seamlessly into the production of 'Work in Progress'. Later, probably in 1924, Joyce established a notebook (VI.B.6) in which he recorded phrases from criticism of *Ulysses*. In discussing the readers of *Ulysses*, then, one must also consider the compilation of 'Work in Progress' as a commentary upon Joyce's earlier reception.

At the very beginning of 'Work in Progress' Joyce hit upon the scheme of collectively grouping reviewers and their reviews (supplied to him by press agencies as well as by individuals, including relatives) which can be seen as an extension of the way that Stephen Dedalus refers to his audience as a collective other. In the early summer of 1923, Ezra Pound advised Herbert Gorman, then preparing his biographical study, to assemble a reply to Joyce's hostile critics: the idea was for Gorman 'to erect some sort of permanent pillory for the GOD damn fools (Jim Douglas, Noyes, Beenet, etc n etcn)'.[24] If this advice was ever passed on to Joyce, Pound and Gorman would have discovered that he was there ahead of them. In October 1922, beginning 'Work in Progress' by rereading *Ulysses* and reading reviews of that novel, Joyce announced to Weaver his intention to fuse the names of several critics so that he could refer to them collectively in the future.[25] He did so under the title 'Noise about Joyce' (*Letters* I, 192), an allusion to the English poet-critic, Alfred Noyes. Then, about a year later, Joyce wrote to Weaver declaring his intention to answer the critics of *Ulysses* in his new work, and this is precisely what he did.[26] A number of critics have discussed Joyce's allusions in 'Work in Progress' to critical responses to *Ulysses*. Ingeborg Landuyt has shown that Joyce referred directly not only to Shane Leslie and Dr Joseph Collins but also to John Middleton Murry, Alfred Noyes, 'Aramis', James Douglas and others.[27] Yet this aspect of Joyce's engagement with his reception is more than a matter of 'replying' to his critics. In Joyce's responses to his professional critics, patrons and ordinary readers, a principle of exhaustion is at stake in which production is drained and consumption renewed, showing not just the social accommodation of writing but also the generative capacity of reception.

If 'Work in Progress' became the 'permanent pillory' that Pound had encouraged, it did so on Joyce's, rather than Pound's, terms. The note-books that comprise the building blocks of 'Work in Progress' form an unstable archive of Joyce's reading (even if the sources are not recorded and often previous loose sheets have been lost); *Finnegans Wake* is the mould of those 'quashed quotatoes' (*FW* 183.22) into a particular medium and design. In achieving this, though, it formulates an 'anarchive', that is, the *Wake* is both a direct line to the notebooks with their records of research, and an anarchic deregulation of that archive, the mutilation of its referentiality in the mutability of its language. What this anarchive accomplishes is the estrangement of historicity: not the annihilation of specificity, but its opening out. By reinscribing readers' responses into his ongoing text, Joyce not only exacted a measure of revenge on the critical establishments but also formed a set of internalised 'readers' for the book – a work that is always reading itself but doing so from particular histor-ical sources. Both the texture and the import of particular readers and readings remains within the work and these can often be traced through the uniquely obtuse reference collection of Joyce's notebooks. Such in-stances should not be taken in isolation as if they were minor point-scoring of a purely personal kind. Instead, as this chapter argues, they are an integral part of a form that was itself a response to shifting modes of reception (and, as the following chapter shows, this engagement was irrevocably political). Joyce was thus able to respond to actual readers while at the same time reformulating those readers and readings into a generic mode that elaborated his engagement with the conditions of his own reception.

Of course, Joyce had taken an interest in the subscriptions to *Ulysses*, not only the famous acceptances (Yeats) and refusals (Shaw), but also some of the less well known ones, including the requests for 'private' post markings. Some later applicants for *Ulysses* thought that the ban would not apply if 'ordered by a physician and plainly marked for a doctor's use'.[28] In *Finnegans Wake*, attempting to deliver the letter (which is also *Ulysses*), Shaun the Post wants to 'collect my extraprofessional postages owing to me by Thaddeus Kellyesque Squire, dr, for nondesirable printed matter' (*FW* 456.29–31). A certain Dr Simon Kelly of Manchester did subscribe to the first edition.[29] Shaw's comments were interesting: despite refusing to subscribe he still recommended that every male Dubliner between fifteen and thirty should be 'forced' to read it (*Letters* III, 50). In chapter I.ii of the *Wake*, the description of HCE's background sets him amid 'our liffeyside people' including 'slips of young dublinos from Cutpurse Row having nothing better to do than . . . weedulicet' or, to read (and weed) *Ulysses* (*FW* 42.25–32). The terms of Shaw's refusal, sent from London, went straight to the heart of his own cultural estrangement: *Ulysses* was simply too close to home. In June 1921 Joyce had proposed that 'something really comic could be written about the subscribers to my tome – a son or nephew of Bela Kun, the British Minister of War Winston Churchill, an Anglican bishop and a leader of the Irish revolutionary movement. I have become a monument – no, a vespasian' (*Letters* III, 46n). The sundry character of the potential readership of *Ulysses* made its impression on Joyce, whose image of himself as a urinal for the use of readers – rather than the image of a grand monument more characteristic of many accounts of modernism – is a signal of the form of reception that his work suggests. Many years previously, in 'The Holy Office', he had referred to 'that motley crew' of would-be readers, but then it was to imply his own superiority; now, however, Joyce both records and rewrites his reception as if to transform the varied and material conditions of actual reading. The suggestion to write about the differing subscribers to *Ulysses* should be seen in tandem with the idea to respond to its critics: *Finnegans Wake* – for all its apparent 'unreadable' language – deepened rather than diminished the interest in (possible) readers.

Of the several reviews of *Ulysses* in which Joyce took a strong interest, that by Shane Leslie in the prestigious, cultured and English *Quarterly Review* stands out. Leslie himself had an eye on his own readers, for around the same time he wrote another piece for the Catholic *Dublin Review* (of which he was editor): each review dismisses *Ulysses* but does so on different grounds, suggesting that Leslie was appealing to his own readers' presumed prejudices. Leslie was an Anglo-Irishman, who had converted to Catholicism and even stood as a Nationalist candidate for Derry in the 1913 general election. The tensions that beset his notion of culture, undoubtedly strained by the War of Independence, are tested by *Ulysses*: on the one hand, readers of the English *Quarterly* are reassured that the centrality of a 'high cultural' tradition remains in place, its common morality and universal literary standards offended but ultimately not threatened by *Ulysses*; on the other hand, readers of the *Dublin Review* are shown *Ulysses* within the context of Irish Catholicism. In the latter case, Joyce appears as a Catholic renegade; in the former, simply as an outsider. Leslie's assumption of different audiences for his own reviews smacks of precisely the sort of essentialism that Joyce's writing so powerfully challenges. Ultimately, Leslie presents a Joyce who fits neither set of (presumed) audiences, Irish Catholic or English 'high cultural'. His evident dislike for European modernism – which he helps to construct as obscure and elitist – helps to show how Joyce is not a writer within an English tradition. By the same token, Leslie's defensiveness on behalf of his adopted faith disqualifies Joyce from being a 'truly' Catholic writer. Instead, there is no ready audience for his work, not even the gullible critics who have been taken in by the 'deliberate bamboozlement of the reader'.[30] In *Finnegans Wake*, it is Shaun the critic who has a 'bamboo-zelem mincethrill voice' (*FW* 515.28). What emerges, perhaps aptly, is a model of Joyce who suits no particular audience and nowhere does this come across more strongly than in the presumptions Leslie makes of his own readers.

In the *Dublin Review*, the offensiveness of *Ulysses* is specifically against Catholicism but in the *Quarterly Review* it is generally against 'all ideas of good taste and morality'. In order to illustrate this affront to common morals, Leslie mentions details from the text at which he thinks Catholics, Puritans and Protestants would all balk. Specifically, he draws the line at 'introducing the names of real people into circumstances of monstrous and ludicrous fiction'. Paradoxically, Leslie actually praised the 'Scylla and Charybdis' episode in which this practice is most evident (as discussed in the previous chapter), saying that it could be reprinted as a separate work. In making this comment, Leslie takes up a previous remark that George Moore had employed the 'artifice' of introducing 'people, still living, by name into his novels. This secured him the double audience of his victims' enemies and friends'.[31] In the *Wake's* language, readers are not mentioned by name but the practice of referring to and transforming actual readings continues. Leslie's pompous objection that 'there are some things which cannot and, we should like to be able to say, shall not be done' became, in the second installment of 'Work in Progress', 'there are certain statements which ought not to be, and one should like to hope to be able to add, ought not to be allowed to be made' (now *FW* 33:19–21).[32] Joyce's rewriting accomplishes a metamorphosis of the self-aggrandising critic into an internal reader of the new work. In addition, as Joyce knew, the practice of referring to actual persons, which Leslie disparaged in *Ulysses*, had also attracted readers – or at least browsers – to that book. A certain James F. Conmee wrote to Joyce from Dublin in 1928 to enquire about purchasing a copy since 'I am told the book tells part of the life of one in whom I am interested. Namely the Rev. Father Conmee SJ.'[33] A similar human enquiry reputedly attracted many more to *Ulysses* and to an extent continues to today.

Noting Joyce's developing engagement with his own reception adds nuance to the familiar caricature of the 'greatly misunderstood' writer suffering form a persecution complex (*FW* 470.01). Joyce's reworking of his reviews, which were sent to him by friends and agencies, can be considered as a sort of reflective exhaustion: his own work and its readers' responses form part of the tired language that must be renewed. The much remarked upon exhaustion of the English language (Leslie had commented on the 'exhausted English speech' and the *Wake* itself offers to 'wipe alley english spooker . . . off the face of the erse' – *FW* 178.6–7) that Joyce's writing displays is particularly germane here for it is intimately bound in with his personal exhaustion.[34] In this respect, Joyce's reviews comprise a sort of narcissistic mirror that supports his self-obsessive writing, no matter how critical those reviews (Leslie's *Quarterly* attack was welcome because it came in a prestigious journal). Joyce's recreation of these responses, which themselves cite his earlier work, continues the exhaustive process of identification – one that is wrapped up in the impossibility of self-expression. A process of responsiveness between writer and reader was built into 'Work in Progress', where each plays the role of Narcissus and Echo.

The construction of identity is dependent upon others' perceptions of the self ('See ourselves as others see us' – *U* 13.1058): the writer writes from his reviews. However, the humanist fantasy of an affable mutual recognition – arguably still echoing in Levinas's ethics of the face-to-face encounter – is never seriously entertained by Joyce.[35] Instead, his reading of others' readings of him implies not acceptance but a two-way glance: back to the historical scene of the response and forward to the readers who are to come. That Joyce stitches these responses (together with other textual fragments) into the *Wake* is both a narcissistic self-creation and a direct confrontation with the conditions of reading – and both of these imply the fragmentation of 'the reading body', that is, of Joyce's reading of himself and of others' readings of him. It is striking how far his letters dwell on these two (related) subjects: his writing (including reviews) and his health. When enquiring about Leslie's *Quarterly* review, for instance, he veers from the topic: 'It is in some valise or trunk but I had bad neuralgia all night or a good part of it and want to write this letter. Did it contain the phrase "U has yet to take its place in the thought and script of mankind"?' (*Letters* I, 194). So rather than resting or retrieving the article himself, Joyce asks Weaver in a long letter about the sales of *Ulysses* and preparations for the third edition. This letter is indicative of the form of exhaustion: the restless point which ensures renewal – of self, of writing. If reception offers a narcissistic mirror, then, it also echoes in the process of production.

III

One aspect of this apparent narcissism as it presented itself to readers was the time Joyce had taken over *Ulysses* and 'Work in Progress', ensuring a personal exhaustion whose auratic aspect will be discussed later in this chapter. The corollary of this elaborate composition was, it seemed, the lack of time available for readers. Without special training, *Ulysses* and 'Work in Progress' would simply take too long to read. Joyce himself was well aware of this complaint and structured it into 'Work in Progress', where it informs not only his depiction of readers but also the form of the text.

Advocating the use of catchphrases in the promotion of *Ulysses* (Larbaud's use of the term 'monologue intérieur' is Joyce's example), Joyce had written to Weaver in 1924, 'They [the reading public] cannot manage more than about one such phrase every six months – not for lack of intelligence but because they are in a hurry' (*Letters* III, 83). This understanding of the plight of the reader should not be taken as a simple siding with the ordinary reader over the specialist. (Nor should it be confused with the tacit criticism of Eglinton, Deasy and others in *Ulysses* for their hurried and over-confident reading: it is precisely their apparent *lack* of reading and judgemental hastiness, rather than any lack of time, that are contrasted with the caution of Stephen and Bloom.) As I will argue, Joyce's understanding of the reader's lack of time did not extend to sympathy, much less empathy.

Joyce did not need critics and patrons to tell him that readers lacked time to read his long books – but they told him anyway. From Paris, Pound estimated the length of *Ulysses* as 'about the size of four ordinary novels' although Joyce himself thought it was more like eight (*Letters* I, 196).[36] Even prior to the publication of *Ulysses*, Richard Aldington in London – in a piece that Joyce read – complained that its serialisation had taken 'an abnormally long time, and that there is some excuse for my impatience'.[37] Beach herself admitted that subscribers had been made to wait 'a long long time'.[38] Michael Healy, Nora's uncle and a supporter of Joyce, had written from Dublin to confirm that *Ulysses* was 'indeed a large book' and to remark on its author's 'great labour'.[39] In Trieste, Stanislaus had offered to lend *Ulysses* to Silvio Benco, who declined by saying 'he would ask me for it when he had time to read it' (*Letters* III, 58). Having spent 'the best part of a fortnight' attempting 'to master *Ulysses*', John Middleton Murry was obliged to concede, rather pompously, 'we should hesitate to say that we understand . . . more than four-fifths of it'. He declared it 'very big . . . hard to read [and] extraordinarily interesting to those who have patience (and they need it)' – a phrase later echoed in *Finnegans Wake* (*FW* 108.8–10).[40] Leslie had likened the 'size and colour' of *Ulysses* to the 'London Telephone Book' and Joyce responded by referring to his 'telephone directory' and the 'serial number of . . . many days or years' it would take to read (*FW* 118.10–13).[41]

When readers did get round to tackling the book they did so with a wariness that anticipated weariness: 'I am reading *Ulysses*', George Moore wrote to Joyce in September 1929, 'I look forward to reading it all winter' (*Letters* III, 194). Virginia Woolf was more seasonal: she read it 'one summer . . . with long lapses of intense boredom'.[42] That the letter in *Finnegans Wake* is never delivered mimics the slow progress of these and Joyce's familial readers: 'I gather that you have not finished it', he reproved his aunt, Josephine Murray, 'Nora will beat you all in the competition. She has got as far as page 27 counting the cover.' By contrast, Josephine should buy 'at once' Lamb's *Adventures of Ulysses*, since 'you can read it in a night' (*Letters* I, 193). As often in Joyce's writing, the familial and personal provides a model for the social and cultural:

readers are always 'too busy'. This 'lack of time for reading' is a crucial aspect in the material situation and critical reception of Joyce's late work: its very exhaustive or comprehensive scale appears to write out the possibility of its ever being read (indeed the 'strain' on the putative reader has become a well-worn interpretation of the experience of reading particularly the final chapters of *Ulysses*[43]).

By acknowledging readers' conditions and complaints, 'Work in Progress' suggests a generic model that recognises the complexities of reception. In particular, the notion of a 'hurried' reader (of *Ulysses* especially) plays a significant formal part in the new work. In Book II of the *Wake*, after the 'mummery' of Butt and Taff, the critical voice of Shaun makes a formal announcement:

A time. And a find time . . . I have just (let us suppraise) been reading in a (suppressed) book – it is notwithstempting by meassures long and limited – the latterpress is eminently legligible, and the paper, so he eagerly seized upon, has scarsely been buttered in works of previous publicity . . . Enough, however, have I read of it, like my good bedst friend, to augur in the hurry of the times that it will cocommend the widest circulation (*FW* 356.16–28).

Among many things, this passage refers to John Long Ltd (who refused to publish *Dubliners*) and to readers' complaints of the time it takes to read. That Shaun has been reading the first edition of *Ulysses* is suggested both by the fine edition and the fact that it has been 'eagerly seized upon' – perhaps by collectors and customs officials as well as readers. The word 'notwithstempting' carries within it: notwithstanding, not with tempting, and *temps* or time. The book, then, takes a 'long' time, but time – like the book – is also 'limited'. The 'hurry of the times' leaves readers ill-prepared: when a book is so glorified in 'previous publicity' and 'ambullished with expurgative plates, replete in information' (*FW* 356.30–1) readers must struggle to 'find time'. This passage also distances any possibility of 'friendship' between writer and reader: a 'good bedst friend' being suspiciously quick to say 'Enough'. Joyce often links the issue of friendship to reading, especially as Wyndham Lewis customarily signed himself an 'ever devoted friend' (*Letters* I, 257) – which Joyce rendered as 'I'm an ever-devouting fiend of his' (*FW* 408.18). Lewis's famous criticism of *Ulysses* – that it was obsessed with time – might in part spring from his own frustration: 'At the end of a long reading of *Ulysses* you feel that it is the very nightmare of the naturalistic method you have been experiencing'.[44]

The apparent lack of time to read 'Work in Progress' bothered many who attempted to defend the notion of an ordinary reader. Principal among these was Harriet Weaver. While many of Joyce's followers withdrew their support for 'Work in Progress' in the mid-to-late 1920s – including Stanislaus, Pound, Lewis, Wells, Weaver herself, and also a number of critics and lesser-known readers – they also often retained their commitment to Joyce the author. Aside from Pound's, it is typical that these rejections make a defence of the 'ordinary' reader and – whether implicitly or explicitly – his or her lack of time.

The following exchange between Weaver and Joyce is emblematic of this process. Coming on top of judgements by Stanislaus – 'unspeakably wearisome' (*Letters* III, 103) – and Pound – 'circumambient peripheriza-tion' (*Letters* III, 145) – Weaver's ambivalence was notable because she was associated less with critical opinion and more with ordinary readers (especially given her so-called 'ordinary edition' that followed Beach's first edition). In 1926, after the first few installments of 'Work in Progress' had been published (but before securing the niche of *transition*), Joyce and Weaver acted the roles of craftsman and patron (*Letters* I, 245). When his 'sample' (*SL* 316) fell short of expectation, Weaver felt pushed into defending – and, in doing so, defining – the ordinary reader through her suggestion of a reader's guide: 'Perhaps you wish him, her and them to disappear from the horizon', she asked, 'otherwise, would it be totally against the grain, your convictions and principles to publish (when the day comes), along with an ordinary edition, also an annotated edition (at double or treble price, say?).'[45] Of course, the offer ('a mere suggestion') was not taken up and instead Joyce 'overworked and overworried . . . took to the sofa again' (*Letters* III, 146) 'in exhaustion'.[46] Her suggestion of an annotated edition (or labour-saving device) anticipates the more recent volumes that have been produced by critics such as Don Gifford and Roland McHugh. Indeed, the latter had initially suggested that his *Annotations to Finnegans Wake* should be interspersed with leaves from the *Wake* to form a composite volume.[47] What the cause of the ordinary reader apparently requires, then, is a further temporal reversal by which exegesis and reading are seen to operate 'simultaneously'. The paradox that what the ordinary reader really needs is the explication of a specialist perpetuates the distinction between types of reader.[48]

According to Adaline Glasheen, Weaver is '*the* model' for Biddy the Hen, who digs up the letter in *Finnegans Wake*, but she is perhaps more obviously recognisable in other allusions.[49] In 1928 she travelled to Paris to reassure Joyce of her 'unconditional support' but only after having earlier worried that he was 'wasting [his] genius' (*Letters* III, 154, n2). In her 'revered majesty' letter in Book IV, ALP remarks 'May all similar douters of our oldhame story have that fancied widming!' (*FW* 616.3–4). Weaver, who hailed from Oldham, might be called the 'old dame' of the *Wake* and one of its doubters whose dedication (German, *Widmung*) was missing.[50] Weaver is also associated with the twelve bar customers in Earwicker's pub, who crop up in various guises throughout the text, for instance as the contributors to *Exagmination*, as the members of a jury and as the twelve disciples. Near the beginning of II.3, the twelve are listed as workers: 'Lorimers and leathersellers, skinners and salters, pewterers and paperstainers, parishclerks, fletcherbowyers, girdlers, mercers, cordwainers and first, and not last, the weavers. Our library is hoping to ye public' (*FW* 312.35–313.2). It was of course partly through Weaver that Joyce's work (itself a sort of library) might be opened to a public. This 'appeal' is made in terms ('ye') that indicate the by-then already out-dated notion of a 'public' readership: the list of working library users is at once the invocation of this idea and the admission of its decline. It has been suggested that Weaver was Joyce's 'ideal reader' because she was also a 'genetic reader', that is, a reader familiar with Joyce's revisions and compositional techniques.[51] Yet it is difficult to see how Joyce held any notion of an ideal reader, having continually to direct, cajole or simply ignore the readers he did encounter. The allusions to her in the *Wake* imply as much.

Joyce's incorporation of Weaver into his writing hints at the problem of her position with its appeal to an ordinariness or normality that Joyce's work shows to be a construct. Defences of the ordinary reader as often implied the contradiction in the idea. Having previously refused to review *A Portrait* citing a lack of time (he then relented), H. G. Wells complained to Joyce in 1928: 'you have turned your back on common men, on their elementary needs and their restricted time and intelligence' – yet he humbly offered himself as a 'typical common reader'.[52] The familiar lament is made that 'a proper appreciation' of the work 'demands so many waking hours of the few thousands I have still to live'. Nonetheless, Wells admits his 'great personal liking' for Joyce and maintains his 'genius'. Notably, his letter begins, 'I have been studying you' – not '*reading* you'. By claiming to save 'Work in Progress' from 'restrictive interruption', but simultaneously rejecting the 'elaborated' writing, Wells exemplifies the paradox of these rejections: he at once calls time on Joyce and asks him to go on.[53] The pretence of the would-be ordinary reader, then, is itself an investment in specialism. This is a restatement of the principle of exhaustion: the point at which the text must be stopped, at which it has become dangerously over-productive, is also the point that marks its necessity and its right to continue.

One month after Wells's letter, an almost identical criticism was levelled at 'Work in Progress' by the English poet and dramatist John Drinkwater. According to Ellmann, Joyce's relations with Drinkwater were quite straightforward: the latter greatly admired his work and, in September 1928, Joyce even considered asking him to write a preface to part of 'Work in Progress'.[54] However, Drinkwater clearly distanced himself and other readers from the ALP section in December 1928. 'You have set your readers a devil of a problem', he says, which 'very few of them are likely altogether to solve.' Drinkwater refers to the 'immense labour' of Joyce's writing and concludes, 'What effect the work will have upon your following I suppose nobody can say . . . in any case this seems to be a relatively unimportant aspect of the business.'[55] On the contrary, Joyce maintained a concern for the conditions of reception, writing such responses into the language of the *Wake*.

While critics and writers laboured in confusion, so did individual readers. Joyce insisted on the inclusion of two letters at the end of *Our Exagmination*: one from the minor poet Vladimir Dixon (discussed later) and another from a self-proclaimed 'common reader', in fact a customer of Shakespeare and Co. called Mrs Kennedy (writing under the pseudonym G. V. L. Slingsby). She mixes reverence with dissatisfaction (a combination similar to the reaction of Wells, Weaver and others) in making the point, 'Whether or not a public can be trained to absorb this kind of thing seems to me extremely doubtful.'[56] Implicitly accepting a specialised readership and the need for time to learn to read the work, she carefully reserves the possibility that such training may prove fruitless. Several letters to Joyce (dated the late 1920s and early 1930s) which have been kept by Sylvia Beach reiterate this point. One, from a Mary O'Callaghan in Ireland, rather nervously remarks, 'still I do not understand "A Work in Progress" . . . I don't quite get all I could from it.'[57] Another reader, Lorentz Bekhoff, admits to being 'always too slow' perhaps because he was also professionally engaged: his series of lectures on Joyce at Oslo University were 'attended . . . by very few people'.[58] Another correspondent writes also on behalf of his wife: 'we can't help but be curious to know *how* to read "Work in Progress". It would need a lot of study. . . . How do you think later generations will view the work?'[59] It is noticeable how many of these readers were concerned with other readers. 'Work in Progress' seems to have always been assumed to be 'for' a future audience rather than current readers. This privileging of a later audience over the current readership has become an established facet of critical thinking on Joyce's reception, but one which, I argue, Joyce's work struggles against.

Joyce was frequently confronted by readers' difficulties, from both ordinary and specialist readers. A letter from 1927 mentions several different readers, among them a 'young man' who called on Joyce in Paris; the critic Desmond MacCarthy (who wrote as 'Affable Hawk' in the *New Statesman*); and another 'man or clergyman'. With the first, Joyce found that the young man knew a lot of the HCE section by heart but 'did not understand many of the words'. With the second, Joyce considered going 'for the last time to explain the piece . . . but let it go'. The third, however, Joyce had only come across as the author of a pamphlet on a prehistoric cave in Penrith, and he wonders 'would [the author] be interested to see t.1 [the first installment of *transition*]? . . . After all, it may interest someone somewhere sometime' (*Letters* I, 254–6). By his own account, Joyce has taken more care with the non-critics than with the critic: MacCarthy will not be replied to, but the young man in Paris was listened to despite (or perhaps because of) his difficulty with the work, and the author of an obscure pamphlet is considered as a possible reader. Sometimes Joyce explains his work, other times he does not. What emerges is an image of the author as promoter but also as someone quite realistically attuned to readers' constraints. While an imaginary 'someone somewhere sometime' is anticipated (like Weaver's 'he, she or them'), Joyce rarely strays far from the material conditions of that distanced and ambivalent readership, what he would later identify as the 'Good Terrafirmaite' (*Letters* I, 284).

IV

Despite the obvious difficulties of reading *Ulysses* and 'Work in Progress', Joyce's rewriting of his reception implies that readers are already in the process of reading: even to say, with Leslie, that the 'massive volume' of *Ulysses* 'must remain impossible to read' is itself a reading of it.[60] The more recent deconstructive account of Joyce's 'impossibility' is a continuation in similar vein. In this sense, that 'lack of time to read' is akin to the deferral of judgement that many critics exercised, in that it pretends to occlude its own pronouncement. Once again an example can be found in one of Leslie's reviews: Joyce was especially interested in the line, 'Time will show what place and influence 'Ulysses' will take in the thought and script of men', which he ensured was reproduced on the circulated 'Extracts of Press Notices'.[61] The phrase is indicative of the ongoing process of reception: its reading was not yet over, nor could it be; more time would always be needed. Over the years, many perplexed reviewers of 'Work in Progress' sought the safety of postponing an opinion. It was 'not possible to pronounce a verdict' but still 'respect-worthy and readable' according to Cyril Connolly; 'its later value we cannot now estimate' warned Leon Edel, 'But that it is worthy of consideration I am certain'; and, for Hamish Miles, 'judgement must stand in suspense'.[62] Implicit in these deferrals of judgement (made in 1929–30) is the traditional liberal call that time will tell, but one of their effects was to sideline Joyce's work as requiring further, specialist study.

The acute awareness of a disjunction between writer and possible public is one of the conditions of Joyce's modernity; one part of this is the history of the accommodation of Joyce as a writer to be studied. It was common for readers of all types to complain of the need for more time and often training as well. For Proust, this objection suggests a dull conservatism: it is the foolish, dreary and socially well-regarded M. de Norpois who opines, 'In this day and age . . . the increasing complexity of modern life leaves one barely any time for reading.'[63] Joyce's – and Proust's – answer might well be that reading is all one does anyway. These complaints can imply the prior existence of an organic age when the social world, including the act of reading, was somehow whole. This assumption seems to lie behind F. R. Leavis's remark in his 1933 review of 'Work in Progress' that 'the "meaning", or an impressive amount of it, can always be worked out at leisure, just as it was worked in'.[64] In turn, this betrays a further assumption of the 'deferral of judgement', for it implies that the 'meaning' can be extracted, that somehow the *time* for reading corresponds to the *ability* to read. It is apparent that Leavis's twinned notions of an English society bound together by its common, living language, and of English studies as a reunifying force, were threatened by 'Work in Progress'. Its uncomfortable accommodation within a shifting and ill-defined emergent institution of English studies was anticipated by many reviewers, such as Gilbert Highet, who pronounced that 'It can be studied . . . but it is impossible to read it'.[65] The pompous professorial voice in chapter 5 of the *Wake* was already there, however, stating that the letter (which is also *Ulysses* and the *Wake* itself) was 'a cosy little brown study all to oneself' (*FW* 114.29–31). The critical and institutional deferment of judgement on 'Work in Progress', while retaining faith in Joyce the author, meant that his last work came to occupy a liminal position as central to literary development but marginal from the 'mainstream' of literary practice. Yet Joyce's rewriting of English implies a different conception of what literature and 'English studies' might be. The *Wake* spells it out: 'You will say it is most unenglish and I shall hope to hear that you will not be wrong about it' (*FW* 160.22–3). As Leavis foresaw, Joyce's reworking of the English language was also a rewriting of its 'reading public' and of the discipline of study.

Published just before Leavis's article, Charles Duff's *James Joyce and the Plain Reader* (which Joyce possessed in his personal library) is indicative of the challenge to criticism that Joyce's work posed. Duff asserts that critics are 'a breed heartily detested by Joyce' and he announces, rather hopefully, that *Ulysses* and *ALP* have 'reached a public well outside the comparatively small section of Joycean devotees or experts in letters'. In short, Joyce's books 'are at last beginning to penetrate the strongholds of the plain reader'.[66] Of course, the very fact of Duff's book removes him from that 'stronghold' and, while it may not have made him detested by Joyce, its defensiveness and tone suggest both the extent of Joyce's appropriation by those 'experts in letters' and the threat that his work was perceived to offer them. It is disturbing what can be said in the name of a 'plain reader': Duff's attempt at popularisation included a distinct racial stereotyping. Joyce was said to have 'the typical Irish mind, but in over-developed forms' and we are told that the 'characteristic qualities of Southern Irish mentality are a restless and often fantastic imagination'.[67] It would be difficult to accept that Joyce was really sympathetic to such 'defences' of the 'plain reader', contrary to Rabaté's claim that Joyce 'continues the vindication of the plain reader's rights' that had been given impetus by Graves and Riding's *Survey of Modernist Poetry*.[68]

By refusing an affability with ordinary readers and the *biens culturels* alike, Joyce's writing ventured towards a difficulty that accorded with a burgeoning and newly professionalised educational market. While today Joyce's work can be touted as a test case for critical theory, it had already been seen in a similar vein in the 1920s and 30s. '*Ulysses* . . . brings to a head all the different questions that have been perplexing literary criticism for some time past,' declared Alfred Noyes in 1922.[69] Indeed, many students applied to Beach for copies of *Ulysses* throughout the 1920s, including several from Cambridge, where Leavis taught it while it was still banned.[70] As a first-year undergraduate at Magdalene College in 1925, William Empson read it to a friend 'for 4 1/2 hours; two chapters'.[71] In 1926, Beach had been told by another Cambridge student that 'some professor there lectured on *Ulysses* and expected every pupil of his to know it like a textbook' (*Letters* I, 246). Not surprisingly, there were objections: in 1931 a disgruntled reader wrote to the London-based (and 'Oxbridge'-dominated) journal *The University* to complain: 'if Culture is not entirely a question of fashion (and it is not), it should be more or less possible to be cultured without being "aware" of Mr Joyce's "existence". In any case, a hundred years ago, nobody knew of Mr Joyce, yet, we presume, Culture had existed then and before then.'[72] What is revealing is not only that Joyce comes to be a test case for the limits of an English studies syllabus but that the syllabus itself is at odds with some notions of 'Culture'. It is evident that Joyce should not be simply accused of a socially conservative or politically evasive institutionalisation. A version of the 'postmodern' denigration of modernist 'museum culture' can be found in Joyce criticism, just as elsewhere others have applauded his radical explosion of the university space, when the significant point is that Joyce's emergence ran in tandem with the development of English as a discipline.[73] It is precisely the arrival of Joyce within such 'debates' that signals the impossibility of divorcing him from their institutional space. Joyce's work both refuses the handshake of recognition while advancing towards an institutional setting that would reinforce the distinction between the specialist and the ordinary reader. In forming part of a new cultural space of reception, in which the formal study of literature begins to shape reading practices, Joyce's work articulates a new form of an older problem in the history of reading: competence.

The revisions to chapter I.5 of *Finnegans Wake* show that the conditions of the consumption of Joyce's last work – and corresponding notions of ordinary and specialised readers – were significant to the production of that work. This chapter was among the first to be written, using especially Notebook VI.B.6, in which Joyce had purposely compiled phrases from reviews of *Ulysses* in early 1924. An early draft of the chapter was published in *Criterion* in July 1925, and it underwent subsequent revisions for *transition* (August 1927) and finally for *Finnegans Wake*. The narrating voice of this episode is professorial in tone, possibly the 'Brotfressor Prenderguest' who was named in 1927. In his revisions, Joyce has his professorial figure distinguish between two forms of reading, corresponding to two types of reader. He invokes both a 'usual sort of ornery josser' (*FW* 109.3) and an 'ideal reader' (*FW* 120.13). The former was first named an 'ordinary fellow'.[74] Late in the revisions, after publication in *transition*, Joyce added a (Bloomian) description of this ordinary reader as 'flatchested fortyish, faintly flatulent . . . given to ratiocination by syncopation in the elucidation of complications' (*FW* 109.2–5). That is, the ordinary reader reasons by a process of contraction in interpreting complex matter: s/he simplifies. In attempting to read the letter, which stands for both *Ulysses* and the *Wake* itself, the professorial voice indicates its interpretive expectations: an ordinary reader ('any fellow of the dime a dozen type') does not have enough time or patience to read 'sufficiently longly' (*FW* 109.1, 109.7). By contrast, the 'ideal reader' is blessed with an 'ideal insomnia'. He reads 'a full trillion times for ever and a night' (*FW* 120.12–14). The professor-figure's invocation of an ideal reader should not be taken too seriously. Instead, Joyce has constructed a professorial voice that has itself constructed a mythical opposition of ordinary vs ideal readers. In this sense, the revisions to this most self-reflexive of chapters betray a sharp awareness of the conditions of reception.

Joyce also implies a criticism of the mediating, professorial voice, which, in the final text, appears to be inconsistent. However, this inconsistency is in fact a developing attitude that emerges over the course of Joyce's revisions. From the first published draft in 1925 Joyce had included in full the well-known plea for patience which echoes the comments of several reviewers of *Ulysses*. 'Now, patience; and remember patience is the great thing, and above all things else we must avoid being or becoming out of patience' (*FW* 108.8–10). This should not be taken, as it often is, as a straightforward request by Joyce to his readers; it is first a conscious echo of actual responses to his work and, moreover, part of a developing engagement with the issue of reception in general, including the critical discourse of the ordinary reader. After the first version was published, Joyce inserted for the *transition* version (1927) the question, 'Sleep, where in the waste is the wisdom?' (now *FW* 114.19–20), echoing a common dismissal and pointing towards the exhaustion of readers and language. The final revisions suggest that professorial patience was increasingly wearing thin: 'there is a limit to all things so this will never do' (*FW* 119.8–9). These embellishments show Joyce making the critical voice in 1.5 increasingly pompous, imprudently levelling the charge that the text is too time-consuming, while continuing to comment upon it.

These revisions also combine to spell out the contradiction in many critics' objections: the pretence to be ordinary readers themselves. On the one hand, this specialist reader who has taken on the task of explication describes himself as 'a worker . . . anxious to pleace averyburies' (*FW* 113.34–5) whereas 'You are a poorjoist, unctuous to polise nopebobbies' (*FW* 113.35–6), and as a consequence 'We cannot say aye to aye' (*FW* 114.1–2). In this case, the professorial critic posits himself on the side of the people whereas 'poor Joyce' can please nobody. The author, Joyce, is thus distinguished from the professional reader in that he is not required to satisfy others. The professional middleman, however, must not only be 'one who deeper thinks' but also must have the book 'finished in a certain time' (*FW* 118.15, 118.8). If the critic is the key cog in the process of dissemination, of course it does not necessarily follow that the line of transmission from author to reader is a smooth one, that 'the writing on the wall will hue it to the mod of men that mote in the main street' (*FW* 118.19–21). The critic's anxiety in I.5 ('anxious to pleace averyburies') may imply that his job is threatened by this text. When he explicates the 'learning betrayed at almost every line's end' (*FW* 120.24), his inconsistency suggests that betrayal may be inherent in learning. Such knowledge of the learning in each line of the document is only 'revealed by a constant labour' (*FW* 120.25–6), suggesting that the professor, who is employed to read, is the nearest to that 'ideal reader' whose 'ideal insomnia' provides the time for such patient and 'constant' application. As seems to be implied, learning also involves a kind of betrayal, so such constant labour may be a fool's quest and a process of exhaustion. In showing how the specialist reader inevitably falls short of his impossible goal, however, the distinction between the 'ordinary' and the 'expert' is *not* necessarily overcome. Instead, 'Work in Progress' exemplifies how the professional construction of readerly 'types' reinforces emergent forms of literary reception. Joyce helps create, even as he undermines, the specialist reader.

This raises a familiar quandary in *Wake* criticism: just what sort of reader does the text presume? Does it tend towards a super-competent 'ideal reader' or an inventive, perhaps solipsistic, reader? Responding to Umberto Eco's rules for a putative 'ideal Joyce Reader' (who 'always has to keep semiotically awake'), Jean-Michel Rabaté has suggested with more leniency that 'we cannot ever condemn "bad" readings . . . The "genrea-der" should not be afraid of misreadings.' This description seems to offer a pragmatic acceptance that the rules are determined by an 'inter-pretive community' while retaining a sense of propriety by holding onto the notion of a 'misreading'. However, if there are no bad readings, only 'better or worse' ones, what do you call a reading which argues that there *are* bad readings?[75] Following Rabaté, a reader who sets out to show the superiority of his or her reading would him/herself be 'bad'. The 'deconstruction of competence' results in an unworkable solipsism, yet it is not necessarily the case that the bad reader must – or, indeed, can – be jettisoned. A reading of Joyce's last work cannot relinquish the notion of competence that informs all reading and its institutions. Admitting that 'I still like him', Derrida defines the 'impatience' of 'the *bad* reader' as 'the reader in a hurry to be determined, decided upon deciding'. Derrida's *J'accuse* might suggest – problematically, and this is oddly reminiscent of Leavis's idea of 'working out the meaning at leisure' – that the 'good' reader is the slowest. I would suggest that Joyce's last work is itself formulated to allow for the bad or 'hurried' (*pressé*) reader.[76] As such, its form is shaped to the possibility of a 'distracted' as well as a 'studied' reception, not from empathy with ordinary readers but as a facet of shifting structures of reception.

If the 'ornery josser' abbreviates but the 'ideal reader' has all time, then the form of Joyce's last work allows for both strategies. Against the charge that 'Work in Progress' was too demanding on time and patience, is the advice given by *Finnegans Wake* itself: the textbook chapter (II.2), in which the twins and Issy are seen reading, offers the cryptic guidance to 'volve the virgil page and view' (*FW* 270.25), referring to *sortes Virgilianae*, the practice of opening Virgil at random and proceeding from any line that catches the eye – as practised on different books with commendable results by St Augustine and Leopold Bloom.[77] This is reinforced a few pages later by the marginal note, 'SORTES VIRGINIANAE' (*FW* 281R). The body of the text thus explains in advance a forthcoming marginal gloss, from which it is characteristically divorced, while the note, itself eye-catching, appears to license its reading in conjunction with any part of the body of the text. On the other hand, the practice of reading even 'SORTES VIRGINIANAE' may well require annotating, and the elucidation of that practice can itself rely upon a near encyclopaedic knowledge of the text.[78]

There is an obvious discrepancy between the 'leisured' reading of a Leavis and the hurried absorption of a notional 'reading public' (those 'men that mote in the main street'?) which may also be seen in the relationship between the length of time Joyce took to write 'Work in Progress' and its accretion of fragmented language with its suitability for select quotation. The *Wake* suggests that even professional readers can be reduced to desperation when it mimics the attitude of the indebted reviewer – and admits its own plundering – in the line 'thanks ever so much for the tiny quote' (*FW* 395.18).[79] At the same time, it seems to appeal to a better, more industrious, reader: 'a tithe of troubles, and is there one who understands me?' (*FW* 627.15). *Finnegans Wake* is well adapted to this bifocal structure of 'sampling versus study', for it both calls for an absolute attention and self-consciously permits the most fleeting of readings. By showing how these two 'types' of reader with their different reading practices are critical constructions in a contemporary discourse of reception, *Finnegans Wake* both invokes and plays between that distinction. It does not 'vindicate' the plain reader, but nor does it uncritically support the specialist.

As I will argue, these different reading strategies can be seen to be aspects of the text's material (and personal) production from states of exhaustion. This chapter concludes by showing how that production was itself indivisible from an aesthetic conundrum: whether the text's language was reproducible or auratic. In doing so, it returns once again to a specific reader, John Eglinton, whose complex cultural antipathy to Joyce bears a striking resemblance to that aesthetic question, which, then, can be seen as also political.

v

For Joyce, writing is a process of exhaustion, of the self and of the language. His sources are the well-worn archetypes of European Culture (Homer, Dante, Shakespeare) but they are also the tired materials of everyday culture (a returned library book, a music-hall cliché, a circulating flyer). He even exhausted his own materials in the process of writing: often notebooks are filled 'end to end hithaways' with lines 'slittering up' and 'slettering down' (*FW* 114.16–18); phrases have 'acquired accretions' (*FW* 114.3–28) as they expand for copying. The notebooks, with their recycled pages and coloured crossings, are an index to many things, but among them surely lies exhaustion, that state where work is unavoidably incomplete but already expended or 'sold out'; that odd amalgam of ceaseless labour and enforced leisure, common to writer and reader. This is not only psychological, but also the form of the world that Joyce salvaged. As John Bishop argues, *Finnegans Wake* is a book about *obscuritas*, and this darkness implies a particular mode of exhaustion – not only of readers and of materials, but also the writer's personal exhaustion.

The silent retort of the apparently inexhaustible Proust to the 'lack of time' was sleeplessly to write all night. Likewise Kafka: 'the only way I can keep going, if at all, is by writing, not through rest and sleep'.[80] Joyce similarly fights time and tiredness with writing, replacing one exhaustion with another until he could claim to Beckett to have 'put the language to sleep'.[81] Exhaustion was a common state for Joyce for roughly a decade from the middle of the 1920s onwards, with Lucia's declining health, his numerous eye operations (plus consumption of painkillers), the composition of the *Wake*, and bouts of drinking all ongoing drains on his resources (not to mention one-off events such as the death of his father, which compounded his depression in early 1932, or the steadily insistent worries such as Nora's threats to leave, the bans on *Ulysses*, Roth's piracy and rejections by former supporters). Joyce wrote to Weaver in 1928,

'I fatigued myself to exhaustion point over ∧a [*FW* III.i]' (*Letters* III, 173). Yet never far behind lies its corollary state – a productive resumption: 'I have returned to a mountain of proofs . . . I am feeling rather lazy about it and will have to give myself some sort of a kick or prod up' (*Letters* III, 177). Jaun has the same sensation in *Finnegans Wake*: 'our greatly misunderstood one we perceived to give himself some sort of a hermetic prod or kick to sit up and take notice' (*FW* 470.1–3). This odd combination of labour and leisure is the very experience of exhaustion whereby work can be neither accomplished nor avoided.

In 1933, in the middle of his difficulties in completing 'Work in Progress', with *Anna Livia Plurabelle* and *Exagmination* released and the critical tide slowly turning, Joyce complained to Larbaud of his recent 'worry, expense and nerves'. 'I wish I had some leisure and that both our minds were free from preoccupation', yet 'I am now hopelessly with the goats' (*Letters* I, 284). (He assumes that Larbaud's mind, like his, is 'preoccupied'.) And Joyce was *on holiday* when he wrote this (though that may be the effect of Torquay). A month after returning to Paris, he began a letter to Weaver, 'I have not stopped working yet.' Again, exhaustion implies contradictory sensations: both the effort of ceaseless striving and enforced recovery – which is less leisure than pain. Joyce's next letter to Weaver, another month on, begins 'I have been sleeping sixteen hours a day for the past three weeks, incapable of thinking, writing, reading or speaking', though nonetheless he manages, 'Here, however is a further installment of news' – roughly 750 words of news (*Letters* I, 286). Writing and sleeping seem to go hand-in-hand; the *Wake* is Joyce's version of sleep-writing. Famously, Joyce told Weaver that a 'wideawake language' would be unsuitable, but only after saying how 'overworked and over-worried' he was (*Letters* III, 146). In addition, his text is littered with calls for sleep – 'Grant sleep in hour's time, O Loud' (*FW* 259.04) – which never quite seem to be granted (and which confuse the critical supposition that the *Wake* is told by a dreaming subject).[82]

Some years earlier Joyce had written to Pound, 'sometimes I find it difficult to keep my eyes open – like the readers of my masterpieces' (*SL* 228). Yet this state is also prefigured in the production of his work. *Ulysses* can serve as a guide. An orthodox critical assumption is that the styles of 'Eumeaus' and 'Penelope' 'reflect' the tiredness of their characters but an organic relation between situation and narrative should not necessarily be trusted given the variety of styles and voices in *Ulysses*. As Derek Attridge has pointed out, 'Eumeaus' can be read as a tireless language which, in a sense, is unstoppable, and Molly's monologue is very much a written, rather than a thought, language. It is one that takes shortcuts with punctuation and graphic emblems but which seems to require a slow reading, reinsertion of punctuation and syntactical rules.[83] The effect is an odd interlacing of roles: if 'Penelope' has been stitched by the omission of signs, its reading silently restores the 'missing' punctuation; it dismantles the language into its component parts, unweaving the thread in order to reassemble it. In this sense, the grammatical reader knits both against and with Molly's writing, combining and pulling away. As with the texture of *Finnegans Wake*, the 'constant labour' of the reader is visible on the page. The process of reception is shown to inhere in the act – and even the appearance – of writing. The *Wake*'s great blocks of condensed print suggest a self-reflexive materiality; the exhausted artefact of the book is displayed in its stodgy form, exhausting the spaces of the page. Even the playful marginalia of II.2 imply less the vivacity of the book than its eventual demise, the inability of the pages to hold their hyperactive text.

Attridge's analysis of 'Penelope' underlines the distance between character and narrative voice, as between author and narrator, yet all the same there does seem to be an uneasily close relationship between the somatic reader and the tortuous writing. Reading has physical consequences, but unlike Barthes' *jouissance* the effects may be rather numbing.[84] Consider Proust, who had to put off a planned reading to a group of friends because his fragile respiratory system could not cope with his own lengthy sentences. David Spurr observes that Proust's unwieldy writing 'forces a transformation even in the *teknè* of silent reading'.[85] (Joyce had suggested that the reader finishes Proust's sentences before the author himself.[86]) A more troubling implication is that Proust projects his own incapacity onto readers, as if the exhaustion of writing is contagious. Joyce does something similar in the language of *Finnegans Wake*, which not only takes up, and returns, the complaints from readers of their own lack of time but also bears the imprint of his own exhaustion in its unpronounceable phrases and its defeat of even the most scrutinous eye. A halting inability to read the thunder words echoes and amplifies the text's 'unbrookable script' (*FW* 123.32–3), with at least one reviewer complaining that 'Work in Progress' was a '*physical* impossibility to read'.[87] After revising 'Shaun the Post' in 1926, Joyce read it 'to a small audience' and admitted to Weaver that 'it produced stupefaction, I think. That evening I was exhausted to the point of idiocy' (*Letters* III, 139). The social attempt to form a readership induces fatigue in both author and listeners/readers; the condition of the language seems to be catching:

'there was a not a snoozer among them but was utterly undeceived in the heel of the reel by the recital of the rigmarole' (*FW* 174.3–4). Joyce's writing and its readers – indeed, even Joyce himself – all appear trapped in an exhaustive cycle: 'becalmed . . . bored, drowsed, bewildered' as one reviewer described 'the reader' of *Ulysses*.[88]

The exhaustion of over-production pertains to an aesthetic problem that can be exemplified by a footnote in the history of Joyce criticism. One of the letters appended to the rear of *Our Exagmination* in 1929 was written in an uncannily familiar language: addressed to 'My Germ's Choice' it explained, in tired puns, how the writer had been able to read 'Work in Progress' only because of a lengthy illness. Signed Vladimir Dixon, this letter was long thought to have been written by Joyce. Beach had annotated the envelope, 'Vladimir Dixon: probably JJ himself'; later, Stuart Gilbert and then Ellmann corroborated the error. In fact, Dixon (1900–1929) was a minor poet of Russian descent then living in Paris, who had previously ordered *This Quarter* (including 'Work in Progress') from Shakespeare & Co. in 1925 and probably also read *transition*.[89] The significance of this anecdote is that the mistake was made and accepted both by people close to Joyce and by some of the most informed later readers his work has enjoyed. It goes to the heart of Joyce's technique which could, it seems, be imitated or reproduced convincingly. This presents a problem for Joyce, and Joyce critics, illustrating how the mode of production is entirely pertinent to the question of reception.

There is a well-known argument of Walter Benjamin's with respect to film, that its potential for a broad and dispersed audience was necessitated by the conditions of film's technological production. Its reproducibility is a feature of the technology and so therefore is the fact that it demands a broad audience. This was a 'distracted' audience, unable to comprehend all that was happening before it so quickly, as opposed to the studied 'absorbed' audience for auratic art.[90] A comparison might be made with the composition of *Finnegans Wake*, whose 'mechanical' language proved so off-putting to many reviewers and so imitable to Dixon. Its self-conscious materiality hints at a Beckettian game of permutations and combinations of syllables, words, phrases, languages. As critics of many generations have admitted, there was something 'maddeningly simplistic' about Joyce's 'pitiless method'. 'Too easy to do and too hard to understand' had been Stuart Gilbert's private comment in his Paris diary.[91]

While Joyce on occasion referred to himself as an engineer and used tunnelling imagery to describe his work, the terms of his notorious approach to James Stephens (to complete 'Work in Progress') are interesting

because they suggest the crucial distinction of *his* 'engine': 'Of course
he would never take a fraction of the time or pains I take' but if 'I showed
him the threads he could finish the design' (*Letters* I, 253).[92] What makes
the difference, in Joyce's terms, is his personal exhaustion (the time and
pains) as this is what helped ensure the exhaustive processing of the text.
There was a confusion in the terms of the approach to Stephens between
the auratic quality of the singular artist and the impersonal, mechanical
character of the language and structure of the text. Before coming up
with Stephens, Joyce had considered that 'There is no such absurd person
as could replace me except the incorrigible god of sleep and no waster
quite so wasteful' (*Letters* I, 252). (Waste and work fit together with an
odd appropriateness.) While the fiction that Stephens could complete
Finnegans Wake (a fiction that Joyce maintained for several years from
1929) was perhaps a necessary crutch, it also both implies the apparent
reproducibility of the method and retains the peculiarity of the individual
artist. Joyce's personal exhaustion remained for him a distinguishing
feature.

   This combination of an auratic humanism and technological reproducibility were further entwined through Joyce's practice of reading his
work, exemplified in the release of his gramophone recording of *Anna
Livia Plurabelle* by the Cambridge Orthological Institute in 1929. Joyce
sent a copy to Stephens – who admired *ALP* – and recommended that
he also make a recording; there was even an idea that they might make a
two-sided disc together (*Letters* III, 203). Despite its poor sales – it sold at
'five discs a year' (*Letters* III, 203) – this record helped promote the idea
that *Finnegans Wake* should be read aloud. C. K. Ogden, whose 'basically
english' (*FW* 116.26) was then in vogue, had helped Joyce with the recording and collaborated on a short piece that was released with the record.
Shortly afterwards, he claimed that without hearing it, 95 per cent of
readers would extract no more than 5 per cent of *ALP*'s significance;
and many others have echoed him, with one reviewer declaring in 1933,
'Work in Progress cannot be understood unless read aloud.'[93] That the
reader was Joyce of course only heightened the auratic illusion: Levin
for one found it a 'captivating phonograph record'.[94] As with many
critical truisms of his work, this idea began with Joyce himself. He had
told Curran, on sending him the first published version of this chapter
in 1925, that it should be read partially aloud, without pausing and
quite quickly.[95] The qualifications here are interesting: a murmur might
still retain the sense of a written text – as in 'wreathing her murmoirs'
(*FW* 387.34) – whilst affecting an incantation. The suggestion that *ALP*

would be read rapidly, without breaking, is symptomatic of a mechanistic, perhaps ritualistic, sense of language, but it also contributes to the power of the individual speaker.

While Joyce's group readings had enhanced the auratic attraction for would-be readers, these events also fed back into the text. Late in 1927, a few days after completing *ALP*, Joyce gave a reading of it to a group of friends and admirers ('a group of "critics"') on whom it 'made a profound impression' (*Letters* I, 260).[96] On 4 November, Joyce wrote to Miss Weaver about the event, noting that his audience comprised 'about 25 people of the world's 1500 million' (*Letters* I, 260). As is often the case with 'Work in Progress', however, the occasion of Joyce's reading has been grafted into the drafts of the text: between the galleys for the aborted publication of *ALP* in *Calendar* (dating from July 1925) and the galleys for *transition* 8 (November 1927), two sentences have been added: 'Will you hold your peace and listen well to what I am going to say now? It might have been ten or twenty to one of the night of Allclose' (now *FW* 207.30–2). This apparently refers to the event of Joyce's reading in its gestures to an audience ('you'), its size ('ten or twenty'), and the date ('All close', All Souls, 2 November). The social events of reception could thus contribute to the ongoing production of the text: their auratic quality merging into the mechanical manipulation of the language. In this way, the means of creating and enabling a potential readership can also be seen as ways by which those events were themselves co-opted into the text: the process of production (the accretion of fragments from an actual reception) coincided with a construction of Joyce's reception (an auratic art that had to be heard) which would remain influential for decades. It is striking how quickly these events became known and how readily critics found that 'his master's voice' allowed a means of 'reading' the apparently unreadable.

VI

A case in point is John Eglinton. Having found his own voice satirised in *Ulysses*, he was in no hurry to read 'Work in Progress'. His 'Glimpse of the Later Joyce' recalls their final meeting at which Eglinton confessed his 'inability to understand' the later work; nonetheless, or perhaps even because of this, Joyce sent him *ALP* on condition that Eglinton would tell him what he thought of it. He never did tell Joyce directly, but published his response in 1935. It is notable for recognising the combination of individuality and reproducibility in Joyce's writing: its desperate

attempt to cling to the former while having to declare the latter is
symptomatic of both Eglinton's own position and the challenge of Joyce's
last work. He declared of its language that 'the word itself had . . . become
a thing'. In observing that there was 'never enough to excite the energy
of continuous attention', he was not complaining of the 'lack of time to
read' but responding to a facet of the book's production. Eglinton went
on, 'It may very well be that this kind of verbal notation is directed to
an order of intelligence likely to become more general.'[97] If, as Benjamin
remarks, at crucial moments an art form aspires to effects that can be
achieved only through the creation of new technology, it might be said
that Eglinton was helped to this insight by reading Joyce in the context
of film.[98] In his earlier review of *Ulysses*, he had noted that 'its infinite
variety is monotonous as only the cinema or hippodrome entertainment
is monotonous'.[99] On the one hand, Eglinton's tacit complaint in 1922
about Joyce's 'cinematic epic' is that it is part of an apparent dehuman-
isation of reading. On the other hand, Eglinton had even earlier (in 1899)
derided Yeats and A. E. for what he saw as their denial of modernity
and in doing so he had associated, as a positive counter-example, 'the
kinematograph' with the *Odyssey*.[100] The curve of Eglinton's response to
emergent film technology, as well as to the possibilities of the new Ireland,
is emblematic of his reaction to Joyce. A complex product of the Revival's
contradictions, Eglinton's personal disillusionment with both the political
climate and modernisation in the 1920s is suggestive of the extent to
which Joyce's work had corresponded with broader shifts in habits of
perception. His response to Joyce, over many years, is indicative of a
personal, political and aesthetic distance.

Eglinton's insight also betrays his presumption: having depersonalised
reading, there is no place for him to invest his response except back onto
the figure of the author whose 'heroic persistence' is duly praised.[101] He
bemoans the distance between reader and writer ('In reading Joyce,
nothing passes from the author's mind to my own') as if the lesson of
'Scylla and Charybdis' was still unlearnt. Eglinton instead fell back on
the assumption that, if *he* was unable to read Joyce, perhaps people who
now knew him could: 'those who appear to understand him – and he is
fortunate in retaining a company of very able henchmen, his interpreters –
are those who enjoy personal relations with him, and have heard him
from time to time, with that accomplished articulation of his, reading
his works aloud.'[102] Eglinton's emphasis on the significance of Joyce's
coterie of friends and helpers is a means of accommodating Joyce within
a given social form: 'racy' Paris was better adapted for this sort of thing.

Indeed, as the Introduction discussed, it has been a long-standing truism of Joyce studies that his last work found an appropriate audience in the Paris of the 1920s and 30s. In Eglinton's case, he subtly accuses Joyce of charlatanism and even an implied thuggery ('henchmen'), both of which might be detected in Joyce's accent, whose 'accomplished articulation', it is implied, has been unnaturally forced. In the end, this is what Eglinton's refusal of Joyce amounts to: a personal dismissal that stands-in for political disenchantment. He finds in 'Work in Progress' an unnatural fusion of the auratic – 'the annoying prominence of his [Joyce's] own idiosyncrasy' – with an experiment that 'seems to belong to the age of the "talkies"'. Joyce is, in Eglinton's phrase, 'a mechanical inventor almost as much as an artist'.[103]

The reception of the *Wake* has often returned to the personal and the auratic – to the author's heroic sacrifice and single-minded creation. While it is a standard facet of biographical studies, this could even be said to be the case in Derrida's interpretation, which universalises the *Wake* as a software encompassing the entirety of Western culture. Claiming it has already read its future readers, Derrida attributes to it the auratic quality of returning our gaze.[104] Evidently, the auratic perception famously described by Benjamin is not easily dismissed (and here Benjamin's own uneasy nostalgia for the auratic comes across in his characterisation of photography as without imagination). The traces of 'aura' run through the *mémoire involontaire* of Proust's account of reading in childhood: for him, childhood reading calls to mind 'the images of the places and the days when we did this reading', not so much the reading-matter itself, and it is in these personal associations that the aura of the object of perception lingers.[105] It is possible to think of the *Wake*'s kaleidoscopic 'recall' of languages, cultures and histories as another form of rejuvenation in which readers' involuntary associations are conjured up by encountering the phantasmal language of the book. Reading in the *Wake* can be thought of as an odd *mémoire involontaire* in which unexpected perceptions offer a temporary and highly speculative 'rejuvenation' of the worlds, the histories, the languages that have constituted its text. Such reading does not of course take in all of the text any more than it takes in all its allusions. Instead, while the scope of the *Wake* appears to suggest an impossible, encyclopaedic recollection, its reading gestures towards a short-lived memory, and in this it creates a generic fusion of epical and novelistic qualities that has the appearance of 'for all time' and the practice of 'for a while'. Indeed, Eglinton's accounts of *Ulysses* seem to be as much his own recollection of the 'places and the days' of his reading

Joyce as an account of what he has read. At the same time, he seems to
have learned to read Joyce in the act of doing so. His final line on Joyce –
that he 'exhibits the disabilities of epic in a world sadly in need of Greek
simplicity and synthesis' – itself exhibits Eglinton's own cultural unease
while grasping a real sense of the thwarted reception for a 'disabled epic'.

The tension between the humanistic and the mechanical is directly
pertinent to the question of reading time and 'reader types'. On the one
hand, Joyce's personal pains 'insure' the value of the text and so its
worthiness to be studied with something approaching 'ideal insomnia' or
'constant labour'. On the other hand, the 'process reproduction' of this
language of the 'tiny quote' demands a fleeting consumption or selective
perusal. The point of Benjamin's analysis of film technology was to show
that the distinction between a 'distracted' (time-pressed, or ordinary) and
'concentrated' (or specialist) audience is inappropriate to the new medium. Benjamin thought that the advent of film (and sport) as reproducible
spectacle makes 'everybody . . . somewhat of an expert' – but he could only
think this on the grounds that 'at the movies [the critic] requires no
attention'.[106] Yet in 'Work in Progress' Joyce's engagement with discourses
of reception, and with actual responses, never fully collapses the distinction between critic-expert and ordinary reader. It does not, therefore,
amount to the 'deconstruction of competence' that Derrida and some
Joyce critics have found. The time-pressed readers of *Finnegans Wake* are a
function of its production which, in turn, ensures its continual reading.

Joyce's writing of reception provides for a historicity of reception – but
a reception that is still an act. Later readers are reminded – or informed –
of earlier ones; more than that, they cannot help but read through those
responses (or versions of them). In one sense, earlier readers *are* the text
that later ones read. In working through these, in our own readings, we
repeat them: one result of our competence is the identification of previous
readers. This emphasis on actual responses both provokes the continuation
of reading (a comment becomes part of the *Wake* and is thus cast into
an indefinite future of other readers) and offers the illusion of a historical
return to the locale of an actual response, as if locating the source were
somehow to grasp the meaning of both its moment and its writing. In this
sense, the *Wake* contains within itself a deceptive *mémoire involontaire*
of its own reception. We trace these reviews but cannot fully recover them.
In displaying our competence, then, we re-encounter the misreadings that
are the prehistory of our own. One should beware the reading of Eglinton:
the initial scene of response has been re-enacted and is now irrecoverable.
So the history of Joyce's reception is in part a fiction of his own writing.

CHAPTER 4

Hypocrisy: Finnegans Wake, hypocrites lecteurs *and the Treaty*

> . . . we were like bro and sis over our castor and porridge. . . He feels he ought to be as asamed of me as me to be ashunned of him. We were in one class of age like to two clots of egg. I am most beholding to him, my namesick, as we sayed it in our Amharican, through the Doubly Telewisher . . . It will pleased me behind with thanks from before and love to self and all I remain here your truly friend. I am no scholar but I loved that man who has africot lupps with the moonshane in his profile, my shemblable! My freer!
>
> (*FW* 489.15–28)

Finnegans Wake is a book that cannot have an epigraph. To do so would set up a relation, even perhaps hint at a genealogy, between text and predecessor, within which an implicit readerly position would also be assumed. An epigraph typically functions as a form of address to the 'competent' reader. Instead, the *Wake*'s citations – as above, to Baudelaire ('– *Hypocrite lecteur, – mon semblable, – mon frère!*'') and others – are gestures and echoes that hint without stating. If, as the previous chapter suggested, the *Wake* contains an 'anarchive' of Joyce's reception, it acts in this way towards all its sources: unable to quote or to represent, it instead transforms and enacts a reading of the myriad texts from which it is drawn. So *Finnegans Wake* performs a kind of hypocritical language, one in which contraries are often expressed (such as ALP's simultaneous indictment and exoneration of HCE) and in which private sources have been publicly transformed. In this sense, the *Wake* is itself a *hypocrite lecteur* and 'shemblable', simultaneously announcing its similarity to, and difference from, the texts it reads.

This chapter explores what a *hypocrite lecteur* might mean in relation to *Finnegans Wake*. I suggest that Joyce constructs a model for the *hypocrite lecteur* from the apparent hypocrisy of some of his actual readers in Ireland, including most notably W. B. Yeats, the 'Doubly Telewisher' or 'W. B. Y. wellwisher', whose complex relationship with Joyce provides a significant model for the writing of reception as it is performed in *Finnegans Wake*. The two writers are not to be regarded as oppositional but more 'like to two clots of egg' – Joyce's rewriting of what Yeats, himself adapting Plato, called 'the yolk and white of the one shell' ('Among School Children'). This relationship is particularly significant given the context in which they once more corresponded: Yeats's reading of *Ulysses* and a possible return by Joyce to Ireland in the early months of the Free State. The publication of *Ulysses* ensured Joyce's continued interrogation of his reception in Ireland, especially given that the nation was at the time divided by the Treaty and Civil War. The citation above shows Shaun, the composite figure of many actual, disapproving readers (Stanislaus, Lewis, etc.) being interviewed by the *Wake*'s internal audience of judges and critics, known as the Four, discussing his relationship with Shem, the autobiographical writer-figure, who has not travelled back to Ireland. These *semblables* and *frères* are both brothers and others. Shaun voices the reservations of all those critics when he says, 'your truly friend. I am no scholar.' At one level, a conventional charge of hypocrisy against Joyce's critics is signalled here by the echo in the first sentence of Wyndham Lewis's private pledge to be an 'ever devoted friend' (*Letters* I, 257). Yet since the second sentence ('I am no scholar') admits the instability of the dislocated reader faced with this language of babble and Babel, it might also be the case that such hypocrisy cannot be helped. More accurately, the distinction between 'sincerity' (as 'truthful intention') and 'hypocrisy' (as double-dealing) has been *overwritten* and a structural hypocrisy has been implied. This is what Joyce does to his respondents: he overwrites them, re-addressing them with his own peculiar stamp. Sending them backwards and onwards to further *hypocrites lecteurs*, Joyce found an analogue for the *Wake*'s overwriting, redirection and change of legitimation of his readers in the operations of the postal service in the foundation of the Free State. In this way, the implication of a dual inscription, and divided reception, is central to this chapter.

Hypocrisy takes on an undecidable form in *Finnegans Wake*, one that echoes and transforms a longstanding political tension for Joyce between concern for his possible readership and the need to write without addressing. If he found in an Irish reading of *Ulysses* a model of hypocrisy that was peculiar to the conditions of the nation, that model also derives from the text: the writing of reception foreplays its betrayal. In that sense, there is a mutually unstable reception enacted between a divided Irish cultural framework and a structurally hypocritical writing. The anxiety of reception that had been endemic to Irish writing – and which helps define a sense of modernity – reaches its climax in *Finnegans Wake* precisely through its continual reading of others' reading and its own refusal of an audience. In this way, Joyce's early concern to have, but not write for, readers (as explored in the previous chapters), finds its fullest form in his last book. What this chapter shows is that this form had a particular contextual inflection.

As the word hypocrisy implies, every critical act of judgement is precisely that: an act.[2] The implication of *Finnegans Wake* that no language, subjectivity or identity is stable or 'truthful' has profound repercussions for the notion of hypocrisy. Since the conventional structure of hypocrisy depends upon a private, known or truthful position (or text) from which a departure has been made, *Finnegans Wake* renders that distinction untrustworthy. In this, it may do no more than, by virtue of its exaggerated intensification, bring out what any writing hints at. In the terms of the *Wake*, hypocrisy is ultimately an unknowable or undecidable term, and this allows Joyce to respond once more to his Irish reception, to dismantle the stage on which it has been performed. If all positions are already profoundly unstable, not only is the distinction upon which hypocrisy depends irrelevant but even bringing the charge of hypocrisy becomes suspect. Such a manoeuvre was not irrelevant to Joyce in the early 1920s as he once more faced the implicit accusation of his own hypocrisy in writing of Ireland from abroad and encountered an apparent hypocrisy from Yeats and others in their attempts to co-opt *Ulysses*. By destabilising hypocrisy, Joyce upsets the conventional depiction of the 'writer abroad' and the 'home audience', at once acknowledging the gap but disallowing a false opposition between them.

Baudelaire's famous invocation of a hypocritical reader is both a performative judgement and another undoing of the notion of hypocrisy. Addressing his volume in the first poem, 'Au Lecteur', Baudelaire announces a fundamental disjunction of modernity, between the apparently de-individuated crowd and the generically-presumed individuality of the lyric poet. At the same time as depicting himself as one of the crowd, sharing their sins, his narrator addresses them through lyric with, it seems, the expectation of not being understood by these readers. If the well-known final line, '– *Hypocrite lecteur, – mon semblable, – mon frère!*', appears to show Baudelaire as both lyric poet and modern reader, it does so, one might say, somewhat hypocritically. That is, he sees his image among the crowd even as he gives voice to the distinction. At the same time that it brings those (br)others together as *frères*, then, the poem opens a chasm between writer and reader: the address to the reader must fail. However, given that the reader has already been explicitly identified as hypocritical, for the address to fail – for it to be misdelivered, or misrecognised – would also confirm the success of the address. The double bind – the inevitable, structural hypocrisy – is that this successful address would appear to undermine its point.

In this way, by announcing an irresolvable dichotomy between author and 'his' public readership, the modern writer begins to thread the difficult line of the 'prosepoem' – a line that Joyce later takes up in his 'poseproem' (*FW* 528.16). Both Baudelaire and Joyce move towards the demarcation of a language and a genre that would fuse the divisions of a 'forked tongue' through the very emphasis on difference. If the disjointed conditions Baudelaire addressed were those of European modernity, witnessed by the poet in the urban crowd, Joyce's echo, seventy years later, speaks to the distinction of the writer from the imagined nation, and of the nation from itself. By playing on the deceptive relationship between the apparent sincerity of the lyric poet and incapacity of the modern reader, Baudelaire's 'Au Lecteur' admits of the gulf that necessarily distinguishes writers from their audience (among whom, nonetheless, he still puts himself). Although the poet names and addresses his *hypocrite lecteur* from the outset, in Joyce's text the hypocritical reader is instead already written into the language and form of the text. For Joyce, there is no dedication or initial address 'to the reader', only the motley assortment of phrasings that make little distinction between those 'laities and gentlenuns' and the 'drear writer' (*FW* 177.08, 476.21).[3] Joyce's reception supposes that a social dialogue is already in place; the readers are already part of the materials of the text.

I

When Joyce began 'Work in Progress' in the Autumn of 1922, he told Weaver that it would be a 'history of the world'. This, at least, is Ellmann's version, one that has powerfully excluded Joyce's continued engagement with Irish cultural politics including his reception here.[4] Yet his first notebook (VI.B.10), predominantly compiled from various newspapers (especially the *Irish Times* and the *Leader* among Irish sources), is often more concerned with recent Irish events rather than with a 'universal history'. Vincent Deane concludes from his analysis of the notebooks that the founding of the Free State and the consequent Civil War 'form a constant background to Joyce's notes in this period'.[5] The apparent transposition of the Irish for the universal is writ large in *Finnegans Wake* (as, indeed in *Ulysses*), and yet the specific historical and textual conditions of Ireland in the early 1920s – with the coincidence of the Treaty and *Ulysses* – provides a crucial context for reading the *Wake*.[6] The mixed reception of these documents would offer a model for Joyce in his new work as he once more returned to readers' responses and finally confronted the cultural politics of his own emigration.

In the years immediately following the formation of an independent Irish state, Joyce's composition of a work whose structural principle is cyclical history would appear to suggest that the disappointment at the terms of that independence, the bitterness of the Civil War, and the drudgery of the new state all consolidated the notion that history (and Irish history in particular) was 'providential warring' in a 'jolting series of prearranged disappointments' (*FW* 107.31–4). To Joyce, then, the narrative of national delivery might be called hypocritical: a series of false performances which Seamus Deane calls a kind of boredom or sameness not only in its repetitive structure but also in its predictable ability to stand in for world history. Joyce's representations of this sort of historical paralysis, Deane argues, lead to a kind of textual paralysis in which no narrative (including a national one) is fully told or achieved. Such a constant deferral is thus a way for Joyce to show how, for instance, a nationalist narrative of Irish history became paralysed and how that narrative itself reproduced further monotony.[7]

This interpretation of Joyce's account of Irish history reads its 'providential warring' according to one meaning of the word *providence* although, as Tony Thwaites has commented, the word refers not only to the hidden guidance and foresight of nature or a deity but also to serendipity.[8] In the first instance, 'providential' means (according to the *OED*) 'characterised by foresight' and prudent arrangement; in the second, it refers to special intercession, one that is 'opportune, lucky'. With both meanings in mind, some significance can also be given to any particular moment at which the historical series appears momentarily to have been suspended. The 'providential warring' of Irish history can be read (as in the orthodox critical account) as an ordained delivery of betrayal and infighting, but also as the inscription, momentarily, of a particular event, an accidental arrest of the 'jolting series' even as it goes on. Such a moment of potential decision came with the Treaty, and, analogously, with *Ulysses*. The reception of these texts would provide a means to the writing of the *Wake*, which in its staging of that reception, shows that 'hypocrisy' and 'providence' are undecidable terms, and which thus continually re-stages the moments of decision faced by their readers. Rather than simply reinscribing the 'paralysis' of Irish history, and the 'betrayal' of the nation, *Finnegans Wake* shows Joyce seeking to move beyond these terms, or, rather, *through* them, towards a staging of the political and literary moment as a potentially 'decisive' one. The decision comes as a response to a different kind of generic question, such as, how can an unreadable text be read?

In the *Wake*, the letter that Shaun attempts to deliver is a synecdoche for Joyce's writing in general and *Ulysses* in particular, but it is also, symbolically, the 1921–2 Treaty *and* the alternative to the Treaty, known as 'Document Number 2', proposed by Eamon de Valera. Throughout the *Wake*, terms used to describe the letter, such as 'documents or document', carry overtones of both the Treaty and de Valera's alternative; and its 'multiplicity of personalities' suggests the seven signatories of the Treaty (*FW* 107.24–5). This 'duplex' document (*FW* 123.30) set the terms over which the 'providential warring' of 'dramdrinker against freethinker' (*FW* 107.31–2) would be conducted. The tension between repetition and singularity in this pattern is reinforced by the apparent date of the letter's postmark, 'the last of the first' (*FW* 111.10). The Treaty came into legal effect in December 1921 and was ratified in January 1922. The letter also refers to 'the general's elections' (*FW* 111.12): the Treaty had established a Provisional Government alongside the Dáil (with largely similar personnel) until the general election of 16 June 1922, which formed the first official Free State government. A pact between Collins and de Valera, sealed the previous month, had little consequence as the elections prevented a clear verdict on the Treaty, spelling the way for Civil War.[9]

The professorial voice that mediates the letter suggests that its readership is similar to that of the Treaty, each struggling to come to terms with the text's confusion:

> while we in our wee Free State, holding to that prestatute in our charter, may have our irremovable doubts as to the whole sense of the lot, the interpretation of any phrase in the whole, the meaning of every word of a phrase so far deciphered out of it, however unfettered our Irish daily independence, we must vaunt no idle dubiosity as to its genuine authorship and holusbolus authoritativeness.
>
> (*FW* 117.34–118.4)

The narrative here has an obvious post-Treaty perspective (this section was first drafted in 1924): 'our 'Irish daily independence' has been 'unfettered' and the 'wee Free State' established, although it is not quite wholesome (with a 'prestatute' in the 'charter' and doubts over 'the whole sense of the lot'). From this perspective, then, the letter is duplicate and duplicitous: both integral and fragmented, authentic and faked.

Towards the end of the letter chapter (I.5), a description is given of the condition of the 'original document': written in 'unbrookable script' with 'no signs of punctuation' although it has been 'pierced . . . by numerous stabs and foliated gashes made by a pronged instrument' (*FW* 123.31–124.3). The condition of the Treaty – which was completed late at night after many revisions – showed similar signs of wear:

> In 1932, when Mr de Valera formed his Government, he disinterred the original Treaty showing the penmarks of excision, revision and so on, to suggest unseemly haste and indecision on the part of the signatories.[10]

John Garvin first proposed that the composite fictional figure of Shaun includes de Valera.[11] In chapter II.4 there is a series of references to de Valera and the documents, and in III.3 the Four refer to 'dogumen number one . . . an illegible downfumbed by an unelgible' (*FW* 482.20–1). The Treaty's revisions – not to mention the ambiguities it threw up – made it arguably illegible, and de Valera's rejection – turning his thumb down – of the Treaty had the consequence of outlawing him, or making him 'unelgible'. However, the composition of Shaun was also influenced by the responses to *Ulysses* of Yeats, a prominent free-stater, who became a kind of postman and whose support might possibly have 'delivered' a version of *Ulysses* to an Irish audience. As the postman for the letter-Treaty-*Ulysses*, Shaun is also its internally divided readership. His failure to deliver the letter does not in itself mean that it goes unread, after all, the *Wake* is the process of reading it. Shaun's inquisition (*FW* 474–554) by the Four – annalists, provinces, gospel writers, the Four Courts (extensively shelled in the Civil War) – is a discussion of that process by which the Four, as the historically divided nation, become internal eavesdroppers, or inscribed readers, of the *Wake* itself.

The role of the Four has not been sufficiently recognised in this respect. They were conceived as four critical readers, seemingly based initially on Yeats, Shaw, Moore and Russell.[12] Joyce later planned a book of four essays on 'Work in Progress'. The Four comprise an omnipresent internal audience, commenting on the progress of the dream, interrogating Shaun about the letter and all the while their continual disagreements and enforced communality offer allegories of the critical reaction to Joyce's own work and of the formation of the nation state. Although Emer Nolan suggests that the Four signal 'a drive towards integration and unification that is by no means politically innocent', in their squabbling incohesion

the Four also illustrate the conditions of reception and the impossibility
of a national audience.[13] Joyce thus projects an Irish readership that is
always inevitably split; but he does so on the basis of particular examples
of reception and not as a necessarily universal 'model'. This is far from
political innocence, but it is not nostalgia or optimism either.

The Letter-Treaty-*Ulysses* divides its readers. Just as the Treaty, itself an
emblem of unity, divided its imagined national audience, so too on a
personal level, *Ulysses* could be said to have acted similarly in Joyce's
relations with Nora. There is a well-known story of Nora and the children
leaving Joyce in spring 1922 with the intention of settling in Galway,
only to return on a train that was ambushed during Civil War skir-
mishes.[14] The role of *Ulysses* in this marital row is instructive, for it is at
once, in Joyce's eyes, the cause of and the solution to their rift. He
pleaded, 'O my dearest, if you would only turn to me even now and read
that terrible book which has now broken the heart in my breast' (*Letters*
III, 63). When euphemistically explaining these events to his aunt nearly
six months later (Nora and children safely restored to Paris), Joyce again
connected Nora's flight to *Ulysses*. Nora had left 'when the edition was
sold out' but now 'the intense excitement . . . caused by the publication
of *Ulysses*' has calmed; the book also conveniently 'explains' the 'slight
confusion' between Joyce and his aunt (*Letters* I, 189–91). It was, however,
also a material cause in their dispute since the valuable, unacknowledged
gift to her of a first edition of *Ulysses* had, it was rumoured, been passed
around Dublin without being read. The dispute between Shem and
Shaun echoes this letter, demanding to know 'Where is that little alimony
nestegg [i.e. *Ulysses*] against our predictable rainy day?' Has it not been
passed around 'a hottentot of dulpeners [Dubliners] crawsick with your
crumbs?' (*FW* 192.32–193.3). Josephine's unacknowledged gift of wedding
cake (the cause of their rift) found its way into the *Wake* letter and earned
Shem the term 'cake-eater!' (*FW* 192.33–4; she is thanked at *FW* III.13–14).
Now in two sold-out editions (published by rivals), *Ulysses*, like the
Treaty, has two versions and features in two family wars: it is the balm
for a split for which it is also responsible, while causing yet another split.
Like the wedding cake, like the Treaty, *Ulysses* bears the economy of the
gift: both settling an account and opening a new one. The serendipity of
the publication of *Ulysses* early in 1922 (shortly followed by an 'ordinary'
edition), just as the Treaty came into effect only to be fiercely opposed,
was never lost on Joyce; however much the Free State disappointed
him, his writing had become historically tied to the fate of Ireland.
Finnegans Wake would *write out* those ties (displaying and purging them),

self-consciously enveloping its apparently undeliverable letter whose fractured readership included Joyce's family, his critics and his divided nation.

If 'providential' Irish history is being paraded as a series of repetitive let-downs, marked by momentary accidents, the letter that circulates in *Finnegans Wake* is a revival on a global scale of one of the founding texts of that history. The 'documents or document' can be seen as both the inauguration of the new following the completion (or achievement) of one narrative, and, at the same time, as a hypocritical betrayal, whether of a particular nationalism (led by de Valera) or of a people oppressed by, first, colonial rule and then by Catholic institutional dogmatism. If the 'documents or document' are/is seen as briefly arresting the ongoing course of Irish history, its readership is faced with a potential decision. *Finnegans Wake* restages the moments of these responses – these 'performative judgements' – as a hypocrisy that is not merely the old narrative of betrayal but instead the 'undecided decision' of the *hypocrite lecteur.*

The possibility that is latent in the *Wake's* symbolic Letter makes it a version of a foundational text. Joyce accords it an epic structure and reach in this respect, more so even than his own *Ulysses*, whose novelistic form and characterisation are tied more closely to a material world.[15] As the untold stories of these texts imply, narratives of nationhood must stay frustrated even as they relate that story; theirs is an *articulation* of that narrative, an exemplification of the fissures opened up by the post-colonial nation in the formation of the state. Likewise, a national audience (the readers appropriate to such a national epic) cannot be either created or revived; and yet the interpretive and social decision that a reader has to make – the possibility that making a decision could be, in a sense, decisive – is replayed by the *Wake*.[16] The much-remarked simultaneity of disintegration and cohesion in its form itself signals the ongoing drive towards nationhood and the obstacles that prevent its self-identity. Joyce's refusal to imagine a national audience is part of his account of the conditions by which that audience has not come about. For this reason it has been important to inscribe an actual readership as a rewritten history of judgement, performance, decision-making. Overwriting the act of reception is thus a restaging of a political (in)decision: the reception of *Ulysses* and the Treaty, like personal letters, shows how the necessary delivery of a text does not mean its arrival. The achievement of Joyce's last work is its creation of a language that is responsible to the writing of such a history: one that carries the actuality and notion of response within itself as part of its defining structure.

The 'providential' character of Irish history – at least in Joyce's version – can be traced through his remodelling of the myth of Leda and the swan as a narrative for those conditions in which a decisive moment could be reached and yet appear undecidable. In a passage from the letter chapter (I.5) – first written in 1924 for publication in *Criterion* (July 1925) – a rendition of the myth borrows from Yeats's poem 'Leda and the Swan', which Joyce had probably read in *The Dial* (June 1924) in its first version.[17] (This was the period when Yeats was attempting to lure Joyce back to Ireland for the Tailteann Games; as discussed below.) In parading the cycles of violence and change, Joyce places his own reception amid an Ireland split by Civil War.

The following paragraph immediately precedes the 'teasy dear' reference in I.5.

> Lead, kindly fowl! They always did: ask the ages. What bird has done yesterday man may do next year, be it fly, be it moult, be it hatch, be it agreement in the nest . . . she knows, she just feels she was kind of born to lay and love eggs (trust her to propagate the species and hoosh her fluffballs safe through din and danger!); lastly but mostly, in her genesic field it is all game and no gammon; she is ladylike in everything she does and plays the gentleman's part every time. Let us auspice it! Yes, before all this has time to end the golden age must return with its vengeance.[18] Man will become dirigible, Ague will be rejuvenated, woman with her ridiculous white burden will reach by one step sublime incubation, the manewanting human lioness with her dishorned discipular manram will lie down together publicly flank upon fleece. No, assuredly, they are not justified, those gloompourers who grouse that letters have never been quite their old selves again since that weird weekday in bleak Janiveer . . . when . . . Biddy Doran looked at literature. (*FW* 112.9–27)

The anagram 'Lead' introduces Leda in a paraphrase of Newman's 'Lead, Kindly Light'. Her rape by Zeus, in the form of a swan, is told in her 'ridiculous white burden' and their lying together. The consequences of this will become a form of 'colonial responsibility' or 'white man's burden'. A cyclical narrative has been revived: what bird (swan, Zeus) has done, man will do. So a bird will 'fly' and man becomes 'dirigible'; 'moult' becomes 'rejuvenated'; 'hatch' becomes 'sublime incubation'; and 'agreement' becomes lying down together in public. This is the cycle that informs the Leda myth. The progeny who resulted from Zeus's relations with Leda were the man-gods and twin sons Castor and Pollux (Yeats was a Pollexfen on his mothers' side; see *FW* 489.16; 431.36, etc.) and the twin daughters Clytemnestra and Helen, who married the brothers Agamemnon and Menalaus respectively. Helen's elopement with Paris of course triggered the Trojan War in which Agamemnon led the Greek forces. On his return, his deception of Clytemnestra was bloodily avenged by her, and so the establishment of society goes hand-in-hand with violence and familial feuds. Yeats's poem, in capturing the moment of the rape of Leda which 'engenders' war and 'Agamemnon dead', also implicitly places the story within the context of its writing. Indeed, on publication in *The Cat and the Moon* in early 1924, the poem was followed by the date of composition, '1923', and then by 'Meditations in Time of Civil War'. Yeats's concerns at the time are all present: the ongoing Civil War, the deaths of personal and political friends; the apparent failures of democracy in the Free State and the implicit 'need' for 'strong' cultural leadership (an increasingly dominant theme in his work).[19] Joyce's engagement with the myth takes up some of these concerns in a more sceptical mode.

The uncomfortable implication in the version of the myth as described by Yeats and others is that Leda may take pleasure from the rape: there is a 'shudder in the loins'; she adopts bird-like features in that her 'vague fingers' echo his 'webbed toes'; and there is the suspicion that she has 'put on his knowledge with his power'.[20] Joyce catches this implication through Leda's knowing and feeling that she was 'born to lay and love eggs [sex?]', in her androgynous 'playing the gentleman's part'. Her relationship with Zeus is 'all game and no gammon' (Greek, *gamos*: marriage), all play and no bonds, but also bitterness without sweetness. Numerous bird allusions – fowl, bird, moult, hatch, nest, lay, eggs, fluffballs, game, down, fleece, grouse – confirm the overwhelming presence of Zeus, but the swan is also later joined by the 'original hen' (*FW* 110.22), Biddy, who has scratched up the Letter-Treaty-*Ulysses* from her midden heap. The introduction of Biddy the Hen, who as the finder of the Letter could be considered its first reader, crucially places the myth of social and cultural revival within the context of its reception. That is to say, Joyce makes the myth a spectacle with an audience. Indeed, it would not be out of keeping with what is known of the letter's contents to say that the story of Leda and the swan is another version of the letter.

Joyce's version of the myth grafts onto it allusions to his own readers to show that *Ulysses* was itself a similar mythic text. Eglinton's review in *The Dial* had doubted whether this 'massive work is of good augury for Irish literature'. It was, Eglinton judged, both a 'masterpiece' and 'a violent interruption of what is known as the Irish literary renasance [sic]'.[21] In fact, Leslie's review in the *Quarterly* had made a not dissimilar claim for *Ulysses* as a 'Clerkenwell explosion in the . . . classical prison of English literature'.[22] These comments – with their overtones of direct political action – suggest that Joyce's work is itself a politically violent and potentially decisive moment (at least, a moment of decision), another mythological version of a narrative of revival as well as an instance of revival within the narrative cycle.

The echo of Eglinton lies in his likening of *Ulysses* to a (poor) augury. In Joyce's version, the Leda myth is explicitly presented in front of an implied audience. The narration confidently announces, 'Let us auspice it!' and concludes that the 'golden age' will return.[23] Since an auspice is an observation of birds for omens, or a prophetic token of especially a fortuitous or happy future, deriving from *avis*, bird, and *specere*, to look, an audience has been invoked. In addition, since 'Let us' suggests also 'letters' (and maybe even Leda) the invitation to read the Letter-Treaty-*Ulysses* in the light of the birds (Zeus-swan and Biddy-hen) is clear. The doubtful 'augury for Irish literature' divined by Eglinton casts him in the role of augur, the Roman religious official assigned the task of reading the birds. An augury then is an auspice, and the term brings to mind that Stephen Dedalus 'watched the birds for augury' in *A Portrait* and *Ulysses* (*U* 9.1206) at the National Library, where he also rebuffed the aloof superiority of Eglinton.

Yet 'augur' is also a verb meaning to usher in, to bring forth, to inaugurate. In this sense, the critic as augur has a decisive role; and inaugural readers face a decision. Does *Ulysses* (or the Treaty) mark a new beginning or a repetition? On the one hand is the shift from an immortal godly being to human life (in all its squalid, squabbling imperfection, exemplified by both the Trojan War and the Civil War), while on the other hand, the Letter-Treaty-*Ulysses* is but a 'violent *interruption*' (in Eglinton's words) and so 'the golden age must return with its vengeance' (*FW* 112.18–19). Joyce also figures himself as part of an audience in *Finnegans Wake* in its most autobiographical section: that is, as a post-war onlooker to the new state. Shem takes a 'tompip peepestrella' through a 'telescope' to see 'whether true conciliation was forging ahead or falling back after the celestious intemperance' (*FW* 178.27–35). Yet the specificity of this position is itself enveloped within a cycle – 'all that has been done has yet to be done and done again' (*FW* 194.10).

Crucially, the augury seems to look both ways, and this is one of Joyce's recurrent points about reception. In *Finnegans Wake*, as opposed to *A Portrait*, the birds are looking back: the event that is being read here is also the 'shock' experienced by 'both' when 'Biddy Doran looked at literature'.

This is a further allusion to a *Ulysses* review: Joseph Collins's *The Doctor Looks at Literature*, published by Doran in 1923 and also cited elsewhere in the *Wake*.[24] The event is inseparable from the audience that looks at it; the augury and its augur, the Letter-Treaty-*Ulysses* and its readers are similarly joined: the meaning of the event of the text is the decision of its reception. The further implication of this is that reception is already worked into the production of literature. This mutually interpretive spectacle, a sort of textual and historical hall of mirrors, dramatises and incorporates readers' responses as itself a further possibly decisive text within a widening historical cycle. By including the responses of Eglinton, Leslie and others within itself, Joyce's writing is positioned as a historical event and its cycle: the *Wake* becomes the particular cultural dynamic of which it is a part.

The 'opening' of the letter, in which its reception has already been prefigured in its writing, through the actual readers of *Ulysses* and the familiar narrative of repetitive enactment, opens a space in which it might be possible to question the seeming inevitability of the providential historical series. This would raise the possibility that the event in question – be it the letter, *Ulysses*, the Treaty, or the rape of Leda – would represent, in its reception, a moment of decision and as such a possibility of change, of locating the accidental with the providential. If the augury also comprises an audience (as when Biddy Doran looked at literature) by becoming a spectacle – that is, if it reads its readership, as Joyce's work consistently does – perhaps the sequentiality of historical determinism can be put under stress and if not broken at least strained. However, this does not signal an optimistic arrival, or the delivery to an audience, but instead suggests a reflection on the conditions of reception and the text's own complicity in the series. Joyce's text keeps in view the moment of decision, and its aftershocks, even as the chance appears lost. By rewriting the 'decisions' – the responses, however, faltering – of his readers and fellow countrymen, Joyce ensures that *Finnegans Wake* enacts a continual, distorting replay of that lost moment. In the *Wake*, the hypocrisy of respondents emerges into a language that both records their 'decisions' and, through a transformation and decontextualisation of them, resumes an ongoing series of like moments. *Finnegans Wake* is a revival of a form of hypocrisy, betrayal and division – terms that in one narrative have characterised Irish history as a series of false returns – and the re-formation of a language in which those terms lose their hidden assumptions of a truth or stability or integrity from which they depart. By restaging his readers' and his own (perceived) hypocrisy into a form that makes hypocrisy an inevitable structural feature of its reception, Joyce is able to overcome the familiar terms ('betrayal', etc.) that have closeted his relationship with Ireland within a straightjacket of oppositions.

III

The question of Joyce's work as an 'augury' for Irish writing and society can be further explored within the context of an apparently hypocritical reading of Joyce by Yeats around the time of the formation of the 'wee Free State' (*FW* 117.34). A correspondence between them developed over two years from summer 1922, some six months after the publication of *Ulysses* (and of course the inauguration of the new State), to summer 1924, when Joyce declined Yeats's conditional invitation to visit 'Irrland's split little pea' (*FW* 171.06). Their rejoinders also comprise Yeats's reading of *Ulysses*, the political circumstances attending his creation of the Tailteann games, and Joyce's responses to him in *Finnegans Wake* (including his allusions to 'Leda and the Swan'). In brief, Joyce transformed Yeats's role into a model of inevitable hypocrisy in the instability of the *Wake* and in the 'two-faced' Free State. Yeats thus figures as emblematic of a condition of reception for Joyce's work: a duplicity that was more than personal and which was structured into the act of reading as an inevitably political enterprise. Although the two are usually seen in oppositional terms, their differences were far from a simple antagonism but formed part of a complex cultural episode which characterised Joyce's reception in Ireland.

In late July 1922, Pound forwarded to Joyce two letters: one was from Lady Gregory addressed to Joyce, requesting that some previous correspondence of theirs be included in a book she was planning; the other letter was from Yeats and addressed to Pound. In effect, this was a coverletter in support of Lady Gregory. Joyce's reply to Lady Gregory asks that all mention of him be omitted from her book since for the past twenty years no one connected with 'the Irish literary movement' has '*publicly*' mentioned him, or his struggle, or his writings (*SL* 290; my emphasis). Nonetheless, he immediately asks her to send thanks to Yeats, whose opinion he values very highly and whom he has always greatly admired, for 'several kind expressions' about *Ulysses*. This is a curious response. In any estimation, Yeats would have to be regarded as the principal figure in the 'movement' which had supposedly ignored Joyce (and of which Joyce is implicitly critical), but Yeats is singled out for his support. Does Joyce dissociate Yeats from the Revival? Or is Joyce perhaps implying a criticism of Yeats for not '*publicly*' praising him and instead being content to send 'kind expressions' in *private* correspondence – in effect, of being a hypocrite. After all, Joyce had accused Yeats of hypocrisy before, both recently – over a possible subscription to *Ulysses* – and back in Dublin, over the Abbey, and over the poet's extravagant praise for Lady Gregory.[25] The implication might be that Yeats is a model of two-faced behaviour, especially in his responses to the work of others.

In Yeats's letter to Pound, which was sent by the latter along with Lady Gregory's request, he praises Lady Gregory's projected volume as 'the most important history there has been of the movement in Ireland which *we all here* belong to' (my emphasis). This in itself cuts off Joyce and supposes a homogeneity of purpose among 'we all here' that did not exist. Indeed this would be a central theme in Joyce's responses: playing upon Yeats's explicit insistence on Joyce's apparent geographical and literary otherness, and noting also the internal contradictions of his Irish reception. For Joyce, such oppositions are easily constructed but less easily borne out by lived conditions (as suggested in 'Scylla and Charybdis'). Yeats continues, 'For our own sake mainly I am very anxious to get Joyce well into that record.' Evidence of a selfish purpose in this approach could hardly have been starker: Yeats's support for Joyce would come at the price of his political appropriation of him.[26] The 'kind expressions' referred to by Joyce in his reply to Lady Gregory were from the latter part of this letter. Yeats goes on to say how he 'admire[s] immensely' *Ulysses*, that it is of 'immense importance', and that he read it 'a few pages . . . at a time as if he [sic] were a poem. Some passages have great beauty, lyric beauty, even in the fashion of my generation.' The effect of this is undone somewhat by the admission that after having read 'a great part' of *Ulysses* 'I . . . gave myself a course of Trollope for a change.' The damage done to Yeats's eyes was, he insists, the result of reading Trollope and not *Ulysses*.[27] Later, in 'Work in Progress', Joyce would not be able to resist this letter's unconscious humour. Its private profession of support evidently pleased Joyce, but he may also have recalled that Yeats had not yet publicly praised *Ulysses*.

The letter in *Finnegans Wake* appears to have been 'signed Toga Girilis, (teasy dear)' (*FW* 112.30). As McHugh suggests, this may indicate a recent graduate of Trinity College: 'toga virilis' is a graduate's gown and TCD is echoed in 'teasy dear'. This phrase might also be understood as an anagrammatic address to 'Dear Yeats' (which is how Joyce addressed his letters to him). If the letter appears to co-sign both Yeats and Trinity College, the fact that Yeats accepted an honorary degree from Trinity in

December 1922 makes this combination seem less odd (despite his quarrels with both Dowden and Dowden's successor, W. F. Trench); and it was at a Trinity debate that Yeats first spoke publicly in praise of *Ulysses*. In addition, it seems that *Ulysses* had already entered Trinity: a relative of Joyce's had checked at the College library only to be told that although it had been ordered for future students it was found on receipt to be nothing but obscenity. It was not catalogued and would be available only to readers who could show they needed to read it on exceptional grounds.[28] The 'Dear Yeats' anagram also signals the poet as a possible recipient of the undeliverable Letter-Treaty-*Ulysses*. In 1935 Joyce had discovered that his recent correspondence to Yeats had gone astray (the 'teasy dear' passage comes amid a paragraph that was added in 1937–8).[29] When he did re-establish contact, Joyce implied that Yeats had not proceeded very far with *Ulysses* at all: if 'Mrs Yeats' would 'unsew the first pages of your *Ulysses*', he would sign them (*Letters* III, 381, 384). Joyce inserted into the *Wake* the allusion to Yeats as a direct addressee (though not necessarily reader) of the letter after discovering the non-delivery of his own letters with their implication of Yeats as a 'non-reader' of *Ulysses*.

Indeed, judging by the many uncut pages of his copy, Yeats had not read much of *Ulysses* at all; although he claimed to be reading it according to something like *sortes virgilianae*, the same method by which the *Wake* is invited to be read, opening at any page. His praise for *Ulysses* in his letter to Joyce is noteworthy for its loaded ambiguity (why '*lyrical* beauty'?): he places it 'even in the fashion of my generation'. There is a hint here that Yeats is attempting to bring Joyce into *his* 'fold' and this attempted private appropriation of him implies a sort of cultural over-writing as well. Yeats could hardly have regarded Joyce as of *his* generation, of which, moreover, he was not necessarily proud. It is precisely the hinted cultural and political attempt to appropriate Joyce that would become the hallmark of Yeats's engagement with his work. The poet's subsequent, highly public, praise for *Ulysses* – sometimes coupled with an admission that he had not really read it – is indicative of the split reception Joyce endured, since Yeats's praise goes hand-in-hand with his own strategic, political aims. For Joyce, then, Yeats's response highlights the problematics of both literary reception and the Free State, embodying its internal fissures. These fissures were not only cultural and religious but also, Yeats's reading implies, generic: he found the novel hard going but was entranced by its lyrical quality. Whereas for many critics, both Irish and British, it was the intense realism of Joyce's prose that made him a writer of Catholic and post-colonial Ireland, Yeats's emphasis on the lyricism of *Ulysses* suggests his continuing suspicion that novelistic 'realism' in fact meant little more than a kind of deathly, moribund, till-grubbing modernisation: precisely the kind of Ireland he resisted. It might be argued, then, that Yeats saw, or thought he saw, in *Ulysses* a generic means of liberation from the prosaic 'things' of the novel (*Ulysses*, as Hugh Kenner observed, is packed with things[30]), whereas it was precisely that 'ordinariness' and socially expressive realism which many others found liberating. These contrary political, cultural and generic readings of *Ulysses* in the context of the Free State would provide an important impetus to the writing of *Finnegans Wake*.

Yeats's letter was the beginning of a correspondence in which he appears as an enthusiastic reader of Joyce's work, allowing Joyce in turn to adopt Yeats as an example of the borders in Irish (post)colonial literary culture. It is not exactly a coincidence that from this period on Yeats was also increasingly engaged in attempting to shape a cultural policy in and for the new Free State (whilst undergoing a further personal, poetic transformation), at one point in 1922 entertaining the apparently realistic hope of becoming the Free State's first Minister of Fine Arts.[31] If he was still in the business of shaping a national audience, it was to be one shaped after his own image, championing the Free State against democracy, violent Republicanism and Catholic censorship. In Paris in January 1922 (with *Ulysses* about to be published) he attended the Irish Race Congress on behalf of the Dáil (when de Valera sent a parallel delegation). Joyce may have recognised in him the busy and important Yeats of two decades before. By the end of the year, their divergent trajectories would be established: Joyce's writing (censored elsewhere) was, thanks to Pound, acquiring its European reputation; Yeats accepting the responsibilities and accolades that would lead him to become that 'smiling public man' as he immersed himself in the capital city's political life.[32] The two might be thought of as something like Wakean inverted twins, or warring brothers.

Following Joyce's sharp letter to Lady Gregory (complaining at the lack of public recognition), Yeats did publicly praise *Ulysses*.[33] In summer 1923, he invited Joyce to Dublin promising a new generation of 'many' admiring readers (*Letters* III, 77) and late that year he praised Joyce at a student debate in Trinity College. The *Irish Times* report of this, which Joyce read, noted how Yeats valued Joyce as having the 'intensity of a great novelist' only to qualify this immediately by admitting that 'The novel was not his . . . *forte*'.[34] So Yeats continued publicly to support Joyce at a time when some, notably Pound and Stanislaus, and the first readers of 'Work in Progress', were either lukewarm or openly hostile. Support of a kind came, then, from a (at best) partial reader. However, its timing was awkward: at the beginning of July 1924, Yeats had re-invited Joyce to Ireland and the *Aonach Tailteann* just as, that summer, Joyce received much personal bad news (the deaths of his Aunt Josephine Murray and John Quinn; Stanislaus's famous despairing letter; a series of cataract operations). In one sense, amid such news, Yeats's support could not have arrived at a better time; Joyce took 'great satisfaction' from this second, more personal invitation (*Letters* III, 100). On the other hand, the context of its arrival might suggest that Joyce would have been a sceptical recipient, alive to its potential 'dangers'. The exchange of letters bears this out: it is characteristically ambiguous, respectful, opportune and wary. This uncertainty comes out in the very invitation: Yeats asks Joyce over but makes it plain that his non-residence will disqualify him from any prize at the festival. This may have been on Joyce's mind when, near the end of the month, he wrote to Larbaud classifying the meanings of 'irlandais' (*Letters* I, 217). In the event, Yeats would go on to praise Joyce above all others.[35]

Yeats's invitation to Joyce in July 1924 to attend the Tailteann games manages to combine both the subtlety and crassness of political maneouvring: it implies that the personal invitation will not be officially sanctioned, and this is then confirmed by a later P.S. saying that the committee has 'all but unanimously' declined to invite him officially as a 'guest of the Nation'. The grounds for this refusal were political and religious: however sophisticated some people in government (like Desmond Fitzgerald) might be, they could not risk offending the Church. As Yeats put it, 'At first the Committee only intended to invite people of other nationalities but at the last moment they decided, for more or less political reasons, to invite Lavery and Shaw. Then the question [arose] of asking other Irishmen.'[36] Joyce's nomination had been blocked principally by 'the Marquis McSwiney, Chamberlain to the Pope' as Yeats described him to Joyce.[37] In his biography of Yeats, Foster remarks that MacSwiney 'might have come out of a Joycean fantasy'; as it happens, there is a strong suggestion of him in *Finnegans Wake* in a passage in which *Ulysses* is mocked in front of the Four who here include one 'Yates' (*FW* 534.15).[38] The 'hole affair is rotten muckswinish'; the Four object, 'Give us your mespilt reception will yous?' (*FW* 535.20–4). The phrasing seems to suggest this incident, especially given Yeats's presence, the inference of misspelling and the split reception in Dublin (on the Mespil Road). The term 'mespilt reception' also implies that a fragmented response only replicates the subjective divisions of the authorial self, and this will have particular implications for Joyce's inscription of Yeats in the pages of *Wake*.

That Joyce anyway declined to attend the Tailteann festival was perhaps predictable, and his eye operation was a useful pretext, but that should not unduly detract from the ramifications of the occasion, which Joyce followed in the newspapers. By inviting Joyce and publicly praising *Ulysses*, Yeats set about provoking the Catholic authorities and the new government into a public debate over censorship through which he hoped to reshape the cultural standing of the Free State.[39] At the same time, he must have realised the extent to which that Government was publicly tied to the Church and that such a debate would backfire into precisely the form of Censorship Bill he feared. Not surprisingly, organs such as the *Catholic Bulletin* were only too happy to engage Yeats in the controversy he sought. This must have had resonance for Joyce: after all *Ulysses* had not been placed on the Index or banned in the Free State (as we have seen, several Dublin bookstores, and one in Belfast, stocked the first edition). Yeats hoped that by organising a cultural festival which honoured writers of diverse opinions he could promote a conception of Irishness which was not only 'not Catholic' but also directly opposed to Church institutions. While provocative to the Catholic establishment, this was also an attempt to promote a public discourse that could be appropriate to his vision of the new State, and Yeats found in Joyce's antagonism to Church piety the perfect exemplar for this project. Yeats's public praise for Joyce was thus always mixed with an emphasis on his 'obscenity': at the Trinity debate he had called *Ulysses* 'as foul as Rabelais' and at the *Aonach Tailteann* he repeated the claim.[40] For his part, Joyce did not shirk the charge and in fact flaunted it: the last phrase was specially singled out for preservation. The flyer of press notices that Joyce gathered for publicity for *Ulysses* emphasised its controversial reception, even citing contrary opinions. Joyce arranged for Eglinton's phrase 'received with enthusiasm by those who provisionally determine literary fame in Ireland' to be juxtaposed with Leslie's 'from Dublin as yet we have heard only jocular contempt'.[41] It might be suggested that such contrariness, within even a single respondent, was typical.

IV

Joyce frames his response to Yeats in *Finnegans Wake* within the context of the Civil War. In doing so, however, this debate is never without a specular attendance, either in the person of Shem overseas or in the frequent interruptions of the omnipresent Four; as with the librarians and Eglinton in *Ulysses*, Joyce frames his scene within an almost theatrical setting, writing-in a series of spectators. As Joyce told Weaver (*Letters* 1, 220), he drew on reports of the Tailteann event in compiling the ending of 'Shem the Penman' (I.7) in which the division between twin-brothers is expressed as a reaction to the Letter-Treaty-*Ulysses*. Shem, as Mercius, is accused by Justius (Shaun) of 'shirking both your bullet and your billet' (*FW* 190.28) and refusing 'to fall in with Plan . . . as all nationists must, and do a certain office . . . in a certain holy office', an open allusion to Joyce's early broadside attacking Yeats as an 'appeaser' of Lady Gregory. The accusation of hypocrisy against Joyce is thus put into the mouth of Shaun, reflecting the reason for Joyce's ineligibility for a Tailteann prize: Shem might work in Ireland and so 'earn from the nation true thanks, right here in our place of burden' (*FW* 190.12–21). In saying this, he echoes the lines of Robert Hand in *Exiles*, who praises Richard only to note how he had departed Ireland 'in her hour of need' (*PE* 245). The hypocrisy of the apparently receptive reader is established in this example of qualified, underhand praise.

Joyce broadened his reception by the Tailteann committee into an image of the 'new Irish stew' (*FW* 190.9), once again establishing *Ulysses* as an augury for the Civil War. Shem's 'dislocated reason' has

cutely foretold . . . by the auspices of that raven cloud, your shade, and by the augury of rooks in parlament, death with every disaster, the dynamatisation of colleagues, the reducing of records to ashes, the levelling of customs by blazes.

(*FW* 189.30–6)

As with all oracles, the point is that it will be misunderstood. Justius accuses Mercius of not accepting the terms of the Treaty: 'your horrible awful poverty of mind so as you couldn't even pledge a crown' (*FW* 192.10). By echoing a notable attack on *Ulysses*, the Treaty is once more likened to Joyce's previous book, not in form but in their reception.[42] Mercius defends himself by declaring that he 'oathily forswore' (*FW* 193.32–3). Of course, this is ambiguous: it may mean that he pledged allegiance to the crown (one of the key issues over which the Treaty's reception was split), or it may mean that he 'forswore' the oath, that is, renounced it. Joyce thus casts *Ulysses* as an augury of the Civil War by likening it to the Treaty: capable of contrary interpretations, it inaugurates a split reception.

Joyce also incorporated more specific responses to Yeats in this passage.[43] The official invitations for the Tailteann games had been addressed to a 'guest of the nation' and in his letter Yeats had used this phrase. At the same time, Yeats had made it clear that Joyce would not be a public 'guest of the nation' but a private one. One possible implication of this, which Joyce was quick to take up in the *Wake*, could be that Yeats stood for Ireland, summoning guests of the nation to his own home: in Book IV he is, clearly ironically, 'the ultimate ysland of Yreland' (*FW* 605.4) in a parody of 'The Lake Isle of Inisfree'. The fantastic character of this island is underscored not only in Yeats's poem but also in the *Wake's* blunt assessment of it as Kevin's bath. If Yeats does not quite convince in the role of public statesman, or national host, it suggests his own divided character. This is reflected in his role as the postman who attempts to deliver the Letter-Treaty-*Ulysses*. Shaun the Post, although also based on de Valera and an assortment of critics, is several times described in terms that directly recall Yeats's letters to Joyce in 1922 and 1924. Joyce was not to be a 'guest of the nation' and nor is Shaun the 'timbreman' who does not have 'the ghuest of innation' (*FW* 414.4, 8). Without the ghost of a notion or a nation, he feels himself betrayed although he has 'Not the phost of a nation' why, 'Nor by a long trollop. I just didn't have the time to' (*FW* 409.6). Trollope, who invented the penny post in his day job as a civil servant (and wrote the bulk of his many novels before breakfast), worked for the Post Office in Ireland. And, as we have seen, Yeats's letter had said that he was reading *Ulysses* alternately with Trollope's novels. The pithy remark, 'not the phost of a nation', sums up the ambiguity of Shaun's position, as invited non-guest, ghost and postman. This phrase also implies the Free State itself, a spectral nation, slowly materialising. Just as Joyce would not be a 'guest of the nation', so Yeats could not be the 'host of the nation'.

Dominic Manganiello repeats the mantra that 'Joyce preferred to be outward-looking' and 'aimed to Europeanise Ireland' as against the 'narrow nationalism' of 'dogmatic and domestic' Shaun (associated with de Valera).[44] This is to go over the grounds of a debate that began around 1920 prior to the completion of *Ulysses* and continued through that decade. On the one hand, Pound had asserted that Joyce was in the line of Flaubert and others; while in Dublin, contrary to Yeats, some were already claiming Joyce as the 'native' writer that Irish Ireland had lacked.[45] In fact, the confining nature of this debate was already being exposed. Thomas MacGreevy (the poet and one of the twelve *Exagmination* critics supervised by Joyce) asserted Joyce's European lineage as part of a specifically Catholic tradition. In doing so, he suggested that an Anglo-Saxon perspective (and an Anglo-Irish one) was cut off from the bulk of an

Irish and European common inheritance.[46] By often alluding to Yeats as a critic of his work and as a national statesman, Joyce is not simply projecting onto him a rejection by Ireland or the worn-out theme of 'betrayal'. Given Yeats's own increasingly marginal position in the Free State, he cannot stand for the nation as a whole; indeed, he represents the impossibility of that very idea. Instead, in the continually shifting cultural grounds of the 1920s, the *Wake* implies that Yeats is emblematic of attempts to appropriate Joyce's writing within a divisive context and not merely to 'expel' it.

V

Joyce's 'overwriting' of his readers' responses, and his structural implication of dual, hypocritical delivery find an interesting parallel in one of the new national institutions: the Post Office or *An Post*. This institution, of immense symbolic, cultural and political significance, was transferred from British to Free State hands, enduring a complex changeover period. Yeats's contribution to Shaun can be further elaborated within this context since it emphasises both the apparent inescapability of divergent readings and the falsity of an apparent opposition. In this sense, subjective positions are themselves fractured – as indeed Yeats recognised of himself in poems like 'Among School Children' – and an inevitable hypocrisy is installed.

The national postal network, immediately prior to 1922, was of course not Irish but British-controlled: red pillar boxes bore the crown and initials of the sovereign and the stamps featured the profile of George V. Yet the election of an unofficial Sinn Féin government and the War of Independence had meant that in many areas of civil life a strange duality already existed. Shaun is not 'the phost of a nation' but he is ghosting the role of national postman. As the stage Irishman Shaun-the-Post, from Boucicault's *Arrah na Pogue*, he is already accustomed to passing between one set of audiences and the other, creating a comic if false reciprocity, both an eloquent artist-figure and a two-dimensional convention. He depicts himself as 'all too unwordy' (*FW* 408.10) and 'the bearer extraordinary of these postoomany missive on his majesty's service' (*FW* 408.13–14), despite the earlier post-Treaty perspective of the description of the letter. Although the *Wake* is no stranger to ancient Irish kingdoms, and the 'magistate' is not only colonial Ireland but also ancient Ireland, the title 'his majesty' would most obviously denote the British monarch. So Shaun here also takes on the persona of a Michael Collins figure, 'a mere mailman of peace' who embodies the letter-Treaty and sends himself through the postal network (*FW* 470.26–30). (Collins, incidentally, had worked as postal clerk in London for two years.) Shaun thus positions himself in opposing camps. There is, then, no national postman and no 'national audience', just as the melodramatic 'delivery' of union that Shaun-the-Post promises, in fact emphasises the divisions within the theatrical audience.[47] Joyce records the political and cultural attempt to create such an enterprise while pointing up its inevitably fractured state. Yeats could hardly have been a better model for this role.

Shaun the Post has 'painted our town a wearing greenridinghued' (*FW* 411.23–4), including, presumably, the postboxes. He has also been 'blazing on the focoal' (*FW* 411.32), which suggests (among other things) that he's been overwriting in Irish, since 'focal [focail]' means 'word[s]'. Thus a green hue replaces the red in deed and phrase. Joyce is echoing a Republican song from the immediate post-Treaty period:

> I'm teaching them Irish and paint their letter-boxes
> All over with green, sure what more can I do?
> For they tell me they want an Irish Republic,
> Without any trimmings of red, white and blue.[48]

Shaun's reference to British control of the postal network recalls the letter, stained by a 'tache of tch . . . a teastain' (*FW* 111.20), that is, embossed by a splash of Maggy's tea, or 'majesty'. The *Wake* suggests that its letter, by being stamped, is 'tainted' in the process of dissemination.

Therefore, the stamps that legitimate the delivery themselves betoken both a divided authority and a split reception. In 1924 Joyce wrote to Weaver describing a stamp that he had seen many times.

Shaun's map: for this see any postage stamp of the Irish Free State. It is a philatelic curiosity. A territorial stamp it includes the territory of another state, Northern Ireland. (*Letters* I, 213)

Joyce had just sent a draft of I.8 to Weaver, containing the phrase 'a sunless map of the world including the moon and stars for Shaun the Post' and shortly afterwards the word 'stamp' replaced 'stars' (*JJA* 48:70). By the time of the second typescript in June 1925 the phrase had become 'a sunless map of the month, including the sword and stamps, for Shemus O'Shaun the Post' (*JJA* 48:79), which is how it stands at *FW* 211.30–1. The stamp Joyce refers to in his letter was from the Free State's first definitives, of which the green 2d edition was the first to be published, on the date of the constitutional establishment of Irish Free State (the first anniversary

Figure 1. 2d stamp from Free State definitives (6 December 1922).

of the signing of the Treaty), 6 December 1922. This stamp (see figure 1) clearly depicts the whole island of Ireland, without showing the border that demarcates the six counties known as Northern Ireland (which had effectively been created in 1919 by Lloyd-George's Amending Act to the Home Rule Bill; a Stormont parliament made the province self-governing from 1920). The 1d and 1 1/2d stamps used the same design, in carmine and claret respectively (the latter was released on Joyce's birthday, 2 February, 1923). In the passage from the *Wake*, there is also a reference to the 1/2d stamp, the third of the four definitives, known as the Sword of Light. There was predictable opposition to these stamps in Belfast and Yeats later expressed disquiet at the new stamps, possibly because of their obvious symbolism, when he came to chair the committee that selected designs for the new coinage in 1926.[49]

These first definitives of 1922–3 had been the product of a sort of Anglo-Irish agreement whereby the dye, plates and gummed paper were assembled at the Royal Mint in London, the plate and paper typographed at Dublin Castle (overseen by the Board of the Inland Revenue), returned to London to be perforated (the Dublin Castle machines not being ready), and then sent back to Ireland for release.[50] So the very stamps that first signalled the emergence of an independent Ireland in the shape of the

Figure 2. 10d Overprint, *Rialtas Sealadac na hÉireann 1922.*

Free State, replacing the visage of the British monarch with national icons, were the product of what might be called a dual legitimation.

An even more telling example of dual authorisation of Irish stamps occurred in 1922 prior to the release of the first Free State definitives. After the creation of the Free State, but before the first official set was available, on 17 February 1922, as an interim measure, the Provisional Government legitimated 'overprints' of the old King George V issues (see figure 2). The same stamps that had previously been issued by the British administration, bearing the head of the monarch, were now released carrying an overprinted statement, *Rialtas Sealadac na hÉireann 1922* (Provisional Government of Ireland, 1922), and were released on 17 February 1922, and later in the same year, after the election, a new overprint read *Saorstát Éireann 1922* (Irish Free State, 1922). Many of these newer overprints were not released until 1923, even though they bore the date 1922. Indeed, the definitive 2d stamp that shows a map of all-Ireland (to which Joyce referred) was released *prior* to most of the overprints. The higher value stamps (2s 6d, 5s, 10s) among this latter set of overprints were in use in Ireland up until 1937, still bearing the date 1922 (and stamps with the map of all-Ireland were in use into the 1960s). Before the official overprints could be produced, however, a number of unofficial ones were set in circulation. Moreover, as the Post Office was not formally handed over to the Irish administration until 1 April 1922 (that is, after the Free State was already in formal existence), all stamps released prior to that date were technically still British: the British still administered the postal network.[51] Strictly speaking, then, it was the British Post Office – directed by the Free State provisional government – that authorised the stamps displaying the King's head and overprinted with the name of the Irish state (in Irish script). As the professorial voice says of the Letter's envelope, 'its face, in all its featureful perfection of imperfection, is its fortune' (*FW* 109.8–9). As this image suggests, the divided community depicted here is also that of the British state: the face of the overprints depicts its fortune as well.

The paradox of Shaun's position, on His Majesty's service, delivering the Treaty, but painting the town and postboxes green and 'blazing on the focal' might be explained by the role of the postal system in this period. This bifocal position also speaks to Joyce's own situation as the 'overwriter' composing 'Work in Progress' by writing over both earlier versions and criticism, 'misappropriating the spoken words of others' (*FW* 108.36) and adding historico-textual layers, offering his own alternative to the English language. The overprints are emblematic of the handover of power and institutions that occurred in the initial phase of the post-colonial period (and, not incidentally, some of the difficulties of any such periodisation). The previous administration was literally written-over by the emerging state, while its distinctive features (including the distinctive features of the King) remained very much in view. Similar periodic, linguistic and legitimating confusion is found in the *Wake*'s 'duplex' letter, whose date both begins and ends, whose language is both simple and illegible, and which is apparently authorised by different parties. It is 'antepostdating the Valgur Eire' (*FW* 256.22–3), both before and after, written over in the vulgar (Irish), signalling 'Eire' as Ireland, which is also the name used by the English for the Republic. Like a tea stain, the stamp's authority seeps through from one layer to the next: the *Wake* suggests that language works in a similar fashion, and perhaps reception could be thought of in this way as well, that is, as the tiered accumulation of readings. Joyce's appropriation of his readers' responses implies just such a historico-textual genealogy.

De Valera's Document No. 2 was described by Michael Collins, in a metaphor by then familiar, as an overprint:

As an improvement on the Treaty, Document No. 2 is not honest . . . It merely attaches a fresh label to the same parcel, or, rather, a label written, of purpose, illegibly in the hope of making belief that the parcel is other than it is.[52]

Joyce used similar terms for his own Letter-Treaty-*Ulysses*, showing that Collins's distinction between an 'honest' language and an 'illegible' language is another false opposition. In 1.7 Shem is described as '*making believe* to read his usylessly unreadable Blue Book of Eccles' (i.e. *Ulysses*) (*FW* 179.26–7, my emphasis). The point seems to be that even when one takes 'awhile to look fact in their face' (*FW* 179.7), the stamped face of the fact may be misleading. Joyce's frequent use of the same overprinting metaphor is suggestive of just how applicable it is to his writing: its obsession with reception as both a structural and a political problem is inseparable from the question of Joyce's departure from Ireland and his unreadiness to return.

The stamp on the letter is possibly the map of the island of Ireland, 'Shaun's map' as Joyce called it; but maybe it is one of the overprinted stamps in circulation around the time of the Treaty. Reading the *Irish Times* at the end of 1922, Joyce noted that the new issue of the Free State 2d stamp was announced with due respect: 'The stamp is a quiet stamp, in which the harmony of the design and the ornamentation of Celtic scrolls and headed outline are well balanced.' Joyce worked the term 'a quiet stamp' from this report into his own more cynical phrase, 'such vitriol of venom a quiet stamp could cover'.[53] In *Finnegans Wake*, the stamp has been overwritten: 'the war is o'er' and ALP is introduced with 'that queen's head affranchisant, a quiet stinkingplaster zeal could cover, prepostered or postpaid!' (*FW* 101.24–5) as if she too has taken on regal visage for postal service in the new state. Shaun himself admits under questioning, 'I am twosides uppish' (*FW* 484.14) and 'marked on me fakesimilar in the foreign' (*FW* 484.34–5), and this may be taken to exemplify not only the condition of the letter-Treaty-text with which he has been entrusted, but also the stamp that authorises its delivery. The confusion of allegiance and chronology all suggest that the conditions for reception are inevitably fractured: this is the condition of Ireland's emergent nation state, and, it is suggested, the inevitable fate of any imagined 'national audience'.

Although Shaun is 'on his majesty's service' (*FW* 408.14), the audience / address for his delivery is also 'Madges Tighe, the postulate auditressee' (*FW* 369.30), suggesting the belatedness and deformation of that 'majesty'. His Majesty may well be too late to receive the letter, *Ulysses* having been published in February 1922, shortly after the formation of the Free State.[54] Yet this royal male also appears to be an Irish woman, Madge, or Maggy ('maggy's tea'), whose authorisation is a tea stain in I.5 and who here calls for a 'cupital tea' (*FW* 369.32). The potential treachery of the postal service has been noted by Enda Duffy, who reproduces a British government notice from the War of Independence calling for secret letters to be sent by informers to a mystery agent.[55] As Duffy observes, there is a strong current of role-playing in such colonial 'missions', and it might be added that the very reproducibility of the emblem of authority, the stamp of the King's head, has a similarly kitsch and performative quality to it. Even if Shaun were to attempt to deliver it to the British monarch he would have trouble reading the address since his language 'hace not one pronouncable teerm . . . to signify majestate, even provisionally' (*FW* 478.11–13). The Shaun section was expanded in revision to include allusions to Joyce's critics: one English reviewer of *Ulysses* had complained that the book lacked both 'reverence for simple majesty' and 'the glory of our written tongue'.[56] Without 'majestate', Shaun is both 'free' and 'illegitimate'. His 'position' (or journey) is thus contradictory or circular: apparently still in the employ of the British monarch, but at the time of the post-Treaty provisional Free State government, 'his majesty' / Maggy is (are) also his addressee(s), yet his language has no word for a monarchic state (and perhaps lacks 'majesty').

Shaun does have 'gumpower' (*FW* 410.25) to stick the stamps and to publish (and possibly, to translate: *An Gum* being the official Free State publishers), but if this 'gunpowder' had been part of the famous Catholic plot to blow up the English parliament in 1605 it is now destined for the Irish Civil War.[57] In Shaun's hands, the letter appears after all to be potentially devastating – as Eglinton and Leslie had warned of *Ulysses*, it was a 'violent interruption' and an 'attempted Clerkenwell explosion' – but its target might have been lost in the translation. In the historical and linguistic slippages that the *Wake* implies, 'ere Molochy wars bring the devil era, a slip of the time between a date and a ghostmark' (*FW* 473.7–9), between date and postmark, lies the 'ghostmark' of the Letter-Treaty-*Ulysses*. Like *Ulysses*, the letter appears to have been written and posted under one jurisdiction, possibly as a challenge to that same authority, only to find itself lost now that the boundaries of power have been redefined.

The readerly demand to 'draw the line somewhawre' (*FW* 292.31–2), that is, to call a halt to reading, has been linked with the fixing of the boundary between Free State and Northern Ireland by the Boundary Commission in 1925 (as a direct consequence of the Treaty). According to Manganiello, Joyce associated the attempts of critics to 'delimit his experiments with the English language' with the 'English' attempt to 'set a limit to the march of his nation'.[58] To say this, however, is to *equate* Joyce's writing with the struggle for independence and to imply that both move towards the manifestation of an essential unity. However, Joyce knew that the country was already deeply split and his concern for his reception spelt out those divisions, which, moreover, were more general conditions elsewhere as well (not only in the 'disunited kingdom' – *FW* 188.16–17). Since Joyce was only too aware of readerly complaints that *Ulysses* was an exhausting book, and of the defences of the ordinary reader, he was already familiar with the readerly and social need to 'draw a line'. In a sense, *Finnegans Wake* makes this a futile need: its lines are already politicised 'ruled barriers along which the traced words, run, march, halt, stumble' (*FW* 114.7–8). Joyce's patent dissatisfaction with both the terms of the Treaty and the Free State (with its repetition of colonial poverty and stultifying pieties) allowed him to go on addressing a condition he knew too well, one in which the act of reading has its own awkward lines.

There would appear to be little substance to ALP's hope, at the close of the *Wake*:

Ourselves, oursouls alone . . . And watch would the letter you're wanting be coming may be . . . Scratching it and patching at with a prompt from a primer . . . Every letter is a hard but yours sure is the hardest crux ever . . . But once done, dealt and delivered, tattat, you're on the map. (*FW* 623.28–35)

Her faith that delivery would put the letter 'on the map' seems to equate the formation of a unified Ireland and a national audience with the successful arrival of her missive. Perhaps a victim of the mailboat accident in December 1921, perhaps delayed by the postal strike in Dublin in the autumn of 1922, or maybe an echo of an unrealised ambition (in the call of *Sinn Féin*), it seems that ALP will go on waiting by the shore, primer at hand, would it ever 'be coming may be'.

Both the stamps that legitimate the Letter-Treaty-*Ulysses* and the audiences that interpret it are split: any attempt to imagine an audience thus stutters in the material conditions of its consumption, conditions which are, moreover, already influenced by the situation of the text's production. The interpretation of the letter, like that of the Treaty, splits the 'audience' it appears to inaugurate. By working the reception of *Ulysses* into this archetype, Joyce suggests that the attempted formation of an audience is always divisive and never determinable.

VI

As this chapter has shown, in *Finnegans Wake* Joyce engaged with the specific terms of Yeats's invitation to Ireland, and, by construing the symbolic Letter as both the Treaty and *Ulysses*, he was able to depict an already divided Irish reception for his work. He did so not as an utter denial of community (national or otherwise), as 'post-structuralist Joyce' would have it, nor as part of an all-too-easy assimilation of difference, as contemporary liberal criticism might say, but as part of his ongoing cultural transformation of the terms of reception.[59] In the words of Deane, Joyce 'is writing towards a community (an Irish community or a readership community) which still did not exist' – this 'communality' would be 'achieved through the very form' of *Finnegans Wake*. Yet even this more subtle reading would cast Joyce as a Yeatsian, striving to formulate the conditions, through writing, in which an Irish audience and nation could come into being.[60] There is indeed a sense in which Joyce's last work writes towards a non-existing Irish readership; and yet it does so not by anticipation – not by modelling an ideal future reader or projecting an appropriate reading position – but by rewriting many of Joyce's own, actual readers. In doing so it points to the historical conditions of reading, which sustain and hinder that reading, and refashions those responses. Joyce writes over actual responses in his own other language, instilling a continual play between elucidating later readers and those who have gone before. This creates a continuation of reading which is therefore the continuation of (a necessarily divided) reception. Such a form establishes the broken communality and ruptured historicity of reading while not reducing its otherness, that is, the process of estrangement from self, text and place that is written into its production. In this way, *Finnegans Wake* is the literary form of the Free State in its deceptive originality, its contrariness, its uncertainty of decision (or decision of uncertainty); the Free State may not have been receptive to this genre of reception but that was perhaps the form it had to take. As Yeats himself would have admitted, if literature and reading are not finished, nor is the nation.

To Joyce, Yeats was a convenient image of the divided reader: 'the Doubly Telewisher' was also '[M]y Shemblable! My freer!' (*FW* 489.21, 489.28) The missing term in the allusion to Baudelaire sums up Yeats's role in the *Wake* as a sort of *hypocrite lecteur*. Yeats's apparent hypocrisy exemplifies the fissured condition of the Free State by treading an uneven path between private opinion, language and belief to public pronouncement, identity, and belonging. Yeats of course well knew this condition (in some ways he saw it as emblematic of the post-colonial Catholic State) and he addressed it directly in part of *The Tower*. Even when writing (in February 1916) of an imperfect national audience, as in 'The Fisherman', he cannot but imagine that this ideal model *will* one day have received his poem.[61] Joyce, however, cannot confidently address such a model: his version of 'the fisherman' is a non-delivering postman who is based on *actual* readers of his work. Yeats himself was one of these, and his distorted inscription in the *Wake* is less the anticipation of a national audience than an imaginative archive of the conditions of its impossibility.

Although Yeats and the terms of his support provided Joyce with a kind of model for an impossible reception, he is not a symbol of mere fickleness: if hypocrisy appears personal it is because it is also structural. The *Wake* also provides a sort of language of the State – a contrary one that seems never to be fully achieved. With Yeats as Joyce's *hypocrite lecteur*, this almost fraternal relationship lies principally in the different approaches each took towards the conditions of reception in Ireland. For Yeats this meant the attempted creation of a national audience, initially with the Irish Literary Theatre and the Abbey as its vehicle, and later through personal poetic symbols of an ideal cultural reception. For Joyce, reception – perhaps especially in Ireland – was inevitably fractured at every level. Whereas Yeats at times took to the public theatre and the political stage as means towards the formation of an audience, and, though only too conscious of the divided society he addressed, nonetheless continued to envisage ideals of cultural unity and versions of a post-colonial national audience (even if only to signal their inevitable fallibility), from the start Joyce inscribed the divisions and incompletion that feature in all his work as emblematic of an always fractured reception amid an irredeemably divided state.[62]

To address these conditions was also to address the image of the writer as reflected across the water, and so the charge of hypocrisy (and narcissism) against Joyce could usefully tally with his implicit accusation against Yeats. By turning the tables on Yeats and bringing his reading of *Ulysses* into the *Wake*, Joyce was able to show that there *were* readers, that the conditions for the absence of a Yeatsian audience were the conditions for a readership of his own work, albeit a necessarily 'broken' one. As ever, a version of this 'readership' was close to hand. In the mid 1930s, Joyce would be entertained and frustrated by Nora's family in Galway, after they sent a series of cryptic letters (including yet more wedding cake). 'These people', he said, 'would be ideal readers for Work in Progress but for the fact that they feel they could do so much better themselves if only they would take the trouble of so doing' (*Letters* I, 392). Although a self-consciously 'unreadable' text, the *Wake* is still a book that can and does have readers. Just as ordinary readers read *Ulysses*, and as the

Letter-Treaty-*Ulysses* gets its force and momentum from being reread in various tones, so the *Wake* is proposed as a text that carefully inflects its 'unreadable' difficulty with an acute knowledge that there were, and are, readers. The very charge of hypocrisy against Joyce was evidence enough of that; and his translation of that charge into a structural feature was deft displacement of the accusation. His development of 'overwriting' not only transformed his readers' responses, thus liberating a space for others, but also formally inscribed a contrary address and a divided society. So Joyce's writing creates the grounds for its own ongoing reception in the very process of recording the conditions of the impossibility of a model audience as its addressee. By displaying and displacing actual responses it clears a space for another reader – one that has been only partially vacated by those lingering readers of the past whose almost lost voices are still occasionally heard: 'mememormee!' (*FW* 628.14).

Using the example of Yeats, among others, Joyce inscribed and transformed actual responses in order to figure reception as a material and historically-embedded facet of textuality and not as a model or an ideal. This attitude is key to Joyce's conceptualisation of reception and fully conforms with his comic aesthetic as with his broadly egalitarian politics. Yeats, on the other hand, could not help but portray an audience in ideal terms even if this invoked a sense of himself as 'not only solitary but helpless'.[63]

A poet is justified not by the expression of himself, but by the public he finds or creates; a public made by others ready to his hand if he is a mere popular poet, but a new public, a new form of life, if he is a man of genius.[64]

This somewhat grandiose, Wordsworthian, statement represents the public leave-taking, rather late in the day (1937), of a national figure.[65] The distinctions that Yeats makes here between the popular writer and the genius, the created audience and the ready public, betray an idealism that Joyce's scenes of reception consistently undercut. Although it has become common to read Joyce-the-modernist as creating his own (future, better) audience, his readers, in the act of reading his work, are predicated on that 'ready public' such as he found it and reworked it in the fiction. For Joyce, any 'new form of life' would be derived initially from the old forms he found about him, including those same critics who had apparently rejected him, Yeats included. Joyce's work is full of revivals but none of them happy, glorious or ideal. He revives his readers as hypocrites, only to show that hypocrisy is a structural facet of reception and of writing.

The *Wake* has instituted a form of reception that is necessarily hypo-critical because it instils contrary responses, like the Treaty and *Ulysses*. In doing so, it pitches reader and writer as mirror-image (br)others, their positions apparently reversible, so that the stable and the unstable text – the truthful opinion and the false showmanship – are indistinguishable.

A letterman does be often thought reading ye between lines that do have no sense at all. I sign myself. With much leg. Inflexibly yours. Ann Posht the Shorn. To be continued. Huck! (*FW* 454.4–7)

In the guise of *An Post*, Shaun-the-Post's mini-letter echoes not only Stanislaus's rejection of 'Work in Progress' as 'pulling the reader's leg' (*Letters* III, 102) but also Joyce's earlier reading of his brother. He had annotated Stannie's diary, 'An' do ye be sittin' up here, scratchin' your arse, an' writin' thim things.'[66] Writer and reader continually occupy each other's positions. The act of reception is thus an informing historical moment, a constituent feature of production, and a partly fictitious record or anarchive; all of which requires 'reading ye between lines'. The point is not only that reading in the present is predicated on past readings but that overwriting, and reading between the lines, produce a reading that is, again, contrary: we are back at Beckett's impasse, in which performance (because reception is already built into it) is always necessar-ily 'To be continued' and at the same time full of stops, points at which a hiccup and an expletive close the book. 'Huck!' indeed.

Afterword

The joke may have been lost somewhat when Joyce first suggested that his work would keep the professors busy for hundreds of years, but now perhaps it is starting to wear a little thin. Generations of readers have been faced with the difficulty – perhaps even the impossibility – of 'saying something new' about Joyce. This problem is structured into Joyce's writing, not only its play on the apparent exhaustion of the English language, but in its engagement with the question of reception. If reading Joyce is also reading in the conditions of his contemporary readers, then the historicity of reception itself becomes a feature of the text. It is in the rewriting of contextual modes of reading and of specific responses that the intimacy of cultural politics to questions of style, language and form can most clearly be seen. The emerging picture of Joyce's work as firmly enmeshed within varying contemporary social discourses (of nationhood, postcolonisation, gender, religious censorship, etc.) is underpinned by showing the extent to which the act of reading was itself a political issue in Joyce's Ireland. His depiction of specific readers and acts of reception allows an analysis of the social conditions in which reading occurs – conditions influenced by forms of national expectation, religious presumption and state formation – as well as a recognition of the very textuality of reading and its resistance to archival capture.

Examination of Joyce's engagement with his contemporary reception also enables a broader understanding of the familiar theme of 'betrayal' as it features in Joyce's writing and biography. It would be misleading to maintain the line (derived from Ellmann and inspired by Stanislaus) that Joyce wrote 'against' certain individuals and 'against' his country. Joyce was not just 'bothered' by some individual criticisms, such as Stanislaus's and Pound's preference for the earlier work, but his work shows that specific readings were part of wider acts of reception. As such, individual responses were implicated in particular social circumstances, from the attempt to instil a national audience for Revival theatre, to the politics of education, to the expectations of an ordinary reader and the controversies of the Free State. It was precisely the manner of his readers' misreadings that spoke to their cultural significance. Yet the rewriting of their responses, and the fictional record of the conditions of reception, signal that the apparently 'unreadable' still asks to be read. The importance of the possibility of being read, especially in Ireland – even if it remains only a possibility – is a key element of Joyce's historical placement.

As Joyce shows, the early ambition of the Literary Revival to form a national audience, in its attempt to create an Irish public for art, misjudged the actual audiences available to it. Joyce's focus on the boredom of actual readers was a means of deflating the ambitious call to a 'people' (in Yeats's term) and instead demonstrating how, for instance, the surveillance of particular religious and political reading strategies could both imply and deny communities of readers. The increasing difficulty of Joyce's work might seem designed to render any communality impossible, as if all reading was already exhausted and inevitably hypocritical. However, the contretemps of the non-address to readers, as shown in the Library episode of *Ulysses*, shows that communities of reception are inevitable, if also problematically constituted. It might be suggested that Joyce's focus on the actualities of reception emphasises the historical grounding of readers and, through the writing of reception, opens a dialogue between text and context, showing how the new is formed in the guise of the old. As such, Joyce's rewriting of readers does not anticipate some future audience (national or otherwise) but points to the conditions through which any such endeavour must work and so implies that readers remain *potential*. In one sense, this is precisely what the act of reception means in Joyce: a potential reading, with possible social meanings. That it remains unachieved is its point. This emphasis on potentiality suggests that the apparently unreadable has a significant political and historical role as that which may yet become articulated.

The central concern of this book – that Joyce's writing was embedded in the manner and significance of its own reception, especially in Ireland – has implications for theories of reception as well as for how we think of Joyce. Having emphasised throughout the preceding chapters the extent to which Joyce records a transformed act of reception into his writing, this study closes by briefly considering the relationship between Joyce's work and one of its most notable later readers, Jacques Derrida. The recent but passing influence of post-structural analysis on Joyce studies over the past three decades and more has supported the claim that Joyce's work anticipates so much (even all) that follows it. The progenitor here is

Derrida, who has cited Joyce as a 'precondition' of deconstruction and suggested that 'we are all his [Joyce's] dream readers'.[1] Despite their apparent disavowal of the authorial subject, these readings are strangely comfortable alongside the older, humanist assumption of Joyce as a 'universal' writer whose work transcends its own time and place. Once again, reader-response theory finds a home here too, with its faith in reading as a means towards 'the possibility that we may formulate ourselves'.[2] Although these interpretive modes differ significantly, they can imply that 'Joyce' has become simply a tool for 'our' use. An alliance of humanist principles with contemporary pragmatism means that 'Joyce' serves as an appropriate educational commodity as if 'we' were his audience.[3] Against the vogue for asserting the 'relevance' of Joyce to our own times – in which current social needs are supposedly met by once again invoking his 'anticipation' of, and need for, a later audience – this Afterword outlines a theory of reception immanent in Joyce's writing.

While not wanting to miscast Derrida as merely a 'textualist' it is still possible to take issue with his optimistic characterisation of both deconstruction and Joyce as the harbingers of a new form of audience. Not unlike Jauss's endorsement of literary texts, which upset generic expectations, Derrida argues that Joyce's work 'invents' its readers who then form a 'special institution' ensuring that 'competence' is a circular achievement.[4] He sees a 'privileged circulation' between Joyce's work and that of deconstruction, and has referred to Joyce on several occasions as a notable example of a similar literary (and theoretical) practice, suggesting that his work is 'one of the most powerful preconditions of deconstruction'.[5] While it can be speculated that in a curious way Joyce's writing of reception looks ahead to, or perhaps preconditions, Derrida's own references to his readers and audiences, it should be clear they are not doing the same thing. If Joyce's work implies a kind of deconstruction of reception (as Derrida might say), it does so in a different way from the work of Derrida, whose references to his readers and audiences imply a hopeful and affirmative possibility, even a 'new enlightenment for the century to come'.[6] In Joyce, the act of reception is a more gloomy affair. Deconstruction implies a textual indefinite audience that is always deferred; on the other hand, Joyce never relinquishes a sense of the local and specific, especially with respect to the conditions of reception that are a part of that work. Without sentimentality, these scenes seem to implore the necessity of a context from which, nonetheless, they have been irrevocably split. The difference might be put like this: in Joyce, the historical has been 'lost' even while it still casts its determining influence; in Derrida, it is always yet to come.

The implied audience that Derrida posits for deconstruction, and indeed for Joyce, is infinite and indefinite. In each case, a 'historical community' is set the task of 'explaining' an infinite textuality, which in turn inevitably undermines that community.[7] This is Derrida's 'deconstruction of reception' and it results in an appeal to the possibility of a later, infinite and indefinite audience. Joyce, on the other hand, although also questioning the structure of reception, is more concerned for the social circumstances within which his writing circulates and the inevitable failure of any co-optation of it.

Derrida has recalled that his own texts were 'unreadable for those at whom they were directed' – that is, at his own 'little milieu' at the école normale supérieure in the 1960s.[8] It is a paradox typical of his work that the moment a determined readership has been signalled, the writing in question is rendered 'unreadable'. This has been a recurring motif in Derrida's writing, which repeatedly invokes a direct addressee only to collapse that reader into an infinite and indefinite audience. This manoeuvre echoes Joyce's inscriptions of reception but with a different emphasis. To rephrase this difference one might repeat a question asked by Pierre Bourdieu, 'can one read . . . without asking what are the social conditions of the possibility of reading?'[9] Joyce's work shows a recognition of the importance of reception as a political and material activity, some of the conditions of which have been described above. It could be suggested that Joyce's difference from deconstruction lies in a scepticism towards a future audience rather than Derrida's more hopeful anticipation of a possible 'new enlightenment'.

In an important interview discussing tentative formulations of 'deconstruction', Derrida characteristically invokes a specific reception (in this case, the academic discourse that reads a ceaseless motif of deconstruction), only to collapse that specificity back into a universal history. He declares, 'What is called "deconstruction" in the sense of a relatively coherent set of discursive rules at a given moment in Western discourse is only a symptom – an effect of deconstruction at work in what one might call history.'[10] This is another way of phrasing the Joyce conundrum: what Derrida would like to call 'Joyce' is the text that undermines the attempts of contemporary critics to name and explain it, a text which gives rise to those critics in the first place. Derrida favours the textuality of deconstruction over its historical formalisation just as, in his view, Joyce's writing always undercuts its commentary. Derrida's framing of the relationship between 'these "real" deconstructions and the apparently academic discourse to which we grant this name', privileges the transhistorical over the specific, so that the latter is just as problematically open-ended as the former: 'What is "today"?' he asks, repeating a manoeuvre made elsewhere.[11] It is on the basis of this ceaselessly operating textual motif of deconstruction that the community which works in that name takes shape; it is the same, he implies, with Joyce's texts, whose deconstruction of competence both authorises and dismantles the authority of the critic. Derrida's emphasis is thus towards reception as an infinite and indefinite textuality.

At several points in his career, Derrida has objected to what Rabaté called the 'naïve' question (when identifying a readership) 'for whom?' He did so in one of his most 'literary' texts, *The Post Card* (which draws significantly on Joyce) and in the earlier and more obviously philosophical essay 'Signature Event Context'. These quite different texts both argue that it is a condition of writing that it be repeatable in the absence of an empirically determinable addressee and that this 'iterability' opens writing for 'any possible user in general'.[12] (The language of 'use' and especially 'work' is a key element of Derrida's account of writing.) Derrida's public/private post card exemplifies the inexhaustible linguistic network and as such 'no rigorous theory of "reception", however necessary it might be, will get to the end of that literature'.[13] This appears to be an admission of the necessity as well as impossibility of a theory of reception. Against this infinite network, as Derrida himself admits elsewhere, it is also structurally necessary that 'one must indeed receive the address of the other at a particular address and in a singular language; otherwise we would not receive it'.[14] At the same time, 'everything depends upon you', upon the reader(s) and yet an addressee 'can never be the object of knowledge'.[15] At stake in Derrida's denial of 'reception' (as he calls it, using inverted commas) is the effacement of any apparently specific addressee within a future audience. 'I annihilate not only what I am saying but also the unique addressee that I constitute, and therefore every possible addressee, and every destination.'[16] The very notion of reception as a history of response, a sort of archive of reading, has been reworked, privileging an infinite and indefinite audience that complements what Derrida sees as the unceasing travail of deconstruction.

In his reading of the *Phaedrus*, Derrida asks of the links that Plato sets up, 'for what reader? at what moment?' only to say that 'to answer such questions in principle and in general will seem impossible; and that will give us the suspicion that there is some malformation in the question itself, in each of its concepts'. By implying that readers cannot be located, Derrida dilutes specific readers into a universal notion of reading. His allusion to 'us' (and, in a footnote, 'the reader') might imply that his writing nonetheless implies a readership, yet his 'suspicion' of the 'concept' of a particular reader and his/her 'moment' is also a refusal to engage with historical reception.[17]

On his own terms, Derrida's appeal to openness among readers is also a call to an ethical responsibility.[18] He labels his insistence on a future in(de)finite audience as an opening to the other. It is implied by some critics that this is also what Joyce's work entails.[19] Yet there is an important relationship between the political and the ethical in the deconstructive configuration of audiences, which is not necessarily the same in Joyce. In Derrida's work, any identification of readers is collapsed into a broader infinite and indefinite audience. This broadly political problem – the apparent impossibility of an identifiable audience or community – goes hand-in-hand with an ethical challenge or appeal to readers not to foreclose the relation between a text or event and its audience or interpreters. This is the undecidable logic of Derrida's 'decision', that is, the necessary and inevitable responsibility: 'the decision, if there is such a thing, must neutralize if not render impossible in advance the who and the what'. For Derrida, this responsibility makes deconstruction 'hyper-politicizing', that is, it 'awakens politicization' by allowing 'us' to rethink democracy.[20] Yet the responsibility implied by deconstruction suggests that readers are asked to forego whatever broadly determinable audience they may (think they) comprise (including any political community) in favour of an infinite and indefinite audience. This has an uncomfortable echo of Iser's liberal implied reader for whom political commitment was a dangerous thing that prevented open reading. Derrida's 'responsibility' similarly forever holds communal politics in abeyance. The most significant thing about Derrida's new 'democracy to come' is that it is always 'to come' (à venir).[21] The call to an ethical responsibility thus takes precedence over any socio-political community. The implied reader of Derrida, then, must give over, or hold always in suspension, membership of any determined social community. This is a strategy in Derrida's work, for all its prestidigitous political procrastination: that readers or readership – and a determinable politics – are willfully suspended in favour of a call to responsibility in the name of audiences to come. In doing so, the familiar refrain of the later audience once more resounds over Joyce's writing.

If, as Derrida implies, a theory of reception demands that both specific reader and later audience be thought in relation to the other, while privileging the latter, then the purpose of my argument has been to show that Joyce maintains the significance of those specific 'local' readers whose responses echo in his work. The tension between the (lost) historical moment and the 'unreadable' text is resolved in an exploration of the social significances of reception. At the same time, I have suggested that Joyce's writing moves towards ways of encoding reception into new generic modes – what might be called a form of responsiveness. This idea of reception as a 'responsiveness' alludes to a sense of reading as an ethical responsibility that Joyce arguably develops in a quite different way from Derrida. For Joyce, reading must still be situated within the particular historical and political conditions of reception.[22] Joyce does not address or imply any particular audience, but he has been careful to record and transform some particular, historical readers and audiences. As such, Joyce's writing does not posit an ideal unreadability but a necessary and inevitably faltering practice of reading in particular circumstances. His work seems to be at pains to point out that reading is not only a difficult and productive performance but also a social act with particular cultural determinations working upon it; moreover, that work inscribes in its own *mal d'archive* a series of representations of actual readers and responses.[23] It is on this basis that an overturning of the critical privilege accorded to the later audience is made possible within Joyce's work. It does so precisely to question the assumptions of certain contemporaneous social discourses that demarcated reception, from the 'ordinary reader' to the 'national audience'. In doing so it also sets out something like an imma-nent theory of reception, but one developed on slightly different terms (despite their apparent similarities) from that of Derrida.

As the previous chapters have argued, the conditions that Joyce en-countered in early twentieth-century Dublin prevented him from ima-gining in his work a model of an audience, or, indeed, of implying a future audience that, either through scholarship or a deconstructive ethics, would have learnt to read it appropriately. Instead, Joyce's work inscribes versions of actual, specific readers as textual traces of historical events and in doing so it performs a restaging of reception. It is for this reason that the orthodox critical presupposition that Joyce demands a future and better audience is limited, for such an audience can only be formed through the hesitations of those earlier readers and their conditions. The act of reception as it is figured in Joyce's work shows how later readers come from, and read through, contemporary readers. His work both displays a concern for the historical situation of its own reading and at the same time displaces the very notion of reception in its critique of the priority accorded to an 'appropriate' audience.[24]

Instead of suggesting that 'we are Joyce's dream readers' it might be said that his writing is haunted by its contemporary readers. Reception is by its nature a question of the past as well as the future. In Joyce, the future does not signal a liberation (Joyce's texts are consistently sceptical towards any site of liberation) but a false revival, even, perhaps especially, after Independence. In a sense, then, his writing remains determinedly provincial, tied to the 'halting' (*D* 5) readings of his contemporaries, still tackling the questions of readership that dogged Irish writing and had been endemic to its political history. At the same time, however, this very 'provincialism' (in Joyce's continual returns to the figure of a local reader and a local context) was also a mark of modernity, of the dislocation of the writer and émigré unable to settle generically or culturally. Perhaps such 'provincialism' can also be understood as a resistance to the reductive political appropriations that were – and sometimes still are – practised upon his work. Not only does it voice the right of that local context to its place on the world stage but in doing so it signals the splits in reception and reading that were already part of Joyce's work.

Joyce's concern with the very real 'failures' of reception amounts to a fictional reworking of the failures of history. The process of 'overwriting' by which actual responses were included and transformed is not the anticipation of an appropriate audience but the predication of a future reading on those past readers' responses. As with Joyce's sense of history – derived from his understanding of Irish history – new readers appear in the garb of the old. Marx's famous lines are apposite: 'the traditions of all the dead generations weigh like a nightmare on the brain of the living'. The 'new' appears only 'in this time-honoured disguise and this borrowed language'.[25] While Marx worries over the impossibility of creation, Joyce's recreation of his contemporary readers' responses carries less *Schadenfreude*. Instead, that practice signals how reception helps form social demarcation, and at the same time rewrites it and so keeps the textuality of reading in play. The notion of reception proposed in this book – and a notion derived from Joyce – is that reception does not simply follow the text but is already part of it: Joyce's writing was produced within circumstances that had already influenced its reading. The act of reception, then, should be seen as part of the context into which Joyce wrote. That his work came to be seen as 'unreadable', and even promoted itself as such, is not a retreat into a purely textual realm, but forms its historical significance. The incorporation of the circumstances of his own reception allowed Joyce to imply the historicity of reception and the social formation of the faltering activity of reading. Joyce's refusal of an audience instilled the possibility of his readers.

Notes

INTRODUCTION: WRITING RECEPTION

1 The following studies provide helpful analytic histories of Joyce criticism in different cultural situations: Patrick Parrinder, 'The Strange Necessity: James Joyce's Rejection in England 1914–30' in *James Joyce: New Perspectives*, ed. Colin MacCabe (Brighton: Harvester Press, 1982) and Jeffrey Segall, *Joyce in America: Cultural Politics and the Trials of Ulysses* (Berkeley: University of California Press, 1993). The most comprehensive overview of the development of Joyce studies is Joseph Brooker, *Joyce's Critics* (Madison: University of Wisconsin Press, 2004).

2 Wolfgang Iser, *The Act of Reading: A Theory of Aesthetic Response* (Baltimore: Johns Hopkins University Press, 1978).

3 Modernity here signals the 'in-between' state of having no audience or public (or belief in the people as a public), and so also lacking shared criteria on which judgement can be made. See Jean-François Lyotard and Jean-Loup Thébaud, *Just Gaming*, trans. Wlad Godzich (Minnesota: University of Minnesota Press, 1985), 11–15.

4 Richard Ellmann, *James Joyce*, new and revised edition (Oxford: Oxford University Press, 1982 [1959]), 3, 744. Joyce wrote advertising jingles for *Anna Livia Plurabelle* and *Haveth Childers Everywhere*; see 616–17n.

5 Herbert Gorman, *James Joyce: A Definitive Biography* (London: John Lane, The Bodley Head, 1941), 339.

6 Lawrence Rainey, *Institutions of Modernism: Literary Elites and Public Culture* (New Haven: Yale University Press, 1998). Rainey's work is discussed in chapter 3 below.

7 Joyce Piell Wexler, *Who Paid for Modernism?* (Fayetteville: University of Arkansas Press, 1997), 65, 72.

8 Jacques Derrida, 'Two Words for Joyce', trans. Geoff Bennington in *Post-Structuralist Joyce: Essays from the French*, ed. Derek Attridge and Daniel Ferrer (Cambridge: Cambridge University Press, 1984), 148.

9 Evelyn Scott, 'Contemporary of the Future', *The Dial* (October 1920), 353–67 (*CH* I, 177–81).

10 Christine Froula, *Modernism's Body: Sex, Culture, and Joyce* (New York: Columbia University Press, 1996), 254. For a discussion of the historical

relationship between Joyce and a 'belated' post-structuralism, see Joe Brooker, 'The Fidelity of Theory: James Joyce and the Rhetoric of Belatedness' in *Joyce's Audiences*, ed. John Nash (Amsterdam: Rodopi, 2002), 201–21.

11 Colin MacCabe, *On the Eloquence of the Vulgar* (London: British Film Institute, 1992), 11.

12 Clearly, there are elements in early Yeats, Eliot, and even Proust, which suggest a 'cultured' future audience as a desirable ideal; however, all these would also appear to recognise the futility of such desire.

13 Colin MacCabe, *James Joyce and the Revolution of the Word* (London: Macmillan, 1979), 156–7. See also, for example, Harry Levin, *James Joyce* 2nd edn (London: Faber, 1963), 121 and Max Eastman, *The Literary Mind* (London: Charles Scrivener, 1931), 102.

14 Seamus Deane, Introduction, *Finnegans Wake* (London; Penguin, 1992), xvii, xlvii. MacCabe had also bemoaned the 'Joyce scholars' who 'form his only audience' (*James Joyce*, 157).

15 Seamus Deane, 'Dead Ends: Joyce's Finest Moments' in *Semicolonial Joyce*, ed. Derek Attridge and Marjorie Howes (Cambridge: Cambridge University Press, 2000), 34.

16 John Carey, *The Intellectuals and the Masses* (London: Faber and Faber, 1992), 20.

17 Deane, Introduction, *Finnegans Wake*, xviii.

18 Marcel Proust, *À la Recherche du Temps Perdu* (Paris: Gallimard, 1999), 73. Paul de Man cites this instance in *Allegories of Reading: Figural Language in Rousseau, Nietzsche, Rilke, and Proust* (New Haven: Yale University Press, 1979), 78.

19 Myles na cGopaleen, 'Cruiskeen Lawn', *Irish Times*, 29 December 1957. Cited in David Powell, 'An Annotated Bibliography of Myles Na Gopaleen's (Flann O' Brien's) "Cruiskeen Lawn" Commentaries on James Joyce', *James Joyce Quarterly* 9:1 (1971), 58.

20 Jacques Derrida, '*ULYSSES* GRAMOPHONE: Hear Say Yes in Joyce', trans. Tina Kendall and revised by Shari Benstock in *James Joyce: The Augmented Ninth*, ed. Bernard Benstock (New York: Syracuse University Press, 1988), 52 (original emphasis).

21 Noam Chomsky's idea of linguistic competence (the ability to apply given conventions or rules to language) lies behind ideas of the 'ideal reader' in reader-response criticism. Derrida sees such competence as a vain pretension to 'neutral, metalinguistic knowledge' ('*ULYSSES* GRAMOPHONE', 52).

22 Derrida, '*ULYSSES* GRAMOPHONE', 48.

23 Derrida, 'Two Words for Joyce', 148.

24 Jean-Michel Rabaté warns against a 'genetic fallacy' although it remains to be seen what qualitative difference genetic criticism will make. *James Joyce and the Politics of Egoism* (Cambridge: Cambridge University Press, 2002), 186.

25 James Fairhall's *James Joyce and the Question of History* (Cambridge: Cambridge University Press, 1993) tends to reduce the historical to the textual and so continues by another means the work of *Post-Structuralist Joyce*. See also Derek Attridge, *Joyce Effects: On Language*, (Cambridge: Cambridge

University Press, 2000) and Rabaté, *James Joyce and the Politics of Egoism*. Historical criticism was for many years largely biographical but more recently some studies have given detailed accounts of Joyce's texts' engagement with specific contextual forms such as nationalism, censorship and ethnography. This more historical criticism, which of course remains firmly interpretive, is exemplified by Andrew Gibson, *Joyce's Revenge: History, Politics, and Aesthetics in 'Ulysses'* (Oxford: Oxford University Press, 2002). For a sensitive account of some of these issues within Joyce's texts, see Margot Norris, *Joyce's Web: the Social Unraveling of Modernism* (Austin: University of Texas Press, 1992).

26 Norris, *Joyce's Web*, 3.
27 See Luke Gibbons, 'Spaces of Time Through Times of Space: Joyce, Ireland and Colonial Modernity', *Field Day Review* 1 (2005), 71–85 and the discussion of historicism in Dipesh Chakrabarty, *Provincializing Europe: Postcolonial Thought and Historical Difference* (Princeton: Princeton University Press, 2000), 3–23.
28 On depictions of reading in Proust and Joyce see David Spurr, *Joyce and the Scene of Modernity* (Gainesville: University Press of Florida, 2002), 88–103.
29 C. L. Innes, 'Modernism, Ireland and Empire: Yeats, Joyce and their Implied Audiences' in *Modernism and Empire*, ed. Howard J. Booth and Nigel Rigby (Manchester: Manchester University Press, 2000), 148. Despite this quibble, I am in broad agreement with Innes's suggestion that in writing *Ulysses*, 'Joyce may have wished to construct an Irish readership that would be ready to identify Bloom as one among themselves . . . A readership growing towards the affirmation of Ireland as an independent nation, writing and reading itself into its own version of history' (153).
30 See Powell, 'An Annotated Bibliography' and James D. Alexander, 'Frank O'Connor's Joyce Criticism', *Journal of Irish Literature* 21:2 (1992), 40–53.
31 Levin, *James Joyce*, 21. See C. P. Curran Collection, University College Dublin Library, CUR ms 6.
32 Ellmann, *James Joyce*, 200–1.
33 Attridge and Ferrer, 'Introduction: Highly Continental Evenements' in *Post-Structuralist Joyce*, 1–2.
34 'Nobody but a Dubliner could appraise its subtlety' – Brian O'Nolan, 'Cruiskeen Lawn', *Irish Times*, 6 June 1957 (cited in Powell, 'An Annotated Bibliography', 57). Frank O'Connor's initial sympathy towards Joyce was expressed in 'Joyce – The Third Period', *Irish Statesman*, 12 April 1930, 114–16. See also Stephen Gwynn, *Irish Literature and Drama in the English Language* (New York: Nelson, 1936).
35 Ellmann, *James Joyce*, 598. (I was pleased to find that when drafting 'Work in Progress' Joyce had consulted a history of the small town that I grew up in.)
36 *Reflections on James Joyce: Stuart Gilbert's Paris Journal*, ed. Thomas F. Staley and Randolph Lewis (Austin: University of Texas Press, 1993), 21.
37 Ezra Pound, 'Paris Letter', *The Dial* LXXII, (June 1922), 6, reprinted in Forrest Read, ed. *Pound/Joyce. The Letters of Ezra Pound to James Joyce, with Pound's Critical Essays and Articles about Joyce* (New York: New Directions, 1967), 197.

38 For a theorisation of a rootlessness which is at home in neither native nor host culture, see Abdul JanMohammed, 'Worldliness-without-World, Homelessness-as-Home: Toward a Definition of the Specular Border Intellectual' in *Edward Said: A Critical Reader*, ed. Michael Sprinker (Oxford: Blackwell, 1993), 96–120. Spurgeon Thompson has argued that Joyce performs this role in 'Joyce as Postcolonial Border Intellectual: A Mediterranean Comparison', Unpublished paper, International James Joyce Symposium, Trieste, 2000.

39 Walter Benjamin, 'The Task of the Translator', in *Illuminations*, ed. Hannah Arendt, trans. Harry Zohn (New York: Schocken Books, 1988), 69.

40 Jean-Michel Rabaté, *James Joyce, Authorized Reader* (Baltimore: Johns Hopkins University Press, 1991), 152.

41 Jacques Derrida, *Politics of Friendship*, trans. George Collins (London: Verso, 1997), 27.

42 John Searle, 'The Logical Status of Fictional Discourse', *New Literary History* 6:2 (1975), 330.

43 Hans-Georg Gadamer, *Truth and Method* (London: Sheed and Ward, 1985) (first published as *Wahrheit und Methode*, 1965), 92.

44 See Hans Robert Jauss, *Toward an Aesthetic of Reception*, trans. Timothy Bahti (Brighton: Harvester, 1982), esp. 'Literary History as a Challenge to Literary Theory', 3–45. As Paul de Man has pointed out in his acute reading of Jauss (also published as an Introduction to Jauss's volume), the transposition of a 'horizon of expectations' to literary history has the benefit of reminding us that 'the historical consciousness of a given period can never exist as a set of openly stated or recorded propositions'. De Man also raises the problem of whether Husserl's theory of the perception of phenomena can be adequately translated to the reading of language. *The Resistance to Theory* (Minneapolis: University of Minnesota Press, 1986), 58, 62.

45 Wolfgang Iser, 'The Reality of Fiction: A Functionalist Approach to Literature', *New Literary History* 6:3 (1975), 26.

46 Iser, *The Act of Reading*, 202.

47 Iser, 'The Reality of Fiction', 34–5.

48 See Brook Thomas, *James Joyce's 'Ulysses': A Book of Many Happy Returns* (Baton Rouge: Louisiana State University Press, 1982) and John Paul Riquelme, *Teller and Tale in Joyce's Fiction: Oscillating Perspectives* (Baltimore: Johns Hopkins, 1983).

49 Studies of forms of 'oppositional reading' include Ross Chambers, *Room for Manoeuvre: Reading (the) Oppositional (in) Narrative* (Illinois: University of Chicago Press, 1991) and Shoshana Felman, *What Does a Woman Want? Reading and Sexual Difference* (Baltimore: Johns Hopkins University Press, 1993). For a historical study of women as readers see Kate Flint, *The Woman Reader, 1837–1914* (Oxford: Oxford University Press, 1993).

50 Michel de Certeau, *The Practice of Everyday Life*, trans. Steven Rendall (Berkeley: University of California Press, 1984). Tony Bennett, 'Texts in History: the Determinations of Readings and their Texts' in *Post-Structuralism and the Question of History*, ed. Derek Attridge, Geoff Bennington and Robert Young (Cambridge: Cambridge University Press, 1987), 63–81.

51 Pierre Bourdieu, 'Reading, Readers, the Literant, Literature' in *In Other Words: Essays Towards a Reflexive Sociology*, trans. Matthew Adamson (Cambridge: Polity Press, 1990).

52 The notion of textual *mise-en-abyme* is explored in Lucien Dällenbach, *The Mirror in the Text*, trans. Jeremy Whiteley and Emma Hughes (Cambridge: Polity Press, 1989).

53 Manfred Pütz, 'The Identity of the Reader in *Finnegans Wake*', *James Joyce Quarterly* 11:4 (1974), 387–94. See also Shari Benstock, 'The Letter of the Law: *La Carte Postale* in *Finnegans Wake*', *Philological Quarterly* 63 (1984), 163–87.

54 Patrick A. McCarthy, 'Reading in *Ulysses*' in *Joycean Occasions*, ed. Janet Dunleavy, Melvin J. Friedman and Michael Patrick Gillespie (Toronto: Associated University Presses, 1991), 15–32 (16). Thomas, *James Joyce's 'Ulysses'*, 162–3.

55 See Fritz Senn, 'Righting *Ulysses*' in *James Joyce: New Perspectives*, ed. Colin MacCabe (Brighton: Harvester Press, 1982), 3–28 and Marilyn French, *The Book as World: James Joyce's 'Ulysses'* (Cambridge, Mass.: Harvard University Press, 1976).

56 Mark A. Wollaeger, 'Reading *Ulysses*: Agency, Ideology, and the Novel' in *Joyce and the Subject of History*, ed. Mark A. Wollaeger, Victor Luftig and Robert Spoo (Ann Arbor: University of Michigan Press, 1996), 97. However sympathetic one might be to that readerly position it is not necessarily that of all readers.

57 Seamus Deane, 'History as Fiction/Fiction as History' in *Joyce in Rome*, ed. Giorgio Melchiori (Rome: Bulzoni Editore, 1984), 137.

58 See Katherine Mullin, *James Joyce, Sexuality and Social Purity* (Cambridge: Cambridge University Press, 2003), 1–27.

59 Frances Ferguson, 'Emma, or Happiness (or Sex Work)', *Critical Inquiry* 28:3 (Spring 2002), 755.

60 Norris, *Joyce's Web*, 31. See Peter Bürger, *Theory of the Avant-Garde*, trans. Michael Shaw (Minneapolis: University of Minnesota Press, 1984).

61 Jacques Derrida, 'Typewriter Ribbon: Limited Ink (2)' in *Without Alibi*, ed. and trans. Peggy Kamuf (Stanford, Ca.: Stanford University Press, 2002), 100.

62 For an example of the challenge to the secure liberal reading subject posed by sensation fiction (such as *The Woman in White*, which Miss Dunne prefers not to read in 'Wandering Rocks'), see D. A. Miller, '*Cage aux folles*: Sensation and Gender in Wilkie Collins's *The Woman in White*' in *Speaking of Gender*, ed. Elaine Showalter (London: Routledge, 1989).

63 A version of this story is told in Flann O'Brien, 'A Bash in the Tunnel' in *A Bash in the Tunnel*, ed. John Ryan (Dublin: Clifton Books, 1970), 18–19.

1 BOREDOM: REVIVING AN AUDIENCE IN *DUBLINERS*

1 A national audience might be tentatively defined as an 'imagined community' that would be suitable and ready to receive the text. See the discussion of the Irish Literary Theatre below. Part of Yeats's project, as initially conceived, was to narrow the gap between his actual audiences and a projected national audience.

2 Ellmann, *James Joyce*, 245–50; Emer Nolan, *James Joyce and Nationalism* (London: Routledge, 1995), 24–36; Deane, 'Dead Ends', 33–6.

3 On Joyce's developing political consciousness, see the Trieste lectures and journalism as well as Kevin Barry's Introduction to *OCPW*. On Joyce and the Revival, see, among others: Terence Brown, *Ireland's Literature* (Mullingar: Lilliput, 1988); Seamus Deane, *Celtic Revivals: Essays in Modern Irish Literature 1880–1980* (London: Faber and Faber, 1985); Nolan, *James Joyce and Nationalism*, 24–54; and John Wilson Foster, *Fictions of the Irish Literary Revival: A Changeling Art* (Syracuse: University of Syracuse Press, 1987).

4 Seamus Deane, *Strange Country* (Oxford: Clarendon Press, 1997), 166. Deane makes the point that Dublin's boredom had a 'striking resemblance' to the inertia felt in 'advanced' countries (168–9).

5 *Ibid.*, 94.

6 *Ibid.*, 167.

7 Ellmann, *James Joyce*, 200.

8 Ellmann reports that Yeats, Gregory and Horniman did not receive copies (*James Joyce*, 200). Joyce's instructions to Stanislaus requested him to 'deliver . . . upon all interested' (*Letters* II, 91).

9 Others to receive the poem included James Cousins, Fred Ryan, G. A. McGinty and O'Leary Curtis.

10 W. B. Yeats, *Collected Poems*, ed. Richard J. Finneran (New York: Collier Books, 1989), 50–51. First published in *The Countess Kathleen and Various Legends and Lyrics* (1892).

11 W. B. Yeats, 'The Fisherman' (February 1916) in *Collected Poems*, 148–9.

12 Seamus Deane, 'Yeats: the Creation of an Audience' in *Tradition and Influence in Anglo-Irish Poetry*, ed. Terence Brown and Nicholas Grene (Basingstoke: Macmillan, 1989), 31–46 (40) and 'National Character and National Audience: Races, Crowds and Readers' in *Critical Approaches to Anglo-Irish Literature*, ed. Michael Allen and Angela Wilcox (Buckinghamshire: Colin Smythe, 1989), 40–52. Elsewhere, Deane argues that Joyce and Yeats were alike in that 'The idea of Ireland still uncreated, awaited its realization' for both writers. *Celtic Revivals*, 100.

13 See Edward A. Bloom and Lillian D. Bloom, *Satire's Persuasive Voice* (Ithaca: Cornell University Press, 1979), 16–23 and Arthur Pollard, *Satire* (London: Methuen, 1970), 73–5.

14 Lady Gregory did admit in 1913 that this 'statement' (as she called it) 'seems now a little pompous'. Lady Augusta Gregory, *Our Irish Theatre: A Chapter of Autobiography* (Gerrards Cross: Colin Smythe, 1972[1913]), 20. See also R. F. Foster, *W. B. Yeats: A Life. I: The Apprentice Mage 1865–1914* (Oxford, Oxford University Press, 1997), 183–5 and Christopher Morash, *A History of Irish Theatre 1601–2000* (Cambridge: Cambridge University Press, 2002), 116.

15 W. B. Yeats, 'Plans and Methods', *Beltaine: The Organ of the Irish Literary Theatre* No.1 (May 1899), 7. The first three numbers reprinted as *Beltaine* (London: Frank Cass and Co. Ltd, 1970).

16 On the ties between the Irish Literary Theatre and constructive Unionism, see Morash, *History of Irish Theatre*, 115–16 and Lionel Pilkington, *Theatre and the State in Twentieth-Century Ireland* (London: Routledge, 2001), 7–12.

17 Edward Martyn, 'A Comparison Between English and Irish Theatrical Audiences', *Beltaine* no. 2 (February 1900), 12. See the discussion of Yeats's 'The Galway Plains' at the end of this chapter.

18 See Ellmann, *James Joyce*, 200; Joseph Valente, *James Joyce and the Problem of Justice* (Cambridge: Cambridge University Press, 1995), 46–8, 245–56; and Susan Swartzlander, 'Multiple Meaning and Misunderstanding: The Mistrial of Festy King', *James Joyce Quarterly* 23:4 (1986), 465–76.

19 *James Joyce*, 200.

20 Joseph Kelly, *Our Joyce: From Outcast to Icon* (Austin: University of Texas Press, 1998), 15.

21 *Ibid.*, 31.

22 *Ibid.*, 62.

23 Hugh Witemeyer, '"He Gave the Name': Herbert Gorman's Rectifications of *James Joyce: His First Forty Years*', *James Joyce Quarterly* 32:3–4 (1995), 524. On generic expectations in one of Joyce's *Homestead* stories, see Katherine Mullin, 'Don't Cry for me Argentina: 'Eveline' and the Seductions of Emigration Propaganda' in *Semicolonial Joyce*, ed. Attridge and Howes, 172–200.

24 Seumas O'Sullivan [James Starkey], *The Rose and Bottle and Other Essays* (Dublin: Talbot Press, 1946), 119–120.

25 That had also been the principal charge against *The Countess Cathleen* in its earlier published version (London, 1892) in which a statue of the Virgin Mary is smashed, though this was revised prior to the first performance.

26 The *Freeman's Journal* claimed that out of 'an audience of four or five hundred' there were 'less than a dozen disorderly boys' who hissed occasionally, 'But the audience, representative of every section of educated opinion in Dublin, was most enthusiastic.' Yeats's friend T. W. Rolleston replied that these dozen boys 'were not exactly "disorderly"' and 'even led the applause' at certain moments. Robert Hogan and James Kilroy, *The Irish Literary Theatre, 1899–1901* (Dublin: The Dolmen Press, 1975), 40–41.

27 This pamphlet, 'The Day of the Rabblement' was quite literally that: it was printed on the same day as the Irish Literary Theatre first staged *Diarmuid and Grania* by Yeats and George Moore along with Douglas Hyde's *Casadh an tSúgáin*, produced by the Keating Branch of the Gaelic League and one of the first plays to be performed in Irish. See Hogan and Kilroy, *Irish Literary Theatre*, 135–6.

28 Deane, *Strange Country*, 167.

29 Pilkington, *Theatre and the State*, 39.

30 See Vincent J. Cheng, *Joyce, Race and Empire* (Cambridge: Cambridge University Press, 1995), 103–10.

31 See Gregory Castle, *Modernism and the Celtic Revival* (Cambridge: Cambridge University Press, 2001), 213–17 and Cheng, *Joyce, Race and Empire*, 151–62.

32 W. B. Yeats, 'J. M. Synge and the Ireland of his Time' in *Essays and Introductions* (New York: Collier Books, MacMillan, 1968), 320–21.

33 Luke Gibbons, 'Romanticism, Realism and Irish Cinema' in *Cinema and Ireland*, ed. Luke Gibbons, Kevin Rockett and John Hill (Syracuse: Syracuse University Press, 1988), 219.

34 *James Joyce and Nationalism*, 62.

35 Synge, *Complete Letters*, ed. Ann Saddlemyer (Oxford, 1983), I, 74. Cited in Morash, *History of Irish Theatre*, 117.

36 See Cheng, *Joyce, Race and Empire*, 128–34 and Michael Levenson, 'Living History in 'The Dead',' in *James Joyce: 'The Dead'*, ed. Daniel R. Schwarz (New York: St Martin's Press, 1994), 163–77.

37 Kevin Barry, Introduction, *OCPW*, xxxi.

38 The Italian text of Joyce's MS is reproduced in *OCPW* (244–59); translation by Conor Deane. Joyce's listeners may already have read an article in *Il Piccolo della Serra* one month prior to this lecture in which he caustically observed the habit of celebrating the dead in Ireland, also using the dramatic metaphor. 'The Irish . . . never fail to show a great reverence for the dead' (*OCPW*, 141). (The funeral in question here was John O'Leary's, which Yeats, also sceptical, declined to attend.) O'Leary was 'the last actor in the turbulent drama that was Fenianism' (*OCPW*, 138). Compare Joyce's view of O'Leary with that of Yeats in 'Poetry and Tradition', *Essays and Introductions*, 246–60.

39 On Joyce's debt to Ferrero see Robert Spoo, *James Joyce and the Language of History: Dedalus's Nightmare* (Oxford: Oxford University Press, 1994), 27–37 and John McCourt, *The Years of Bloom: James Joyce in Trieste 1904–1920* (Dublin: Lilliput, 2000), 67–70.

40 Stanislaus Joyce, *My Brother's Keeper*, ed. Richard Ellmann (London: Faber and Faber, 1982), 187. Leerssen says that this play was the 'height' of 'recon-ciliation between Yeats and the nationalists'. Joep Leerssen, *Remembrance and Imagination: Patterns in the Literary and Historical Representations of Ireland in the Nineteenth Century* (Cork: Cork University Press, 1996), 212.

41 *The Playboy of the Western World* was preceded on stage by *Riders to the Sea*, which the audience attended respectfully. In 1903, Joyce had been one of the first to read *Riders* (he criticised it to Synge).

42 Christopher Morash, 'All Playboys Now: The Audience and the Riot' in *Interpreting Synge*, ed. Nicholas Grene (Dublin: Lilliput, 2000), 135–51, and Morash, *History of Irish Theatre*, 126–7.

43 She wears a brooch marked by 'an Irish device' (*D* 187). The symbol of Inghinidhe na hÉireann was a silver replica of the Cavan Brooch. See Foster, *Fictions of the Irish Literary Revival*, 151.

44 Foster, *Fictions of the Irish Literary Revival*, 163, 169. See also Luke Gibbons, ''Some Hysterical Hatred': History, Hysteria and the Literary Revival', *Irish University Review* 27:1 (1994), 7–23.

45 Stanislaus Joyce, *The Dublin Diary of Stanislaus Joyce*, ed. George Harris Healey (London: Faber and Faber, 1962), 74

46 Leerssen, *Remembrance and Imagination*, 220.

47 While part of the *Playboy* audience struck up 'God save the King' another part 'simultaneously' sang 'God save Ireland'. Morash, 'All Playboys Now: The Audience and the Riot', 146.

48 *James Joyce and Nationalism*, 24–36. See also Benedict Anderson, *Imagined Communities: Reflections on the Origin and Spread of Nationalism* (London: Verso, 1992).

49 Walter Benjamin, 'The Storyteller' in *Illuminations*, ed. Hannah Arendt, trans. Harry Zohn (New York: Schocken Books, 1988), esp. 91–101.

50 For a discussion of this blank space in a comparison of Joyce's text with John Huston's film, see Kevin Barry, *The Dead* (Cork: Cork University Press, 2001), 67–80.

51 Benjamin, 'On Some Motifs in Baudelaire', in *Illuminations*, 188.

52 For instance, Burke in *In the Shadow of the Glen* or old Mahon in *Playboy*. See Leerssen, *Remembrance and Imagination*, 222–3 and Deane, *Celtic Revivals*, 53.

53 *Joseph Holloway's Abbey Theatre: A Selection from his Unpublished Journal 'Impressions of a Dublin Playgoer'*, ed. Robert Hogan and Michael J. O'Neill (Illinois: Southern Illinois University Press, 1967), 17.

54 J. M. Synge, *Complete Plays*, ed. Ann Saddlemyer (Oxford: Oxford University Press, 1995), 25. Stanislaus Joyce, *Dublin Diary*, 75.

55 Arthur Power, *Conversations with James Joyce* (Dublin: Lilliput, 1999), 44–5.

56 Norris, *Joyce's Web*, 101. On possible inscribed reader-figures in 'The Dead' see *Joyce's Web*, 97–118 and Ross Chambers, *Story and Situation: Narrative Seduction and the Power of Fiction* (Minneapolis: University of Minnesota Press, 1984), 181–204.

57 'Dead Ends', 34.

58 Joyce's review of Stephen Gwynn's *Today and Tomorrow in Ireland* (a book lauding the Revival) appeared in the *Daily Express* with the final line added by Longworth, reassuring us that it was 'admirably bound and printed'. Joyce's last review for the *Daily Express* famously ends with the line, 'the binding of the book is as ugly as one could reasonably expect' (*OCPW* 66, 99). That Gabriel by contrast 'loved to feel the covers . . . of newly printed books' (*D* 188) clearly suggests an intertextual ironic distancing of him.

59 'If Homer were alive today. . .' W. B. Yeats, 'The Galway Plains' [1903], in *Essays and Introductions* (New York: Macmillan, 1961), 303. Yeats's review of *Cuchulain of Muirthemne* is alluded to in Don Gifford with Robert J. Seidman, *'Ulysses' Annotated: Notes for James Joyce's 'Ulysses'* (Berkeley: University of California Press, 1988; 2nd edn), 254. Gifford says that 'Homer is Mulligan's contribution' (254) but given the pertinence of Yeats's Preface the allusion may well have originated here.

60 'The Galway Plains', in *Essays and Introductions*, 213–14.

61 W. B. Yeats, 'Preface to the First Edition of *The Well of the Saints*', in *Essays and Introductions*, 299. Joyce possessed a copy of this in Trieste and, although the introduction is missing from the book as it now sits in Texas, he may well have read it. See Michael Patrick Gillespie with Erik Bradford Stocker, *James*

Joyce's Trieste Library: A Catalogue (Austin: Harry Ransom Humanities Research Centre, 1986), 234.
62 Benjamin, 'The Storyteller', 100.

2 SURVEILLANCE: EDUCATION, CONFESSION AND THE POLITICS OF RECEPTION

1 National Library of Ireland (NLI) ms 36,639/8/C.
2 The term 'confessor' may apply either to someone who confesses their faith or to a priest who hears confession. It is used in the latter case here, although its ambiguity is pertinent to the argument.
3 Foucault uses the term surveillance to distinguish between a subject–object perception (specular) and a mutual perception (as in the surveillance of a panopticon). Michel Foucault, *Discipline and Punish*, trans. Alan Sheridan (New York: Pantheon Books, 1977), 77.
4 H. G. Wells, *The Nation*, 24 February 1917, 710, 712 (*CH* I, 87–8).
5 Ellmann, *James Joyce*, 414.
6 Anon., *Everyman*, 23 February, 1917, 398 (*CH* I, 85).
7 Thomas Kettle, *Freeman's Journal*, 1 June 1907, n.p. (*CH* I, 37).
8 John Eglinton, 'Dublin Letter', *The Dial* LXXIII (October 1922), 434. A handwritten partial copy of this article, which was sent to Joyce, now resides in Harriet Shaw Weaver's papers at the British Library, Add. 57346 f. 169. One of the most significant Irish responses to *Ulysses*, it is inexplicably omitted from Deming's *Critical Heritage*. The last phrase is from John Eglinton, *Irish Literary Portraits* (London: MacMillan, 1935), 133.
9 John Eglinton, 'Irish Letter', *The Dial* LXXXVI (May 1929), 417–20 (*CH* II, 459).
10 Joseph Hone, 'Letter from Ireland', *London Mercury* v (January 1923), 306–8 (*CH* I, 298).
11 See Senia Pašeta, *Before the Revolution: Nationalism, Social Change and Ireland's Catholic Elite* (Cork: Cork University Press, 1999), 41.
12 See Joyce's addition to the typescript of a Radio Eireann broadcast in 1938. National Library of Ireland, *The James Joyce–Paul Leon Papers in the National Library of Ireland: A Catalogue*, compiled by Catherine Fahy (National Library of Ireland, 1992), 205.
13 See Kevin Sullivan, *Joyce Among the Jesuits* (New York: Columbia University Press, 1958), 172–3 and Donal McCartney, *UCD: A National Idea. The History of University College Dublin* (Dublin: Gill and Macmillan, 1999), 17–24.
14 Queen's College, Belfast secured its independence from the new national institution and Trinity College maintained its unique position.
15 R. D. Anderson, 'Universities and Elites in Modern Britain', *History of Universities* 10 (1991), 229.
16 John Hutchinson, *The Dynamics of Cultural Nationalism: The Gaelic Revival and the Creation of the Irish Nation State* (London: Allen and Unwin, 1987), 226, 269–71.

17 Similar conditions applied to women teachers. One of the most prominent campaigners for equal educational rights, Mary Hayden, achieved some notoriety when her election to a fellowship in English at University College was prevented by Fr Delany, the College President. (She eventually secured a lectureship in modern Irish history.) See Mary M. Macken, 'Women in the University and the College: A Struggle within a Struggle' in *Struggle with Fortune*, ed. Michael Tierney (Dublin: Browne and Nolan, 1954), 142–65, and McCartney, *UCD: A National Idea*, 77–8.

18 Ellmann reports that Joyce also attended some law lectures. *James Joyce*, 140.

19 'Solicitors and their Profession', *The Clongownian* (Christmas 1897). Cited in Hutchinson, *Dynamics of Cultural Nationalism*, 299, n24.

20 See Fr William Delany, *Irish University Education: A Plea for Fair Play* (Dublin: Browne and Nolan, 1904), 20.

21 See also Colleen Lamos, 'James Joyce and the English Vice', *Novel: A Forum on Fiction* 29:1 (1995), 19–26.

22 See Gillespie, *James Joyce's Trieste Library*, 46.

23 Roy Gottfried, 'The Audiences for Joyce's Autobiographies' in *Joyce's Audiences*, ed. Nash, 75.

24 Letter from J. F. Byrne to Joyce, 19 August 1904 cited in Ellmann, *James Joyce*, 162n.

25 Unpublished letter from C. P. Curran to Joyce, 17 February 1917. Special Collections, University College Dublin, CUR L349 a-b-c. The letter is summarised in *Letters* II, 391 n2.

26 See the discussion of these texts in Joshua Wilner, *Feeding on Infinity: Readings in the Romantic Rhetoric of Internalization* (Baltimore: Johns Hopkins University Press, 2000), 6–9. The address to readers as a generic feature of autobiographical writing is discussed by Paul de Man, 'Autobiography as De-Facement', *The Rhetoric of Romanticism* (New York: Columbia University Press, 1984), 67–81.

27 'Je l'ay voué à la commodité particuliere de mes parens et amis.' Michel de Montaigne, 'To the Reader' [1580] in *The Complete Works*, trans. Donald M. Frame (New York: Alfred A. Knopf, Everyman's Library, 2003), 2. (Wilner gives a less formal translation, *Feeding on Infinity*, 119.)

28 See Wilner, *Feeding on Infinity*, 9.

29 Jean-Jacques Rousseau, *The Confessions*, trans. J. M. Cohen (London: Penguin, 1953[1781]), 17. See Derrida's analysis of de Man's reading of the *Confessions* in 'Typewriter Ribbon: Limited Ink (2)', 71–161 (esp. 98–125).

30 This insight is rather let down by the subsequent observation that the book is concerned with life in 'a Jesuit school and Trinity College'. [Anon.], *Literary World*, 1 March 1917, 43 (*CH* I, 91).

31 See Stanley Cavell on the style of 'self-dialogue' in Wittgenstein's *Investigations* (which itself begins with Augustine's *Confessions*): 'in confessing you do not explain or justify, but describe how it is with you. And confession, unlike dogma, is not to be believed but tested, and accepted or rejected. Nor is it the occasion for accusation, except of yourself.' Stanley

Cavell, *Must We Mean What We Say?* (Cambridge: Cambridge University Press, 1976), 71.

32 Stanislaus Joyce, *The Dublin Diary*, 14.

33 Stanislaus Joyce's diary cited in Ellmann, *James Joyce*, 148.

34 Derrida, *Politics of Friendship*, 1, 22. Montaigne uses this expression to describe 'ordinary and customary friendships' as opposed to 'sovereign and masterful friendship'. Montaigne, 'Of Friendship' [1572–80], *The Complete Works*, 171. For a view of friendship as a potentially positive experience in Joyce, see Jacques Aubert, 'On Friendship in Joyce', *Joyce Studies Annual* (1995), 3–9.

35 The words 'flag-practices with phrases' are marked in crayon for revision.

36 William Shakespeare, *Hamlet*, III.iv, lines 152, 154. *The Riverside Shakespeare* (Boston: Houghton Mifflin, 1974), 1169. See also Derrida, 'Typewriter Ribbon', 88.

37 Joyce's own mother, Mary Jane (May) Murray had a respectable musical training as a child. She is a peculiarly silent figure in both Ellmann's biography and Brenda Maddox's *Nora* (Boston: Houghton Mifflin, 1998), where little is recorded beyond her pregnancies. See also Bonnie Kime Scott, *Joyce and Feminism* (Brighton: Harvester Press, 1984), 56–60. In conversation with Curran in 1964, her daughter May recalled her as musical and intelligent, 'ready to discuss literature or serious subjects with Jim' (CUR ms 6, UCD).

38 This is noted in a discussion of Joyce's educational context in Scott, *Joyce and Feminism*, 39–44.

39 Peter Costello discusses models for Emma Clery in *James Joyce: The Years of Growth 1882–1915* (London: Kyle Cathie Ltd, 1992), 185–93. Marion Eide discusses this scene in *Ethical Joyce* (Cambridge: Cambridge University Press, 2002), 57–62.

40 See Froula, *Modernism's Body*, 49.

41 On the varying religious contexts of censorship as Joyce encountered it in *A Portrait*, see Mullin, *James Joyce, Sexuality and Social Purity*, 83–115.

42 Eide, *Ethical Joyce*, 144–5. The various meanings of envoy / *envoi* are discussed by Alan Bass in his glossary to Jacques Derrida, *The Post Card: From Socrates to Freud and Beyond*, trans. Alan Bass (Chicago: University of Chicago Press, 1987), xxi.

43 The text was probably written in 1912–14 and copied out by Joyce in 'fair hand'. Although shown to Richard Ellmann by Stanislaus Joyce in the 1950s, when Ellmann drew on it for his biography, it was not published until 1968.

44 The most extensive recovery of Amalia Popper is in Vicki Mahaffey, 'Fascism and Silence: The Coded History of Amalia Popper', *James Joyce Quarterly* 32:3/4 (1995), 501–22. The dates of Popper's lessons are uncertain. See also Ellmann, *James Joyce*, 342 and McCourt, *The Years of Bloom*, 203.

45 The letters a and p appear next to each other 35 times. Mahaffey says that the hat and umbrella at the end of the text resemble the letters a and p respectively. *States of Desire* (Oxford: Oxford University Press, 1998), 151.

46 Valente refers to the narrator's 'erotic imperialism' over She (whom Valente calls Amalia). *James Joyce and the Problem of Justice*, 113. See also Henriette Lazaridis Power, 'Incorporating *Giacomo Joyce*', *James Joyce Quarterly* 28:3 (1991), 623–30.

47 McCourt, *The Years of Bloom*, 198.

48 *Il Piccolo*, 12 November, 1912. Cited in McCourt, *The Years of Bloom*, 192.

49 John Quinn, 'James Joyce. A New Irish Novelist', *Vanity Fair* (May 1917), 128 (*CH* 1, 104).

50 Valente, *James Joyce and the Problem of Justice*, 121.

51 This 'lady of letters' seeks Stephen's Alphabet books. McCourt (*The Years of Bloom*, 203) says Popper was 'worthy of the title' and Valente (*James Joyce and the Problem of Justice*, 122) remarks that the phrase shows 'professional regard'. However, it was a put-down to someone who dabbled in the literary. In Dublin, Joyce hated the phrase. A 'man of letters' was 'exactly what my brother was striving heroically not to be' wrote Stanislaus (*My Brother's Keeper*, 205).

52 W. B. Hodgson, *Errors in the Use of English* (Edinburgh: David Douglas, 1885).

53 Although only Eglinton, Best and Mulligan are present when Stephen makes this silent observation, I take 'these' to refer to the group initially assembled for the Shakespeare discussion.

54 Gregory Castle sees this episode as a 'scathing critique' by Stephen Dedalus of 'revivalist modes' and, for Len Platt, the group with whom Stephen argues are 'the Anglo-Irish revivalists'. Castle, *Modernism and the Celtic Revival*, esp. 219–22; and Platt, *Joyce and the Anglo-Irish* (Amsterdam: Rodopi, 1998), 74. This reading maintains a longer tradition begun with the aid of Magee/Eglinton himself, who called *Ulysses* as a 'violent interruption' of the Revival and directly contrary to its main tenets. 'Dublin Letter', *The Dial* LXXIII (October 1922), 437.

55 Clare Hutton, 'Joyce and the Institutions of Revivalism', *Irish University Review* 33:1 (2003), 116–32.

56 Eglinton, *Irish Literary Portraits* (London: Macmillan & Co. Ltd., 1935), 132, 136, 137.

57 John Eglinton, 'Dublin Letter', 436.

58 *Irish Literary Portraits*, 148.

59 Eugene Sheehy's recollection cited in James Meenan, ed. *Centenary History of the Literary and Historical Society of University College Dublin 1855–1955* (Tralee, 1955), 86. See Ellmann, *James Joyce*, 136.

60 C. P. Curran, cited in Sullivan, *Joyce Among the Jesuits*, 198.

61 Rev. J. Darlington, MA, FRUI, 'The Catholicity of Shakspere's Plays: A Lecture', *New Ireland Review* 8 (December 1897), 241–50 and (January 1898), 304–10 (305, 307, 305, 306, 243, 305). Darlington's essay was first noted as a source for Joyce in Weldon Thornton, *Allusions in Ulysses* (Chapel Hill: University of North Carolina Press, 1968) and its contrast of Platonism and Aristotelianism was briefly discussed in Richard M. Kain, '"Your Dean of Studies" and his Theory of Shakespeare (*U* 205.15)', *James Joyce Quarterly* 10:2 (1973), 262–3.

62 Darlington, 'The Catholicity of Shakspere's Plays: A Lecture', 305.

63 C. P. Curran, *James Joyce Remembered* (Oxford: Oxford University Press, 1968), 26, 38. Curran suggests that a key source for Joyce's Thomism was a well-known student textbook (as used by J. F. Byrne): Joseph Rickaby, SJ, *General Metaphysics* (London, 1980; 3rd edn. 1898).

64 In exams, candidates were tested on their knowledge of English language – verse scansion and use of grammar – and of literature, notably Shakespeare, Macaulay's essays, and *The Warwick Library*. See Royal University of Ireland, *Calendar for the Year 1899* and Neil R. Davison, 'Joyce's Matriculation Examination', *James Joyce Quarterly* 30:3 (1983), 393–409. This English syllabus persisted for several decades, as Declan Kiberd shows in 'Irish Readers in an English Frame', *Studies in Literary Imagination* 30 (1997), 119–26. See also my discussion of this disciplinary context in 'Reading Joyce in English', in *Joyce on the Threshold*, ed. Anne Fogarty and Timothy Martin (Gainesville: University Press of Florida, 2005), 110–31.

65 See McCartney, *UCD: A National Idea*, 213–14.

66 See Platt, *Joyce and the Anglo-Irish*, 73–86.

67 See John Henry Newman, *The Idea of a University: Defined and Illustrated*, ed. I. T. Ker (Oxford: Clarendon Press, 1976); Thomas Docherty, 'Newman, Ireland and Universality', *Boundary 2* 31:1 (2004), 73–92; and Seamus Deane, *Foreign Affections: Essays on Edmund Burke* (Cork: Cork University Press / Field Day, 2005), 147–67.

68 Edward Dowden, *Irish Unionists and the Present Administration* (Dublin: Irish Unionist Alliance, n.d. [c. 1904]).

69 *Irish Literary Portraits*, 133.

70 Stephen Gwynn, *Experiences of a Literary Man* (London: Thornton Butterworth, 1926), 64.

71 Ernest A. Boyd, *Appreciations and Depreciations: Irish Literary Studies* (Dublin: Talbot Press, 1917), 149.

72 George Moore recalls 'walking home with John Eglinton from Professor Dowden's' in *Hail and Farewell* (Gerrards Cross: Colin Smythe, 1985), 345.

73 John Eglinton, 'Irish Letter', 417–20.

74 Gibson, *Joyce's Revenge*, 66.

75 Edward Dowden, *Shakespere: A Critical Study of his Mind and Art* (London: Henry S. King and Co., 1875), 8. This volume went into numerous editions over the following decades.

76 Dowden, 'Edmund Spenser: Poet and Teacher' in *The Complete Works in Verse and Prose of Edmund Spenser* (privately printed, London, 1882–4), vol. I, 315, cited in David Gardiner, *Befitting Emblems of Adversity: A Modern Irish View of Edmund Spenser from W. B. Yeats to the Present* (Omaha, Nebraska: Creighton University Press, 2001), 63–71.

77 *Shakespere: A Critical Study*, 160; *Introduction to Shakespeare* (London: Blackie & Son Ltd., 1893), 34. Gibson suggests that behind this emphasis on English 'fact' lay Arnold's Celticism. *Joyce's Revenge*, 66–7.

78 Dowden, Introduction, *New Studies in Literature* (London, 1895), cited in his letter to the *Daily Express*, 25 January 1895. Dowden was responding to a letter from T. W. Rolleston which accused him of having an English, rather than Irish, literary canon.

79 See William M. Schutte, *Joyce and Shakespeare: A Study in the Meaning of 'Ulysses'* (New Haven: Yale University Press, 1957), 141–2.

80 John Eglinton, 'Dublin Letter', *The Dial* LXXII (June 1922) 619–22 (*CH* I, 271); *Irish Literary Portraits*, 146.

81 *Shakespere: A Critical Study*, 131, 160.

82 *Introduction to Shakespeare*, 19.

83 *Introduction to Shakespeare*, 111.

84 See Gibson, *Joyce's Revenge*, 68–76.

85 NLI ms 36,639/8/B; NLI ms 36,639/8/A.

86 See, for example, Platt, *Joyce and the Anglo-Irish*, 82.

87 Moore, *Hail and Farewell*, 207–58. See also P. J. Mathews, *Revival: The Abbey Theatre, Sinn Féin, the Gaelic League and the Co-operative Movement* (Cork: Cork University Press, 2003), 66–76.

88 Gwynn, *Irish Literature and Drama in the English Language*, 199; cited Schutte, *Joyce and Shakespeare*, 31–2. C. P. Curran, 'Memories of University College, Dublin: The Jesuit Tenure, 1883–1908' in *Struggle with Fortune*, ed. Tierney, 222.

89 Gwynn, *Experiences of a Literary Man*, 64–5. J. F. Byrne, *Silent Years: An Autobiography with Memoirs of James Joyce* (New York: Farrar, Straus and Young, 1953), 58–9.

90 Ellmann, *James Joyce*, 140.

91 Joyce may also have been aware that June 1904 saw the foundation of Cumann na Leabharlann (the Library Association). See Mary Casteleyn, *A History of Literacy and Libraries in Ireland* (Brookfield, Vt.: Gower, 1984).

92 *Irish Literary Portraits*, 134.

93 Compare the sense of 'historical destiny' that retroactively appropriates 'The Dead' in John Huston's film version; plus Andras Ungar, *Joyce's Ulysses as National Epic* (Gainesville: University of Florida Press, 2002) and Enda Duffy, *The Subaltern 'Ulysses'* (Minneapolis: University of Minnesota Press, 1994). For a different view, see David Lloyd, *Anomalous States: Irish Writing and the Post-Colonial Moment* (Dublin: Lilliput, 1993), 110.

94 See Maud Ellmann, 'The Ghosts of *Ulysses*' in *James Joyce: The Artist and the Labyrinth*, ed. Augustine Martin (London: Ryan, 1990), 193–228.

95 See NLI ms 36,639/8/B.

96 *Joyce's Web*, 94.

97 Compare Russell's remark that Joyce's poems 'might have been written by almost any young versifying sentimentalist'. Eglinton, *Irish Literary Portraits*, 142.

98 See also Gibson, *Joyce's Revenge*, 28–30.

99 Ellmann, *James Joyce*, 277.

100 The final stages of *Giacomo Joyce* and the first stages of this chapter may well have overlapped. The composition of *Exiles* and of the final pages of *A Portrait* were also around this time. The theme of cultural and national severance and belonging runs through them all.

101 See Gibbons, 'Spaces of Time Through Times of Space', 71–85.

3 EXHAUSTION: *ULYSSES*, 'WORK IN PROGRESS' AND THE ORDINARY READER

1 Theodor Adorno, *Prisms*, trans. Samuel and Shierry Weber (Cambridge, Mass.: MIT Press, 1990), 150. Benjamin, 'The Image of Proust' in *Illuminations*, 202.

2 Letter from Franz Leonard to Joyce, 9 December 1926. Sylvia Beach Papers, Princeton University Library, Box 119, Folder 9. Henceforth cited as SBPP.

3 Carey, *The Intellectuals and the Masses*, 20.

4 Derrida, '*ULYSSES* GRAMOPHONE', 52.

5 See Andreas Huyssen, *After the Great Divide: Modernism, Mass Culture, Postmodernism* (Bloomington: Indiana University Press, 1986) and Rainey, *Institutions of Modernism*.

6 *Institutions of Modernism*, 55–6.

7 *Ibid.*, 44.

8 According to Mark S. Morrisson, 'neither' the *Little Review* nor *The Egoist* 'conforms to the commonplace understanding of modernist little magazines as turning their backs on audiences and publishing for the select few', owing to their use of mass-market magazines' advertising techniques. *The Public Face of Modernism: Little Magazines, Audiences and Reception, 1905–1920* (Madison: University of Wisconsin Press, 2001), 134.

9 Laura Barnes has transcribed part of Beach's *Ulysses* subscribers' notebook (at the Harry Ransom Humanities Research Centre), with a census of the first edition, in Glenn Horowitz, *James Joyce: Books and Manuscripts* (New York: Glenn Horowitz Bookseller, Inc., 1996), 111–34. Hereafter cited as Horowitz, Beach Notebook.

10 Edward L. Bishop, 'The "Garbled History" of the First-Edition *Ulysses*', *Joyce Studies Annual* (1998), 3–36.

11 Sylvia Beach, 'The Ulysses Subscribers' (n.d.), SBPP Box 123, Folder 16.

12 According to Beach's list of buyers, at least twenty-four copies of the first edition were on sale through four Dublin bookshops in the first few months after publication: Fred Hanna on Nassau Street took six (one at 350 francs, five at 150); Hodges Figgis, also Nassau Street, took four (two each at 350 and 150 francs); the Irish Book Shop on Dawson Street took one of the 350 franc copies, two at 250 francs and ten of the cheapest 150 franc run, making thirteen in total; and Combridge of Grafton Street took one of the cheapest run. (Bishop gives slightly different figures.) In March and April, buyers of the cheapest version were increasingly less likely to be recorded by Beach, so some figures may be underestimated. See Horowitz, Beach Notebook, plus other subscription books in SBPP Box 63.

13 The following readers in Ireland were sent copies by Beach (copy no. in brackets; 150 francs unless stated): Miss J.[?] Whitfield of Cabra Park, Dublin (167; 250 francs), Constantine Curran (309), M. J. McManus (313), Rt Hon. L. A. Waldron (378), John J. Nolan (609), Lennox Robinson (751), Thomas Kiersey (819), Hubert Murphy (930), W. B. Yeats (939). See SBPP Boxes 63, 132–3 and Horowitz, Beach Notebook.

14 Letter from Kenneth J. Dickinson, Newcastle, 5 March 1922. SBPP Box 132, Folder 6.

15 Sylvia Beach draft memoir, SBPP Box 121, Folder 4. Sisley Huddleston, '*Ulysses*', *Observer*, 5 March 1922, 4 (*CH* I, 216). See Bishop, 'The "Garbled History" of the First-Edition *Ulysses*', 25.

16 SBPP, Box 123, Folder 10.

17 Virginia Woolf, *The Diary of Virginia Woolf, Vol. V: 1936–1941*, ed. Anne Olivier Bell (London: Hogarth Press, 1984), 353.

18 Letters dated 31 January, 10 June (annotated by Beach), 9 August, 1927. SBPP Box 119, Folder 9.

19 Valéry Larbaud, 'James Joyce', *Nouvelle Revue Française* 18 (April 1922), 385–405 (*CH* I, 258).

20 Huddleston, *CH* I, 216, 213.

21 A reproduction of this slip appears in Jane Lidderdale and Mary Nicholson, *Dear Miss Weaver: Harriet Shaw Weaver 1876–1961* (London: Faber and Faber, 1970), facing 176.

22 The first notice is reproduced in Melissa Banta and Oscar A. Silverman, eds. *James Joyce's Letters to Sylvia Beach, 1921–1940* (Bloomington: Indiana University Press, 1987), 107. The second is in SBPP Box 123, Folder 2.

23 Harriet Shaw Weaver Collection, British Library, Add. 57358. f.8 Hereafter cited as HSWC.

24 Letter from Pound to Weaver, 4 July 1923. HSWC Add. 57353 f.96.

25 Letter from Joyce to Weaver, 4 October 1922. HSWC Add. 57346 f.167. Part of this letter is reproduced at *Letters* III, 67.

26 Letter from Joyce to Weaver, 23 December 1923. HSWC Add. 57347 f.128.

27 See Ingeborg Landuyt, 'Joyce Reading Himself and Others' in *Joyce's Audiences*, ed. Nash, 141–52 and *Finnegans Wake Notebooks at Buffalo*, VI.B.6, ed. Vincent Deane, Daniel Ferrer and Geert Lernout (Turnhout, Belgium: Brepols, 2002).

28 Letter from Norman L. Madson, Los Angeles, 22 January 1927, SBPP Box 132, Folder 15.

29 SBPP Box 132, Folder 13. Dr Kelly received a 150 francs copy, no.731. Horowitz, Beach Notebook.

30 Shane Leslie, '*Ulysses*', *Quarterly Review*, 238 (October 1922), 228. See my discussion in '"Irish Audiences and English Readers": the Cultural Politics of Shane Leslie's Reviews of *Ulysses*' in *Joyce, Ireland, Britain*, ed. Andrew Gibson and Len Platt (Gainesville: University Press of Florida, 2006 forthcoming).

31 Leslie, '*Ulysses*', 222.

32 Leslie, '*Ulysses*', 225.

33 SBPP Box 132, Folder 5.

34 [Shane Leslie] Domini Canis, '*Ulysses*', *Dublin Review*, 171 (July, August, September 1922), 113.

35 In this sense, my argument runs counter to the reinvention of Joyce as a modern liberal. On Levinas and Joyce see Eide, *Ethical Joyce*.

36 Pound, 'Paris Letter' in Read, ed. *Pound / Joyce*, 198.

37 Richard Aldington, 'The Influence of Mr James Joyce', *English Review* (April 1921), 333–41 (*CH* I, 186).

38 Beach, 'The *Ulysses* Subscribers'.

39 Letter from Michael Healy to Joyce, 13 March 1922. SBPP, Box 119, Folder 9. Healy had been sent one of five covered unnumbered copies of the first edition reserved for close family and friends.

40 John Middleton Murry, review, *Nation & Athenaeum* (22 April, 1922), 124–5 (*CH* I, 197, 195).

41 Leslie, *Quarterly Review*, 219.

42 Woolf, *Diary of Virginia Woolf, Vol.* V: *1936–1941*, 353.

43 S. L. Goldberg, *James Joyce* (New York: Grove Press, 1962), 95. See the more sympathetic understanding in David Hayman, '*Ulysses*': *The Mechanics of Meaning* (Madison: University of Wisconsin Press, 1982), 2nd edn, 82.

44 Wyndham Lewis, *Time and Western Man* (New York: Harcourt Brace, 1928), 78. Joyce's responses to Lewis's criticisms of *Ulysses* are discussed in David Hayman, 'Enter Wyndham Lewis Leading Dancing Dave: New Light on a Key Relationship', *James Joyce Quarterly*, 35:4–36:1 (1998), 621–31.

45 From an uncollected letter, Weaver to Joyce, 20 November 1926, cited in Ellmann, *James Joyce*, 584.

46 Ellmann, *James Joyce*, 584.

47 Roland McHugh, *Annotations to Finnegans Wake* (London: Routledge & Kegan Paul, 1980), vi. This suggestion was silently withdrawn in the revised edition of 1991.

48 The same notion can be seen in the *Saturday Review of Literature*'s double spread on 'How to Enjoy James Joyce's Great Novel *Ulysses*', 10 February 1934, 474. See Suman Gupta, 'A Random House Advertisement', *James Joyce Quarterly*, 30:4/31:1 (1993), 861–8. It is also a feature of Joyce's own instinct for publicity: he imagines critics' phrases filtering down to a busy public (*Letters* III, 74); he sanctioned the (partial) release of his 'schema' for *Ulysses*, and supervised the twelve essayists of *Our Exagmination*.

49 Adaline Glasheen, *Third Census of Finnegans Wake* (Berkeley: University of California Press, 1977), 77.

50 McHugh, *Annotations*, 616, calls Oldham a 'suburb of Manchester' and notes *Widmung*.

51 Rabaté, *James Joyce and the Politics of Egoism*, 182–3.

52 Ellmann, *James Joyce*, 414.

53 Different versions of this letter are cited in Ellmann, *James Joyce*, 607–8 and *Letters* I, 274–5: the phrase 'typical common reader' is 'typical male' in the *Letters*.

54 Ellmann, *James Joyce*, 591, 603, 605, 616–17. See also Banta and Silverman, *Joyce's Letters to Beach*, 143.

55 Letter from John Drinkwater to Joyce, London, 3 December 1928. SBPP, Box 119, Folder 9.

56 G. V. L. Slingsby, 'Writes a Common Reader' in Samuel Beckett et al., *Our Exagmination Round His Factification for Incamination of Work in Progress* (Paris: Shakespeare and Company / London: Faber and Faber, 1972 [1929]), 190.

57 Letter to Joyce, 24 November 1927. SBPP Box 119, Folder 1.

58 Letter to Joyce, 12 December 1929. SBPP Box 119, Folder 3.

59 Letter from John Melville to Joyce (n.d.). SBPP Box 119, Folder 9.

60 Leslie, *Quarterly Review*, 219.

61 *Ibid.*, 233.

62 Cyril Connolly, 'The Position of Joyce', *Life and Letters* (April 1929), 273–90 (*CH* II, 403). Leon Edel, 'New Writers', *Canadian Forum* (June 1930), 329–30 (*CH* II, 408). Hamish Miles, review, *Criterion* (October 1930), 188–92 (*CH* II, 507). The critical reception of 'Work in Progress' became more respectful and cautiously welcoming from the late 1920s, after publication of *Anna Livia Plurabelle* in 1928 and *Our Exagmination* the following year.

63 Proust, *In the Shadow of Young Girls in Flower*, 47 (Gallimard, 379).

64 F. R. Leavis, 'Joyce and "The Revolution of the Word"', *Scrutiny* 2:2 (1933), 196.

65 Gilbert Highet, 'The Revolution of the Word', *New Oxford Outlook* 1:3 (February 1934), 288–304.

66 Charles Duff, *James Joyce and the Plain Reader* (London: Desmond Harmsworth, 1932), 21, 72.

67 *Ibid.*, 23.

68 *James Joyce and the Politics of Egoism*, 150.

69 Alfred Noyes, 'Rottenness in Literature', *Sunday Chronicle* (29 October, 1922), 2 (*CH* I, 274).

70 See SBPP Boxes 132–3. Alistair McCleery, 'Naughty Old Leavis', *Times Higher Educational Supplement*, 13 September 1991, 18.

71 Empson's diary cited by John Haffenden, *William Empson: Volume 1: Among the Mandarins* (Oxford: Oxford University Press, 2005), 102.

72 J. Stewart Cook, 'Universities and the Things That Matter', *The University* (Michaelmas 1931), 19.

73 See the discussion of MacCabe's *James Joyce and the Revolution of the Word* in the Introduction, and Patrick McGee, 'Joyce's Pedagogy: *Ulysses* and *Finnegans Wake* as Theory' in *Coping with Joyce*, ed. Morris Beja and Shari Benstock (Columbus: Ohio State University Press, 1989), 212–13.

74 James Joyce, 'Fragment of an Unpublished Work', *Criterion*, 3:2 (July 1925), 500.

75 Umberto Eco et al. *The Limits of Interpretation* (Bloomington: Indiana University Press, 1990), 151. Rabaté, *James Joyce and the Politics of Egoism*, 207.

76 *J'accuse* suggests not just accusation but also showing and defining. Derrida, *The Post Card*, 4; *La Carte Postale* (Paris: Flammarion, 1980), 8. Original emphasis.

77 Augustine was converted on opening Paul's Epistles and silently reading where his eye alighted on a knowing denunciation of sexual desire, finding the passage personally appropriate. Augustine was led to this conversion by a child's voice repeating over and over, 'Pick up and read, pick up and read.' The effect of that reading was that 'I did not now seek a wife.' Saint Augustine, *Confessions*, trans. Henry Chadwick (Oxford: Oxford University Press, 1991), 8:12 (29–30), 152–4. Bloom also reads *Sweets of Sin* from 'where his finger opened' (*U* 9.607).

78 McHugh, *Annotations*, 218. See John Bishop, *Joyce's Book of the Dark* (Madison: University of Wisconsin Press, 1986), 305–16.

79 This is redolent of those reviews that either used 'catchphrases' such as Joyce had encouraged or cited the text at length to avoid commentary. It possibly alludes also to a particular occasion. In a letter to Caresse Crosby from Frank Croninshield of *Vanity Fair* in August 1929 – a letter which Joyce read and annotated for her reply – Croninshield thanks her for *Tales Told of Shem and Shaun* and asks 'Would it be a good idea to use little quotations from it in Vanity Fair?' (*Letters* III, 193). This is the only one of nine questions not answered by Joyce. The phrase was introduced to *Finnegans Wake* in checking the second typescript in August 1938. See *JJA* 56: 200.

80 Elias Canetti, *Letters to Felice. Kafka's Other Trial* (London: Penguin, 1978), 550.

81 Ellmann, *James Joyce*, 546.

82 On this supposition see Attridge, *Joyce Effects*, 133–55.

83 *Ibid.*, esp. 98–106.

84 See Roland Barthes, *Le Plaisir du Texte* (Paris: Éditions du Seuil, 1973).

85 Spurr, *Joyce and the Scene of Modernity*, 96.

86 See Ellmann, *James Joyce*, 509 and Jean-Yves Tadié, *Marcel Proust: A Life*, trans. Euan Cameron (London: Penguin, 2000), 765.

87 Affable Hawk [Desmond McCarthy], 'Current Literature', *New Statesman* XXIX (14 May, 1927), 151 (*CH* I, 376). Original emphasis.

88 Holbrook Jackson, '*Ulysses* à la Joyce', *To-Day* (June 1922), 47–9. (*CH* I, 199).

89 See Thomas A. Goldwasser, 'Who Was Vladimir Dixon? Was He Vladimir Dixon?', *James Joyce Quarterly* 16:3 (1979), 219–23 and John Whittier-Ferguson, 'The Voice Behind the Echo: Vladimir Dixon's Letters to James Joyce and Sylvia Beach', *James Joyce Quarterly* 29:3 (1992), 511–33.

90 Benjamin, 'The Work of Art in an Age of Mechanical Reproduction' in *Illuminations*, 244 n.7.

91 Rabaté, *James Joyce and the Politics of Egoism*, 182. Gilbert, *Reflections on James Joyce*, 20–1.

92 *SL* 304; Ellmann, *James Joyce*, 543.

93 C. K. Ogden, 'The Joyce Record', *Psyche* 2:1 (1930), 95–6. Anon., 'What is Poetry?', *New Britain* 8 (Nov. 1933), 784. More recently, see Michel Butor, 'Crossing the Joycean Threshold', *James Joyce Quarterly* 7:3 (1971), 160–77.
94 Levin, *James Joyce*, 149.
95 Curran ms 22, UCD.
96 Joyce read from an advance copy of *transition* 8 (November 1927). *Anna Livia Plurabelle* (New York: Crosby Gaige, 1928) became the most successful section of 'Work in Progress' with Joyce's reviewers, readers and friends, which was as well since he had declared it was a piece 'on which I am prepared to stake everything' (*Letters* III, 163).
97 *Irish Literary Portraits*, 156–7. Similarly, an anonymous reviewer remarked on the need for 'new technical devices to prevent its [prose's] exhaustion.' Review of *ALP*, *Times Literary Supplement*, 20 December 1928, 1008 (*CH* II, 394).
98 'The Work of Art' in *Illuminations*, 237. In *The Mechanic Muse* (Oxford: Oxford University Press, 1978), Hugh Kenner discussed the 'verbal technologies' (110) of modernism without referring to film. See also Thomas L. Burkdall, *Joycean Frames: Film and the Fiction of James Joyce* (London: Routledge, 2001).
99 Eglinton, 'Dublin Letter', *The Dial* (October 1922), 436. This phrase also appeared on the flyer of press notices advertising *Ulysses*.
100 John Eglinton, 'Mr Yeats and Popular Poetry', in *Literary Ideals in Ireland* (London: Fisher Unwin, 1899), 43. Cited in Luke Gibbons, *Transformations in Irish Culture* (Cork: Cork University Press, 1996), 165.
101 Eglinton, 'Dublin Letter', 437.
102 Eglinton, *Irish Literary Portraits*, 156–7.
103 *Ibid.*, 158, 155–6.
104 Derrida, 'Two Words for Joyce' in *Post-Structuralist Joyce*, ed. Attridge and Ferrer, 148–9. See Benjamin, 'On Some Motifs in Baudelaire' in *Illuminations*, 188.
105 Marcel Proust, 'On Reading' [1906], trans. and ed. Jean Autret and William Burford in Proust, *On Reading Ruskin* (New Haven and London: Yale University Press, 1987), 110.
106 'The Work of Art' in *Illuminations*, 231, 240–41.

4 HYPOCRISY: *FINNEGANS WAKE, HYPOCRITES LECTEURS* AND THE TREATY

1 Charles Baudelaire, *Les Fleurs du Mal* (Boston: David R. Godine, 1982 [1857]), 184.
2 The Greek *hupokrisis*, meaning the playing of a theatrical part, derives from *Hypo-* meaning under or lower and *krinein* meaning to decide or to judge. Modern English 'hypocrisy', deriving from *hupokrisis* therefore suggests the performative function of judgement. Through judge (*kritēs*), *krinein* also provides the root for criticism.

3 In contrast, James M. Cahalan claims that 'Joyce speaks directly to his readers.' '"Dear Reader" and "Drear Writer": Joyce's Direct Addresses to his Readers in *Finnegans Wake*', *Twentieth Century Literature*, 41:3 (1995), 306–18 (308).

4 Ellmann, *James Joyce*, 537.

5 Vincent Deane, Introduction, *The Finnegans Wake Notebooks at Buffalo*, *Notebook* VI.B.*10*, ed. Vincent Deane, Daniel Ferrer and Geert Lernout (Turnhout, Belgium: Brepols, 2001), 11.

6 Discussions of Civil War references in the *Wake* include: John Garvin, *James Joyce's Disunited Kingdom and the Irish Dimension* (Dublin: Gill and Macmillan, 1976); Dominic Manganiello, *Joyce's Politics* (London: Routledge, 1980), 174–89; Nolan, *James Joyce and Nationalism*, 141–3; David Pierce, 'The Politics of *Finnegans Wake*', *Textual Practice*, 2:3 (1988), 367–80; and Thomas C. Hofheinz, *Joyce and the Invention of Irish History: 'Finnegans Wake' in Context* (Cambridge: Cambridge University Press, 1995), 35–8.

7 *Strange Country*, 167–8.

8 Tony Thwaites, *Joycean Temporalities: Debts, Promises and Countersignatures* (Gainesville: University Press of Florida, 2001), 171–2.

9 See Tom Garvin, *1922: The Birth of Irish Democracy* (Dublin: Gill and Macmillan, 1996), 42.

10 John Garvin, *James Joyce's Disunited Kingdom*, 141.

11 Garvin first made this claim in *The Irish Times*, 26 April, 1947 and elaborated it in *James Joyce's Disunited Kingdom*, 133–44.

12 Thomas E. Connolly, *James Joyce's Scribbledehobble: The Ur-Workbook for 'Finnegans Wake'* (Evanston, Ill.: Northwestern University Press, 1961), 104.

13 *James Joyce and Nationalism*, 142.

14 Ellmann, *James Joyce*, 534–5.

15 See Georg Lukàcs, *The Theory of the Novel*, trans. Anna Bostock (Cambridge, Mass.: The MIT Press, 1990), esp. 56–69.

16 Compare Ungar: 'national identity . . . impossible for the generation alive in 1922, has self-evident coherence' for later generations. *Joyce's Ulysses as National Epic*, 8.

17 'Leda and the Swan' was first published in *The Dial* LXXVI (June 1924). It later appeared in *The Cat and the Moon and Certain Poems* (1924), and *To-Morrow* (August 1924); it was revised for *A Vision* (1925, 1937) and *The Tower* (1928). It cannot be said for certain when Joyce first read Yeats's poem or in which version, although he did read *The Dial* at this time. The first introduction to *Finnegans Wake* of the paragraph cited here (*FW* 112.9–27) seems to have been in early 1925 (February–March) since it was not part of the original drafting of two sections that became 1.5 and was first inserted as a handwritten addition to the typescript being prepared for the *Criterion* version (published July 1925). See 47471b-59v and 61v (*JJA* 46:338–9) and 47473–11 (*JJA* 46:328). At this point the 'Lead. . .' paragraph became a link between the earlier two sections to form a composite first integrated draft of 1.5. Textual and circumstantial evidence implies Joyce did read Yeats's poem in *The Dial* in 1924 and

then parodied it in this paragraph, but in any case he would have been familiar with the myth, possibly in its Homeric version, and there are a number of allusions to it scattered throughout the *Wake*. The paragraph was corrected on proofcopy in April 1925 for publication in *Criterion*. Unusually, its first published version is almost identical to its final form in the *Wake*. In August 1927, the revised *transition* version of this chapter made no changes to this paragraph (except for misspelling 'at' as 'ad' in the final line). The only changes for *Finnegans Wake* are the late proofcopy correction of that misspelling, the alteration of 'age' to 'Ague' (line 20) and the addition of the short parenthetical remark at line 26.

18 A loaded word for Joyce. Stanislaus had ended his lengthy denunciation of 'Work in Progress' and the latter stages of *Ulysses* with the comment, 'I write rarely but with a vengeance' (*Letters* III, 106).

19 Yeats himself placed the poem in a broader context of Hobbes and the French Revolution, yet in writing it, he says, 'all politics went out of it' such that his 'conservative readers', as he was told, 'would misunderstand the poem'. *The Cat and the Moon* (Dublin: The Cuala Press, 1924), 37. See also Elizabeth Cullingford, *Yeats, Ireland and Fascism* (London: Macmillan, 1981), 130 and Declan Kiberd, *Inventing Ireland* (London: Jonathan Cape, 1995), 314–15.

20 W. B. Yeats, *The Yeats Reader*, ed. Richard J. Finneran (London: Palgrave Macmillan, 2002; rev. edn.), 481 and 102–3. This edition gives the versions from *The Dial* LXXVI(June 1924) and *The Tower* (1928). The lines cited here are common to both. The role and motivation of Helen is similarly ambiguous in some versions of the story. Marjorie Howes argues that Yeats 'had put the violence back into a scene that was frequently figured more as a seduction than a rape'. See *Yeats's Nations: Gender, Class and Irishness* (Cambridge: Cambridge University Press, 1996), 119–20.

21 'Dublin Letter', *The Dial* LXXIII(October 1922). These phrases were included on Joyce's flyer of press extracts advertising *Ulysses*.

22 *Quarterly Review*, 234.

23 The words 'auspice it!' were a correction made to the second typescript of the *Criterion* version in July 1925, where they replace the scratched-through word 'hope'. See 47473–74 (*JJA* 46:377).

24 See David Hayman, 'Dr J. Collins Looks at J. J.: The Invention of a Shaun for I.7' in *Joyce and Popular Culture*, ed. R. Brandon Kershner (Gainesville: University Press of Florida, 1996), 89–101.

25 Joyce had mistakenly thought that Yeats would not be taking out an 'official' subscription to the first edition (*Letters* III, 51) but would subscribe anonymously. In fact, Yeats did subscribe and was sent copy no. 939 on 3 March 1922 (Horowitz, Beach Notebook, 132). As Joyce knew and appreciated, Yeats had also been instrumental in arranging for a Royal Literary Fund grant for Joyce in summer 1915. Foster implies Yeats may not have read much of *A Portrait* (then in serialisation) when citing it to Edmund Gosse in support of the award, and this is corroborated by an unpublished letter from Yeats to Pound (dated 11 February 1917) to say he was only then nearly finishing the book. See

R. F. Foster, *W. B. Yeats: A Life*, vol. II: *The Arch-Poet, 1915–1939* (Oxford: Oxford University Press, 2003), 13 and Robert Scholes, *The Cornell Joyce Collection* (Ithaca: Cornell University Press, 1961), 203.

26 In 1914, Yeats had volunteered Joyce when Pound requested an Irish poet who could contribute verse to an anthology 'unlike his [Yeats's] own'. Ezra Pound, 'James Joyce: To His Memory' [1941] rep. in Read, ed., *Pound / Joyce*, 269.

27 Unpublished letter from Yeats to Pound, 27 July, 1922. Series IV, Box 14, James Joyce Collection, Cornell University Library. (Foster reproduces fragments of the same letter, including some of the above, in *W. B. Yeats: A Life*, vol. II, 260.)

28 'Extract from a Private Letter from a Relative in Dublin', 29 March 1922. HSWC Add. 57346 f.102.

29 See *JJA* 49:153 and 49:443.

30 As Kenner notes, one of those things is text. *The Stoic Comedians: Flaubert, Joyce, Beckett* (Berkeley: University of California Press, 1974), 50–5.

31 As it turned out, no such post was created. The controversy over the return of the Hugh Lane pictures was perhaps Yeats's chief political concern at this time. See Foster, *W. B. Yeats: A Life*, vol. II, 208, 273.

32 Yeats, 'Among School Children' (first published in *The Dial*, August 1927). These accolades included the Nobel Prize for 1923 after Desmond Fitzgerald had rashly promised to have Joyce nominated (*Letters* III, 61).

33 Yeats had, however, unknown to Joyce, already defended him from the political sniping of Edmund Gosse behind the private doors of the Savile Club in London at the end of 1922. See Foster, *W. B. Yeats: A Life*, vol. II, 708.

34 [Anon.], 'The Modern Novel. An Irish Author Discussed', *Irish Times*, 9 November, 1923, 4. (*CH* I, 290). A copy is at SBPP Box 123, Folder 5. Foster discusses this occasion in the context of literary and geographical borders in 'The National and the Normal', *Dublin Review* 2 (Spring 2001), 46–65 (esp. 55–9).

35 Yeats's plan to revive the legendary *Aonach Tailteann* had been conceived in 1922 but its enactment was postponed until 1924 by the Civil War. It was to be a cross between an Olympic-style athletic competition and a cultural conference. The *Aonach Tailteann* merits only a footnote in Ellmann's biography (*James Joyce*, 566–7).

36 Unpublished letter from Yeats to Joyce, 1 July 1924. Series IV, Box 14, James Joyce Collection, Cornell University Library. Foster cites some of this letter (but gives the date as 1 June). The final guest list included a Persian poet-prince, the Swedish foreign minister and Ranji, the famous Indian cricketing prince who played for Cambridge University, Sussex and England and owned Ballynahinch Castle in Connemara. See Foster, *W. B. Yeats: A Life*, vol. II, 263. On Ranji see Narinder Kapur, *The Irish Raj* (Antrim: Greystone Press, 1997), 55–65.

37 Yeats to Joyce, 1 July 1924.

38 Foster, *W. B. Yeats: A Life*, vol. II, 264. MacSwiney may also be in 'Shunny MacShunny' (*FW* 475.29). Glasheen suggests Peter Paul MacSwiney, Lord

Mayor of Dublin in 1875 and cousin of Joyce's mother, and Terence MacSwiney, the Lord Mayor of Cork, whose death on hunger strike in 1920 affected Joyce. See Glasheen, *A Third Census*, 180.

39 The other organisers of the Tailteann festival clearly had differing views from Yeats about its purpose: the Chairman, J. J. Walsh (the Postmaster General) thought the games were about 'racial pride, national outlook, love of the Homeland' (*Irish Times*, 4 August 1924; cited Foster, *W. B. Yeats: A Life*, vol. II, 264). Yeats was less certain, comparing the new nation to a young man come of age 'of whom it is impossible to say if he is a wise man or a fool' (*Irish Independent*, 4 August 1924. Cited Foster, *W. B. Yeats: A Life*, vol. II, 265). It is apparent from Yeats's invocation of Mussolini and his draft notes cited by Foster that he was warning against the consequences of democracy. When it came to the literary prizes, presented at the Royal Irish Academy, Yeats made it clear that Joyce's non-residence had excluded him but praised *Ulysses* as the best prose by any Irishman since Synge. On the backlash against Yeats, led by the *Catholic Bulletin*, see Foster, *W. B. Yeats: A Life*, vol. II, 267–8.

40 *Irish Times*, 9 November, 1923, 4; *Irish Statesman*, 28 August, 1924. An annotated copy of the *Irish Times* report, making clear which words were used by Yeats, and which by others, resides in the Beach papers. It was apparently used in preparing advertising material for *Ulysses*. SBPP Box 123, Folder 5.

41 Eglinton, 'Dublin Letter', *The Dial* LXXIII (October 1922), 435; Leslie, 'Ulysses', *Quarterly Review*, 225.

42 This is a fitting context for Woolf's snobbish dismissal of Joyce ('the comparative poverty of the writer's mind') in her review-essay of, among others, *A Portrait* and the serialised *Ulysses*. Virginia Woolf, 'Modern Novels', *Times Literary Supplement*, 10 April 1919, 189–90 (*CH* I, 126).

43 There are many other passages containing clusters of allusions to Yeats. For instance, he appears in the fable of the Ondt and the Gracehoper (*FW* 418–19), commonly seen as Joyce's reply to Wyndham Lewis.

44 Manganiello, *Joyce's Politics*, 189.

45 See Ezra Pound, 'James Joyce et Pécuchet', *Mercure de France*, CLVI: 575 (1 June 1922), 307–20, reprinted in Read, ed. *Pound / Joyce*, 200–11; and C. P. Curran, 'Anna Livia Plurabelle', *Irish Statesman* (16 February, 1929), 475–6. As Terence Brown argues, Joyce was re-appropriated as a realist as against the apparent 'anachronism' of Yeats. See 'Yeats, Joyce and the Irish Critical Debate' in *Ireland's Literature: Selected Essays* (Mullingar: Lilliput, 1988), 77–80.

46 See Brown's discussion of MacGreevy's writing in *The Irish Statesman* in 'Yeats, Joyce and the Irish Critical Debate', pp. 79–90; and Thomas MacGreevy, 'The Catholic Element in *Work in Progress*' in *Our Exagmination*, 117–28. He also attacks English converts such as Newman and Manning.

47 The staging of *Arrah na Pogue* met with limiting conditions according to where it played: 'The Wearing of the Green' was banned from productions throughout the British Empire.

48 Garvin, *1922*, epigraph.

49 Foster, *W. B. Yeats: A Life*, vol. II, 322.

50 James A. Mackay, *Eire: The Story of Eire and Her Stamps* (London: Philatelic Publishers, 1969), 89. The fullest discussion of the overprints is in Mackay but see also James A. Hill, *The Overprinted Stamps of Ireland*, Harry Hayes Philatelic Study no. 27 (Batley, W. Yorks: Harry Hayes, 1976).

51 In the early years of the Free State the following existed in postal circulation: the first definitive stamps of the Republic; overprints of British stamps; British franked stationery (postcards and envelopes) and postage due labels; and IRA stamps issued in Cork. See Mackay, *Eire: The Story of Eire and Her Stamps*, 61–72.

52 Michael Collins, *The Path to Freedom* (Cork, 1922). Cited by Manganiello, *Joyce's Politics*, 181.

53 This source has been identified by the editors of the *Finnegans Wake Notebooks at Buffalo*, Notebook VI.B.*10* (Deane, Ferrer and Lernout). See VI.B.10.065, which cites *Irish Times*, 6 December 1922; and 47471b-29 in *JJA* 46:049.

54 Possibly George V had already read some of Joyce's work: Joyce had appealed to him when attempting to publish 'Ivy Day' (enclosing the offending passage) and received a reply form his secretary to say that 'His Majesty' could not express an opinion in such cases. Perhaps the British monarchy could be associated with literary indecision? See Ellmann, *James Joyce*, 314–15.

55 See Duffy, *The Subaltern 'Ulysses'*, 24. For Duffy, *Ulysses* is just such a secret document, but a determinately subversive one. It is, he says, '*the* book of Irish postcolonial independence' (1).

56 S. P. B. Mais, 'An Irish Revel: And Some Flappers', *Daily Express*, 25 March 1922, n.p. (*CH* I, 191). This review was also excerpted on the advertising flyer for *Ulysses*.

57 The syllable 'gum' was added late in revisions (*JJA* 60:209). *An Gum* was founded in 1925 to print books in Irish. Often, these were translated from English.

58 Manganiello, *Joyce's Politics*, 78. Cf. Rabaté, *James Joyce and the Politics of Egoism*, 209.

59 See Phillipe Sollers: 'Dans ce qu'il [Joyce] écrit, il n'y a *plus que des différences*: il met donc en question toute communauté (on appelle ça son 'illisibilité').' 'Joyce et Cie', *Tel Quel* 64 (1975), 15–24 (16). More recently, Christy L. Burns argues for the co-optation of Joyce as a post-nationalist writer in 'Parodic Irishness: Joyce's Reconfigurations of the Nation in *Finnegans Wake*', *Novel*, 31:2 (1998), 237–55.

60 Deane, 'History as Fiction / Fiction as History', 139–40. See also *Celtic Revivals*, 99–100.

61 See Deane, 'Yeats: the Creation of an Audience', 36 and the discussion of Yeats in chapter 1 above.

62 Of course, Yeats arrived at a cynical frustration towards the Free State just as Joyce did, although they approached this conclusion from different paths.

63 He admits this immediately after a famous description of 'a nation, as distinguished from a crowd of chance comers, bound together by these

parallel streams of thought'. W. B. Yeats, 'More Memories', *The Dial*, LXXIII (July 1922), 64–5.

64 Yeats, Introduction, *Essays and Introductions*, x.

65 An '*original*' writer, Wordsworth famously declares, has 'the task of *creating* the taste by which he is to be enjoyed'. William Wordsworth, 'Essay Supplementary to the Preface' [to *Poems*, 1815] in *The Prose Works of William Wordsworth*, ed. W. J. B. Owen and Jane Worthington Smyser (Oxford: Clarendon Press, 1974), 3 vols., III, 80 (lines.692–4).

66 Stanislaus Joyce, *Dublin Diary*, 104.

AFTERWORD

1 Jacques Derrida cited by Ellen Carol Jones in *James Joyce: The Augmented Ninth*, ed. Bernard Benstock (New York: Syracuse University Press, 1988), 77; and '"This Strange Institution Called Literature": An Interview with Jacques Derrida' in *Acts of Literature*, ed. Derek Attridge (New York: Routledge, 1992), 74.

2 Iser, *The Implied Reader*, 294.

3 'Studying the difficult ways in which Joyce explored Irish history also enables us to open up new and affirmative dimensions of historical experience in ourselves.' Hofheinz, *Joyce and the Invention of Irish History*, 3.

4 Derrida, '"This Strange Institution Called Literature"', 74.

5 Cited by Jones in *James Joyce: The Augmented Ninth*, ed. Benstock, 77.

6 Jacques Derrida, *Specters of Marx*, trans. Peggy Kamuf (New York: Routledge, 1994), xx.

7 I have developed this point in 'Deconstruction's Audiences: "A New Enlightenment for the Century to Come"?', in *Paragraph: A Journal of Modern Critical Theory* 23:2 (2000), 119–35.

8 Jacques Derrida, 'Politics and Friendship: An Interview with Jacques Derrida', transcribed by Cecile Rivoallan, trans. Robert Harvey, in *The Althusserian Legacy*, ed. E. Ann Kaplan and Michael Sprinker (London: Verso, 1993), 188, 200.

9 Bourdieu, 'Reading, Readers, the Literant, Literature', 94.

10 Derrida, 'Politics and Friendship', 226.

11 *Ibid.* Compare the following passage from '*Différance*': '*différance*, which is neither a word nor a concept, strategically seemed to me the most proper one to think . . . what is most irreducible about our "era". Therefore I am starting, strategically, from the place and time in which "we" are, even though . . . it is only on the basis of *différance* and its "history" that we can allegedly know who "we" are, and what the limits of an "era" might be.' *Différance* in *Margins of Philosophy*, trans. Alan Bass (Sussex: Harvester, 1982), 7.

12 'Signature Event Context' in *Margins of Philosophy*, 315.

13 *The Post Card*, 71. The French term *réception*, which Derrida uses in quotation marks (*La Carte Postale*, 79) signifies also receipt (as of a commodity).

14 *Politics of Friendship*, 27.

15 *The Post Card*, 71, 174.
16 *Ibid.*, 33.
17 Derrida, *Dissemination*, trans. Barbara Johnson (London: Athlone Press, 1981), 96.
18 See Simon Critchley, *The Ethics of Deconstruction* (Oxford: Blackwell, 1992).
19 See Valente, *James Joyce and the Problem of Justice*.
20 Jacques Derrida, 'Remarks on Deconstruction and Pragmatism', trans. Simon Critchley, in *Deconstruction and Pragmatism*, ed. Chantal Mouffe (New York: Routledge, 1996), 84–5.
21 *Ibid.*, 83.
22 Compare Marion Eide's, *Ethical Joyce*, which posits a Derridean and Levinasian reading of ethics in Joyce's work.
23 Derrida, 'Typewriter Ribbon', 100.
24 Compare Barthes' desire for a reading practice that would have no 'order of entrance', in which 'the "first" version of a reading must be able to be its last'. Roland Barthes, *S/Z*, trans. Robert Howard (London: Jonathan Cape, 1974), 15.
25 Karl Marx, 'The Eighteenth Brumaire of Louis Bonaparte', in Karl Marx and Frederick Engels, *Selected Works* (Moscow: Progress Publishers, 1969) vol. I, 398.

Bibliography

The following library collections have been consulted:

Sylvia Beach Papers, Department of Rare Books and Special Collections, Princeton University Library.
James Joyce Collection, National Library of Ireland.
C. P. Curran Papers, Special Collections, University College Dublin.
Harriet Shaw Weaver Collection, The British Library.

Adorno, Theodor. *Prisms.* Trans. Samuel and Shierry Weber. Cambridge, Mass.: MIT Press, 1990.
Alexander, James D. 'Frank O'Connor's Joyce Criticism'. *Journal of Irish Literature* 21:2 (1992), 40–53.
Anderson, Benedict. *Imagined Communities: Reflections on the Origin and Spread of Nationalism.* London: Verso, 1992.
Anderson, R. D. 'Universities and Elites in Modern Britain'. *History of Universities* 10 (1991), 225–50.
Anon., 'What is Poetry?' *New Britain* 8 (Nov. 1933), 784.
Attridge, Derek. *Joyce Effects: On Language, Theory and History.* Cambridge: Cambridge University Press, 2000.
Attridge, Derek, and Daniel Ferrer, eds. *Post-Structuralist Joyce: Essays from the French.* Cambridge: Cambridge University Press, 1984.
Attridge, Derek, and Marjorie Howes, eds. *Semicolonial Joyce.* Cambridge: Cambridge University Press, 2000.
Aubert, Jacques. 'On Friendship in Joyce'. *Joyce Studies Annual* (1995), 3–9.
Augustine. *Confessions.* Trans. Henry Chadwick. Oxford: Oxford University Press, 1991.
Banta, Melissa, and Oscar A. Silverman, eds. *James Joyce's Letters to Sylvia Beach, 1921–1940.* Bloomington: Indiana University Press, 1987.
Barry, Kevin. *The Dead.* Cork: Cork University Press, 2001.
Barthes, Roland. *Le Plaisir du Texte.* Paris: Éditions du Seuil, 1973.
    S/Z. Trans. Robert Howard. London: Jonathan Cape, 1974.
Baudelaire, Charles. *Les Fleurs du Mal.* [1857]. Boston: David R. Godine, 1982.
Beach, Sylvia. *Shakespeare and Company.* New York: Harcourt Brace, 1959.

Beckett, Samuel, et al. *Our Exagmination Round His Factification for Incamination of Work in Progress*. [1929]. London: Faber and Faber, 1972.

Benjamin, Walter. *Illuminations*. Ed. Hannah Arendt. Trans. Harry Zohn. New York: Schocken Books, 1988.

Bennett, Tony. 'Texts in History: The Determinations of Texts and Their Readings'. In Derek Attridge, Geoff Bennington and Robert Young, eds., *Post-Structuralism and the Question of History*. Cambridge: Cambridge University Press, 1987.

Benstock, Bernard, ed. *James Joyce: The Augmented Ninth*. New York: Syracuse University Press, 1988.

Benstock, Shari. 'The Letter of the Law: *La Carte Postale* in *Finnegans Wake*'. *Philological Quarterly* 63 (1984), 163–87.

'The Printed Letters in *Ulysses*'. *James Joyce Quarterly* 19:4 (1982), 415–29.

Bishop, Edward L. 'The "Garbled History" of the First-Edition *Ulysses*'. *Joyce Studies Annual* (1998), 23–35.

Bishop, John. *Joyce's Book of the Dark*. Madison: University of Wisconsin Press, 1986.

Bloom, Edward A., and Lillian D. Bloom. *Satire's Persuasive Voice*. Ithaca: Cornell University Press, 1979.

Bourdieu, Pierre. 'Reading, Readers, the Literant, Literature'. *In Other Words: Essays Towards a Reflexive Sociology*. Trans. Matthew Adamson. Cambridge: Polity Press, 1990.

Boyd, Ernest A. *Appreciations and Depreciations: Irish Literary Studies*. Dublin: Talbot Press, 1917.

Brooker, Joseph. 'The Fidelity of Theory: James Joyce and the Rhetoric of Belatedness'. In Nash, ed., *Joyce's Audiences*.

Joyce's Critics. Madison: University of Wisconsin Press, 2004.

Brown, Terence. 'Yeats, Joyce and the Irish Critical Debate'. *Ireland's Literature: Selected Essays*. Mullingar: Lilliput, 1988.

Bryson, Mary E. 'Dublin Letters: John Eglinton and *The Dial*, 1921–29'. *Éire-Ireland* 24:4 (1994), 132–48.

Bürger, Peter. *Theory of the Avant-Garde*. Trans. Michael Shaw. Manchester: Manchester University Press, 1984.

Burkdall, Thomas L. *Joycean Frames: Film and the Fiction of James Joyce*. New York: Routledge, 2001.

Burns, Christy L. 'Parodic Irishness: Joyce's Reconfigurations of the Nation in *Finnegans Wake*'. *Novel: A Forum on Fiction* 31:2 (1998), 237–55.

Butor, Michel. 'Crossing the Joycean Threshold'. *James Joyce Quarterly* 7:3 (1971), 160–77.

Byrne, J. F. *Silent Years: An Autobiography with Memoirs of James Joyce*. New York: Farrar, Straus and Young, 1953.

Cahalan, James M. '"Dear Reader" and "Drear Writer": Joyce's Direct Addresses to his Readers in *Finnegans Wake*'. *Twentieth Century Literature* 41:3 (1995), 306–18.

Canetti, Elias. *Letters to Felice* with *Kafka's Other Trial*. London: Penguin, 1978.

Carey, John. *The Intellectuals and the Masses*. London: Faber and Faber, 1992.

Casteleyn, Mary. *A History of Literacy and Libraries in Ireland*. Brookfield, Vt.: Gower, 1984.

Castle, Gregory. *Modernism and the Celtic Revival*. Cambridge: Cambridge University Press, 2001.

Cavell, Stanley. *Must We Mean What We Say?* Cambridge: Cambridge University Press, 1976.

Chakrabarty, Dipesh. *Provincializing Europe: Postcolonial Thought and Historical Difference*. Princeton, N. J.: Princeton University Press, 2000.

Chambers, Ross. *Room for Manoeuvre: Reading (the) Oppositional (in) Narrative*. Illinois: University of Chicago Press, 1991.

  Story and Situation: Narrative Seduction and the Power of Fiction. Minneapolis: University of Minnesota Press, 1984.

Cheng, Vincent J. *Joyce, Race and Empire*. Cambridge: Cambridge University Press, 1995.

Connolly, Thomas E. *James Joyce's Scribbledehobble: The Ur-Workbook for 'Finnegans Wake'*. Evanston, Ill.: Northwestern University Press, 1961.

Cook, J. Stewart. 'Universities and the Things That Matter', *The University*, Michaelmas 1931, 18–20.

Costello, Peter. *James Joyce: The Years of Growth 1882 – 1915*. London: Kyle Cathie, 1992.

Critchley, Simon. *The Ethics of Deconstruction*. Oxford: Blackwell, 1992.

Cullingford, Elizabeth. *Yeats, Ireland and Fascism*. London: Macmillan, 1981.

Curran, C. P. 'Anna Livia Plurabelle'. *Irish Statesman*, 16 February, 1929, 475–6.

  'Memories of University College, Dublin: The Jesuit Tenure, 1883–1908'. In Tierney, ed., *Struggle with Fortune*.

  James Joyce Remembered. Oxford: Oxford University Press, 1968.

Dällenbach, Lucien. *The Mirror in the Text*. Trans. Jeremy Whiteley and Emma Hughes. Cambridge: Polity Press, 1989.

Darlington, Rev. Joseph. 'The Catholicity of Shakspere's Plays: A Lecture'. *New Ireland Review* 8 (December 1897), 241–50; (January 1898), 304–10.

Davison, Neil R. 'Joyce's Matriculation Examination'. *James Joyce Quarterly* 30:3 (1983), 393–409.

Deane, Seamus. *Celtic Revivals: Essays in Modern Irish Literature 1880–1980*. London: Faber and Faber, 1985.

  'Dead Ends: Joyce's Finest Moments'. In Attridge and Howes, eds., *Semicolonial Joyce*.

  Foreign Affections: Essays on Edmund Burke. Cork: Cork University Press / Field Day, 2005.

  'History as Fiction / Fiction as History'. In Giorgio Melchiori, ed., *Joyce in Rome*. Rome: Bulzoni Editore, 1984.

  'Introduction' to James Joyce, *Finnegans Wake*. London: Penguin, 1992.

  'National Character and National Audience: Races, Crowds and Readers'. In Michael Allen and Angela Wilcox, eds., *Critical Approaches to Anglo-Irish Literature*. Buckinghamshire: Colin Smythe, 1989.

Strange Country: Modernity and Nationhood in Irish Writing Since 1790. Oxford: Clarendon Press, 1997.

'Yeats: The Creation of an Audience'. In Terence Brown and Nicholas Grene, eds., *Tradition and Influence in Anglo-Irish Poetry.* Basingstoke: Macmillan, 1989.

De Certeau, Michel. *The Practice of Everyday Life.* Trans. Steven Rendall. Berkeley: University of California Press, 1984.

De Man, Paul. 'Autobiography as De-Facement'. *The Rhetoric of Romanticism.* New York: Columbia University Press, 1984.

'Reading (Proust)'. *Allegories of Reading: Figural Language in Rousseau, Nietzsche, Rilke, and Proust.* New Haven: Yale University Press, 1979.

The Resistance to Theory. Minneapolis: University of Minnesota Press, 1986.

Delany, William. *Irish University Education: A Plea for Fair Play.* Dublin: Browne and Nolan, 1904.

Deming, Robert H., ed. *James Joyce: The Critical Heritage,* 2 vols. *Volume I: 1907–1927; Volume II: 1928–1941.* London: Routledge and Kegan Paul, 1970.

Derrida, Jacques. *La Carte Postale.* Paris: Flammarion, 1980. *The Post Card: From Socrates to Freud and Beyond.* Trans. Alan Bass. Chicago: University of Chicago Press, 1987.

Dissemination. [1972]. Trans. Barbara Johnson. London: Athlone Press, 1981.

Margins of Philosophy, [1972]. Trans. Alan Bass. Sussex: Harvester, 1982.

'Politics and Friendship: An Interview with Jacques Derrida'. Transcribed by Cecile Rivoallan. Trans. Robert Harvey. In E. Ann Kaplan and Michael Sprinker, eds., *The Althusserian Legacy.* London: Verso, 1993.

Politics of Friendship. Trans. George Collins. London: Verso, 1997.

'Remarks on Deconstruction and Pragmatism'. Trans. Simon Critchley. In Chantal Mouffe, ed., *Deconstruction and Pragmatism.* New York: Routledge, 1996.

Specters of Marx. Trans. Peggy Kamuf. New York: Routledge, 1994.

'"This Strange Institution Called Literature": An Interview with Jacques Derrida'. In Derek Attridge, ed., *Acts of Literature.* New York: Routledge, 1992.

'Two Words for Joyce'. Trans. Geoff Bennington. In Attridge and Ferrer, eds., *Post-Structuralist Joyce.*

'Typewriter Ribbon: Limited Ink (2)'. *Without Alibi.* Ed. and trans. Peggy Kamuf. Stanford, Ca: Stanford University Press, 2002.

'ULYSSES GRAMOPHONE: Hear Say Yes in Joyce'. Trans. Tina Kendall, revised by Shari Benstock. In Bernard Benstock, ed., *James Joyce: The Augmented Ninth.* New York: Syracuse University Press, 1988.

Docherty, Thomas. 'Newman, Ireland, and Universality'. *Boundary 2,* 31.1 (2004), 73–92.

Dowden, Edward. *Introduction to Shakespeare.* London: Blackie & Son Ltd, 1893.

Irish Unionists and the Present Administration. Dublin: Irish Unionist Alliance, n.d. [c. 1904].

Shakespere: A Critical Study of his Mind and Art. London: Henry S. King and Co., 1875.

Duff, Charles. *James Joyce and the Plain Reader.* London: Desmond Harmsworth, 1932.

Duffy, Enda. *The Subaltern 'Ulysses'.* Minneapolis: University of Minnesota Press, 1994.

Eco, Umberto, et al. *The Limits of Interpretation.* Bloomington: Indiana University Press, 1990.

Eglinton, John [W. K. Magee]. 'Dublin Letter'. *The Dial* LXXII (June 1922), 619–22.

'Dublin Letter'. *The Dial* LXXIII (October 1922), 434–7.

'Irish Letter'. *The Dial* LXXXVI (May 1929), 417–20.

Irish Literary Portraits. London: Macmillan & Co. Ltd, 1935.

Literary Ideals in Ireland. London: Fisher Unwin, 1899.

Eide, Marian. *Ethical Joyce.* Cambridge: Cambridge University Press, 2002.

Ellmann, Maud. 'The Ghosts of *Ulysses*'. In Augustine Martin, ed., *James Joyce: The Artist and the Labyrinth.* London: Ryan, 1990.

Ellmann, Richard. *Eminent Domain: Yeats Among Wilde, Joyce, Pound, Eliot and Auden.* Oxford: Oxford University Press, 1970.

James Joyce. Oxford: Oxford University Press, new and revised edition 1982.

Fairhall, James. *James Joyce and the Question of History.* Cambridge: Cambridge University Press, 1993.

Felman, Shoshana. *What Does a Woman Want? Reading and Sexual Difference.* Baltimore: Johns Hopkins University Press, 1993.

Ferguson, Frances. 'Emma, or Happiness (or Sex Work)'. *Critical Inquiry* 28:3 (2002), 749–79.

Fitch, Noel Riley. *Sylvia Beach and the Lost Generation: A History of Literary Paris in the Twenties and Thirties.* New York: Norton, 1983.

Flint, Kate. *The Woman Reader, 1837–1914.* Oxford: Oxford University Press, 1993.

Foster, John Wilson. *Fictions of the Irish Literary Revival: A Changeling Art.* Syracuse: University of Syracuse Press, 1987.

Foster, R. F. *W. B. Yeats: A Life. Volume I: The Apprentice Mage 1865–1914.* Oxford: Oxford University Press, 1997. *Volume II: The Arch-Poet, 1915–1939.* Oxford: Oxford University Press, 2003.

'The National and the Normal'. *Dublin Review* 2 (2001), 46–65.

Foucault, Michel. *Discipline and Punish.* Trans. Alan Sheridan. New York: Pantheon Books, 1977.

French, Marilyn. *The Book as World: James Joyce's 'Ulysses'.* Cambridge, Ma.: Harvard University Press, 1976.

Froula, Christine. *Modernism's Body: Sex, Culture and Joyce.* New York: University of Columbia Press, 1996.

Gadamer, Hans-Georg. *Truth and Method.* London: Sheed and Ward, 1985.

Gardiner, David. *Befitting Emblems of Adversity: A Modern Irish View of Edmund Spenser from W. B. Yeats to the Present.* Omaha, Nebraska: Creighton University Press, 2001.

Garvin, John. *James Joyce's Disunited Kingdom and the Irish Dimension.* Dublin: Gill and Macmillan, 1976.

Garvin, Tom. *1922: The Birth of Irish Democracy*. Dublin: Gill and Macmillan, 1996.

Gibbons, Luke. 'Romanticism, Realism and Irish Cinema'. In Luke Gibbons, Kevin Rockett and John Hill, eds., *Cinema and Ireland*. Syracuse: Syracuse University Press, 1988.

'"Some Hysterical Hatred": History, Hysteria and the Literary Revival'. *Irish University Review* 27:1 (1994), 7–23.

'Spaces of Time Through Times of Space: Joyce, Ireland and Colonial Modernity'. *Field Day Review* 1 (2005), 71–85.

Transformations in Irish Culture. Cork: Cork University Press, 1996.

Gibson, Andrew. *Joyce's Revenge: History, Politics, and Aesthetics in 'Ulysses'*. Oxford: Oxford University Press, 2002.

Gifford, Don with Robert J. Seidman. *'Ulysses' Annotated: Notes for James Joyce's 'Ulysses'*. Berkeley: University of California Press, 2nd edn 1988.

Gilbert, Stuart. *Reflections on James Joyce: Stuart Gilbert's Paris Journal*. Ed. Thomas F. Staley and Randolph Lewis. Austin: University of Texas Press, 1993.

Gillespie, Michael Patrick with Erik Bradford Stocker. *James Joyce's Trieste Library: A Catalogue*. Austin: Harry Ransom Humanities Research Centre, 1986.

Glasheen, Adaline. *Third Census of 'Finnegans Wake'*. Berkeley: University of California Press, 1977.

Glowinski, Michal. 'Reading, Interpretation, Reception'. *New Literary History* 11:1 (1979), 75–83.

Gogarty, Oliver St John. *As I Was Going Down Sackville Street*. [1937]. Dublin: O'Brien Press, 1994.

Rolling Down the Lea. London: Constable, 1950.

Goldberg, S. L. *James Joyce*. New York: Grove Press, 1962.

Goldwasser, Thomas A. 'Who Was Vladimir Dixon? Was He Vladimir Dixon?' *James Joyce Quarterly* 16:3 (1979), 219–23.

Gorman, Herbert. *James Joyce: A Definitive Biography*. London: John Lane, The Bodley Head, 1941.

James Joyce: His First Forty Years. London: Geoffrey Bles, 1926.

Gottfried, Roy. 'The Audiences for Joyce's Autobiographies'. In Nash, ed., *Joyce's Audiences*.

Gregory, Lady Augusta. *Our Irish Theatre: A Chapter of Autobiography*. [1913]. Gerrards Cross: Colin Smythe, 1972.

Gupta, Suman. 'A Random House Advertisement'. *James Joyce Quarterly* 30:4/ 31:1 (1993), 861–8.

Gwynn, Stephen. *Experiences of a Literary Man*. London: Thornton Butterworth, 1926.

Irish Literature and Drama in the English Language: A Short History. London: Nelson, 1936.

Haffenden, John. *William Empson. Volume I: Among the Mandarins*. Oxford: Oxford University Press, 2005.

Hayman, David. 'Dr J. Collins Looks at J. J.: The Invention of a Shaun for 1.7'.
    In R. Brandon Kershner, ed., *Joyce and Popular Culture*. Gainesville:
    University Press of Florida, 1996.
    'Enter Wyndham Lewis Leading Dancing Dave: New Light on a Key
    Relationship'. *James Joyce Quarterly* 35:4–36:1 (1998), 621–31.
    'Ulysses': The Mechanics of Meaning. Madison: University of Wisconsin Press,
    2nd edn 1982.
Highet, Gilbert. 'The Revolution of the Word'. *New Oxford Outlook* 1:3
    (February 1934), 288–304.
Hill, James A. *The Overprinted Stamps of Ireland*. Harry Hayes Philatelic Study
    no 27. Batley, W Yorks: Harry Hayes, 1976.
Hofheinz, Thomas C. *Joyce and the Invention of Irish History: 'Finnegans Wake' in
    Context*. Cambridge: Cambridge University Press, 1995.
Hogan, Robert, and James Kilroy, eds. *The Irish Literary Theatre, 1899–1901*.
    Dublin: The Dolmen Press, 1975.
Holloway, Joseph. *Joseph Holloway's Abbey Theatre: A Selection from his Unpub-
    lished Journal 'Impressions of a Dublin Playgoer'*. Ed. Robert Hogan and
    Michael J. O'Neill. Illinois: Southern Illinois University Press, 1967.
Holub, Robert C. *Crossing Borders: Reception Theory, Poststructuralism, Decon-
    struction*. Madison: University of Wisconsin Press, 1992.
Horowitz, Glenn. *James Joyce: Books and Manuscripts*. New York: Glenn
    Horowitz Bookseller, Inc., 1996.
Howes, Marjorie. *Yeats's Nations: Gender, Class and Irishness*. Cambridge:
    Cambridge University Press, 1996.
Hutchinson, John. *The Dynamics of Cultural Nationalism: The Gaelic Revival and
    the Creation of the Irish Nation State*. London: Allen and Unwin, 1987.
Hutton, Clare. 'Joyce and the Institutions of Revivalism'. *Irish University Review*
    33:1 (2003), 116–32.
Huyssen, Andreas. *After the Great Divide: Modernism, Mass Culture, Postmodern-
    ism*. Bloomington: Indiana University Press, 1986.
Innes, C. L. 'Modernism, Ireland and Empire: Yeats, Joyce and their Implied
    Audiences'. In Howard J. Booth and Nigel Rigby, eds., *Modernism and
    Empire*. Manchester: Manchester University Press, 2000.
Iser, Wolfgang. *The Act of Reading: A Theory of Aesthetic Response*. Baltimore:
    Johns Hopkins University Press, 1978.
    The Implied Reader. Trans. Wilhelm Fink. Baltimore: Johns Hopkins Univer-
    sity Press, 1974.
    'The Reality of Fiction: A Functionalist Approach to Literature'. *New Literary
    History* 6:3 (1975), 7–38.
    'Ulysses and the Reader'. *Prospecting*. Baltimore: Johns Hopkins University
    Press, 1989.
JanMohammed, Abdul. 'Worldliness-without-World, Homelessness-as-Home:
    Toward a Definition of the Specular Border Intellectual'. In Michael
    Sprinker, ed., *Edward Said: A Critical Reader*. Oxford: Blackwell, 1993.

Jauss, Hans Robert. *Aesthetic Experience and Literary Hermeneutics.* Trans. Michael Shaw. Minneapolis: University of Minnesota Press, 1982.

Toward an Aesthetic of Reception. Trans. Timothy Bahti. Brighton: Harvester, 1982.

Joyce, James. *A Portrait of the Artist as a Young Man.* [1916]. Ed. Seamus Deane. London: Penguin, 1992.

'Continuation of a Work in Progress'. *transition* 5 (1927), 15–31.

Critical Writings. 1959. Ed. Richard Ellmann and Ellsworth Mason. Ithaca: Cornell University Press, 1989.

Dubliners. [1914]. Ed. Terence Brown. London: Penguin, 1992.

Finnegans Wake. [1939]. London: Faber and Faber, 3rd edn, rep. 1988.

'Fragment of an Unpublished Work'. *Criterion* 3:2 (1925), 498–510.

Giacomo Joyce. Ed. Richard Ellmann. New York: Viking Press, 1968.

James Joyce Archive. Ed. Michael Groden, et al. New York: Garland Publishing, 1977–9.

Letters of James Joyce, vol. I. Ed. Stuart Gilbert. New York: Viking Press, 1957; reissued with corrections 1966.

Letters of James Joyce, vols. II–III. Ed. Richard Ellmann. New York: Viking Press, 1966.

Occasional, Critical and Political Writing. Ed. Kevin Barry. Translations by Conor Deane. Oxford: Oxford University Press, 2000.

Poems and Exiles. Ed. J. C. C. Mays. London: Penguin, 1992.

Selected Letters of James Joyce. Ed. Richard Ellmann. London: Faber and Faber, 1975.

Stephen Hero. [1944]. Ed. John J. Slocum and Herbert Cahoon. Grafton Books, 1977.

Ulysses. [1922]. Ed. Hans Walter Gabler, et al. New York: Random House, 1986.

The Finnegans Wake Notebooks at Buffalo, Notebook VI.B.6. Ed. Vincent Deane, Daniel Ferrer and Geert Lernout. Turnhout, Belgium: Brepols, 2001.

The Finnegans Wake Notebooks at Buffalo, Notebook VI.B.10. Ed. Vincent Deane, Daniel Ferrer and Geert Lernout. Turnhout, Belgium: Brepols, 2002.

Joyce, Stanislaus. *The Dublin Diary of Stanislaus Joyce.* Ed. George Harris Healey. London: Faber and Faber, 1962.

My Brother's Keeper. [1958]. Ed. Richard Ellmann. London: Faber and Faber, 1982.

Kain, Richard M. '"Your Dean of Studies" and his Theory of Shakespeare (*U* 205.15)', *James Joyce Quarterly* 10:2 (1973), 262–3.

Kelly, Joseph. *Our Joyce: From Outcast to Icon.* Austin: University of Texas Press, 1998.

Kenner, Hugh. *The Mechanic Muse.* Oxford: Oxford University Press, 1978.

The Stoic Comedians: Flaubert, Joyce, Beckett. Berkeley: University of California Press, 1974.

Kiberd, Declan. 'Irish Readers in an English Frame'. *Studies in Literary Imagination* 30 (1997), 119–26.

Inventing Ireland. London: Jonathan Cape, 1995.

Lamos, Colleen. 'James Joyce and the English Vice'. *Novel: A Forum on Fiction* 29:1 (1995), 19–26.

Landuyt, Ingeborg. 'Joyce Reading Himself and Others'. In Nash, ed., *Joyce's Audiences*.

Leavis, F. R. 'Joyce and "The Revolution of the Word"'. *Scrutiny* 2:2 (September 1933), 193–201.

Leerssen, Joep. *Remembrance and Imagination: Patterns in the Literary and Historical Representations of Ireland in the Nineteenth Century*. Cork: Cork University Press, 1996.

[Leslie, Shane], Domini Canis. 'Ulysses'. *Dublin Review* 171 (July, August, September 1922), 112–19.

Leslie, Shane. '*Ulysses*'. *Quarterly Review* 238 (October 1922), 219–34.

Levenson, Michael. 'Living History in "The Dead"'. In Daniel R. Schwarz, ed. *James Joyce, 'The Dead'*. New York: St Martin's Press, 1994.

Levin, Harry. *James Joyce*. London: Faber, 1963; 2nd edn.

Lewis, Percy Wyndham. *Time and Western Man*. New York: Harcourt Brace, 1928.

Lidderdale, Jane, and Mary Nicholson. *Dear Miss Weaver: Harriet Shaw Weaver 1876–1961*. London: Faber and Faber, 1970.

Lloyd, David. *Anomalous States: Irish Writing and the Post-Colonial Moment*. Dublin: Lilliput, 1993.

Lukàcs, Georg. *The Theory of the Novel*. [1920]. Trans. Anna Bostock. Cambridge, Mass.: The MIT Press, 1990.

Lyotard, Jean-François and Jean-Loup Thébaud. *Just Gaming*. Trans. Wlad Godzich. Minnesota: University of Minnesota Press, 1985.

MacCabe, Colin. *James Joyce and the Revolution of the Word*. London: Macmillan, 1979.

ed., *James Joyce: New Perspectives*. Brighton: Harvester Press, 1982.

On the Eloquence of the Vulgar. London: British Film Institute, 1992.

MacGreevy, Thomas. 'The Catholic Element in *Work in Progress*'. In Beckett, et al. *Our Exagmination*.

Mackay, James A. *Eire: The Story of Eire and Her Stamps*. London: Philatelic Publishers, 1969.

Macken, Mary M. 'Women in the University and the College: A Struggle Within a Struggle'. In Tierney, ed., *Struggle with Fortune*.

Maddox, Brenda. *Nora*. Boston: Houghton Mifflin, 1998.

Mahaffey, Vicki. 'Fascism and Silence: The Coded History of Amalia Popper'. *James Joyce Quarterly* 32:3/4 (1995), 501–22.

'*Giacomo Joyce*'. In Zack Bowen and James F. Carens, eds., *A Companion to Joyce Studies*. Westport, Conn.: Greenwood Press, 1984.

States of Desire. Oxford: Oxford University Press, 1998.

Manganiello, Dominic. *Joyce's Politics*. London: Routledge, 1980.

Martyn, Edward. 'A Comparison Between English and Irish Theatrical Audiences'. *Beltaine* 2 (February 1900), 11–13. Rep. *Beltaine*. London: Frank Cass and Co. Ltd, 1970.

Marx, Karl. 'The Eighteenth Brumaire of Louis Bonaparte'. Karl Marx and Frederick Engels. *Selected Works*, vol. i. Moscow: Progress Publishers, 1969.

Mathews, P. J. *Revival: The Abbey Theatre, Sinn Féin, the Gaelic League and the Co-operative Movement.* Cork: Cork University Press, 2003.

McArthur, Murray. 'The Example of Joyce: Derrida Reading Joyce'. *James Joyce Quarterly* 32:2 (1995), 227–43.

McCarthy, Patrick A. 'Joyce's Silent Readers'. In Bonnie Kime Scott, ed., *New Alliances in Joyce Studies*. Newark: University of Delaware Press, 1988.

'Reading in *Ulysses*'. Janet Dunleavy, Melvin J. Friedman and Michael Patrick Gillespie, eds., *Joycean Occasions*. Newark: University of Delaware Press, 1991.

McCartney, Donal. *UCD: A National Idea. The History of University College Dublin.* Dublin: Gill and Macmillan, 1999.

McCleery, Alistair. 'Naughty Old Leavis'. *Times Higher Educational Supplement.* 13 September 1991, 18.

McCourt, John. *The Years of Bloom: James Joyce in Trieste 1904–1920.* Dublin: Lilliput, 2000.

McGee, Patrick. 'Joyce's Pedagogy: *Ulysses* and *Finnegans Wake* as Theory'. In Morris Beja and Shari Benstock, eds., *Coping with Joyce.* Columbus: Ohio State University Press, 1989.

McHugh, Roland. *Annotations to 'Finnegans Wake'.* London: Routledge and Kegan Paul, 1980. Rev. edn. Baltimore: Johns Hopkins University Press, 1991.

Meenan, James, ed., *Centenary History of the Literary and Historical Society of University College Dublin 1855–1955.* Tralee, 1955.

Michelfelder, Diane P. *Dialogue and Deconstruction: The Gadamer–Derrida Encounter.* New York: State University of New York Press, 1989.

Mierlo, Wim van. 'Reading Joyce in and out of the Archive'. *Joyce Studies Annual* (2002), 32–63.

Miller, D. A. '*Cage aux Folles*: Sensation and Gender in Wilkie Collins's *The Woman in White*'. In Elaine Showalter, ed., *Speaking of Gender.* London: Routledge, 1989.

Montaigne, Michel de. 'Of Friendship'. [1572–80]. *The Complete Works.* Trans. Donald M. Frame. New York: Alfred A. Knopf, Everyman's Library, 2003.

Moore, George. *Hail and Farewell.* [1911]. Buckinghamshire: Colin Smythe, 1985.

Morash, Christopher. *A History of Irish Theatre 1601–2000.* Cambridge: Cambridge University Press, 2002.

'All Playboys Now: The Audience and the Riot'. In Nicholas Grene, ed., *Interpreting Synge.* Dublin: Lilliput, 2000.

Morrisson, Mark S. *The Public Face of Modernism: Little Magazines, Audiences and Reception, 1905–1920.* Madison: University of Wisconsin Press, 2001.

Mullin, Katherine. 'Don't Cry for me Argentina: "Eveline" and the Seductions of Emigration Propaganda'. In Attridge and Howes, eds., *Semicolonial Joyce. James Joyce, Sexuality and Social Purity*. Cambridge: Cambridge University Press, 2003.

Nash, John. 'Deconstruction's Audiences: "A New Enlightenment for the Century to Come"?' *Paragraph: A Journal of Modern Critical Theory* 23:2 (2000), 119–35.

'"Irish Audiences and English Readers": the Cultural Politics of Shane Leslie's Reviews of *Ulysses*'. In Andrew Gibson and Len Platt, eds. *Joyce, Ireland, Britain*. Gainesville: University Press of Florida, 2006.

'Reading Joyce in English'. In Anne Fogarty and Timothy Martin, eds., *Joyce on the Threshold*. Gainesville: University Press of Florida, 2005.

Nash, John. ed. *Joyce's Audiences*. Amsterdam and New York: Rodopi, 2002.

National Library of Ireland. *The James Joyce–Paul Leon Papers in the National Library of Ireland: A Catalogue*. Compiled by Catherine Fahy. National Library of Ireland, 1992.

Newman, John Henry. *The Idea of a University: Defined and Illustrated*. [1852]. Ed. I. T. Ker. Oxford: Clarendon Press, 1976.

Nolan, Emer. *James Joyce and Nationalism*. London: Routledge, 1995.

Norris, Margot. *Joyce's Web: The Social Unraveling of Modernism*. Austin: University of Texas Press, 1992.

O'Brien, Flann. 'A Bash in the Tunnel'. In John Ryan, ed., *A Bash in the Tunnel*. Dublin: Clifton Books, 1970.

O'Connor, Frank. 'Joyce – The Third Period'. *Irish Statesman*. 12 April 1930, 114–16.

Ogden, C. K. 'The Joyce Record', *Psyche* 2:1 (1930), 95–6.

Ong, Walter J. 'The Writer's Audience is Always a Fiction'. *PMLA* 90.1 (1975) 9–22.

O'Sullivan, Seumas [James Starkey]. *The Rose and Bottle and Other Essays*. Dublin: Talbot Press, 1946.

Parrinder, Patrick. 'The Strange Necessity: James Joyce's Rejection in England 1914–30'. In MacCabe, ed., *James Joyce: New Perspectives*.

Pašeta, Senia. *Before the Revolution: Nationalism, Social Change and Ireland's Catholic Elite*. Cork: Cork University Press, 1999.

Pierce, David. 'The Politics of *Finnegans Wake*'. *Textual Practice* 2.3 (1988), 367–80.

Pilkington, Lionel. '"Every Crossing Sweeper Thinks Himself a Moralist": The Critical Role of Audiences in Irish Theatre History'. *Irish University Review* 27:1 (1997), 152–65.

Theatre and the State in Twentieth-Century Ireland. London: Routledge, 2001.

Platt, Len. *Joyce and the Anglo-Irish*. Amsterdam: Rodopi, 1998.

Pollard, Arthur. *Satire*. London: Methuen, 1970.

Potts, Willard. *Joyce and the Two Irelands*. Austin: University of Texas Press, 2000.

Pound, Ezra. *Pound / Joyce: The Letters of Ezra Pound to James Joyce, with Pound's Essays about Joyce*. Ed. with commentary by Forrest Read. New York: New Directions, 1967.

Powell, David. 'An Annotated Bibliography of Myles Na Gopaleen's (Flann O' Brien's) "Cruiskeen Lawn" Commentaries on James Joyce'. *James Joyce Quarterly* 9:1 (1971), 50–62.

Power, Arthur. *Conversations with James Joyce*. Ed. Clive Hart. Dublin: Lilliput, 1999.

Power, Henriette Lazaridis. 'Incorporating *Giacomo Joyce*'. *James Joyce Quarterly* 28:3 (1991), 623–30.

Pratt, Mary Louise. 'Interpretive Strategies / Strategic Interpretations: on Anglo-American Reader Response Criticism'. *Boundary 2* 11:1–2 (1982/1983), 201–31.

Proust, Marcel. *À La Recherche du Temps Perdu*. [1913–22]. Paris: Quarto Gallimard, 1999.

In the Shadow of Young Girls in Flower. [1913]. Trans. James Grieve. London: Penguin, 2002.

'On Reading'. [1906]. Trans. and ed. Jean Autret and William Burford. *On Reading Ruskin*. New Haven: Yale University Press, 1987.

Pütz, Manfred. 'The Identity of the Reader in *Finnegans Wake*'. *James Joyce Quarterly* 11:4 (1974), 387–94.

Rabaté, Jean-Michel. *James Joyce, Authorized Reader*. Baltimore: Johns Hopkins University Press, 1991.

James Joyce and the Politics of Egoism. Cambridge: Cambridge University Press, 2002.

Joyce Upon the Void: The Genesis of Doubt. London: Macmillan, 1990.

Rabinowitz, Peter J. 'Truth in Fiction: A Re-examination of Audiences'. *Critical Inquiry* 4:1 (1977), 126–40.

Rainey, Lawrence. *Institutions of Modernism: Literary Elites and Public Culture*. New Haven: Yale University Press, 1998.

Riquelme, John Paul. *Teller and Tale in Joyce's Fiction: Oscillating Perspectives*. Baltimore: John Hopkins, 1983.

Rousseau, Jean-Jacques. *The Confessions* [1781]. Trans. J. M. Cohen. London: Penguin, 1953.

Scholes, Robert. *The Cornell Joyce Collection*. Ithaca: Cornell University Press, 1961.

Schutte, William M. *Joyce and Shakespeare: A Study in the Meaning of 'Ulysses'*. New Haven: Yale University Press, 1957.

Scott, Bonnie Kime. *Joyce and Feminism*. Brighton: Harvester Press, 1984.

Searle, John. 'The Logical Status of Fictional Discourse'. *New Literary History* 6:2 (1975), 319–32.

Segall, Jeffrey. *Joyce in America: Cultural Politics and the Trials of 'Ulysses'*. Berkeley: University of California Press, 1993.

Senn, Fritz. 'Habent sua fata'. *James Joyce Quarterly* 27:1 (1989), 132–4.

'Righting *Ulysses*'. In MacCabe, ed., *James Joyce: New Perspectives*.

'*Ulysses* and Its Audience'. In Morris Beja, Phillip Herring, David Norris and Maurice Harmon, eds., *James Joyce: The Centennial Symposium*. Urbana: University of Illinois Press, 1986.

212

Bibliography

Shakespeare, William. *Hamlet. The Riverside Shakespeare.* Boston: Houghton Mifflin, 1974.

Slingsby, G. V. L. 'Writes a Common Reader'. In Beckett, et al., *Our Exagmination.*

Sollers, Phillipe. 'Joyce et Cie'. *Tel Quel* 64 (1975), 15–24.

Spoo, Robert. *James Joyce and the Language of History: Dedalus's Nightmare.* Oxford: Oxford University Press, 1994.

Spurr, David. *Joyce and the Scene of Modernity.* Gainesville: University Press of Florida, 2002.

Sullivan, Kevin. *Joyce Among the Jesuits.* New York: Columbia University Press, 1958.

Swartzlander, Susan. 'Multiple Meaning and Misunderstanding: The Mistrial of Festy King'. *James Joyce Quarterly* 23:4 (1986), 465–76.

Synge, J. M. *Complete Plays.* Ed. Ann Saddlemyer. Oxford: Oxford University Press, 1995.

Tadié, Jean-Yves. *Marcel Proust: A Life.* Trans. Euan Cameron. London: Penguin, 2000.

Thomas, Brook. *James Joyce's 'Ulysses': A Book of Many Happy Returns.* Baton Rouge: Louisiana State University Press, 1982.

Thompson, Spurgeon. 'Joyce as Postcolonial Border Intellectual: A Mediterranean Comparison'. Unpublished paper. International James Joyce Symposium, Trieste, 2000.

Thwaites, Tony. *Joycean Temporalities: Debts, Promises and Countersignatures.* Gainesville: University Press of Florida, 2001.

Tierney, Michael, ed. *Struggle with Fortune.* Dublin: Browne and Nolan, 1954.

Ungar, Andras. *Joyce's 'Ulysses' as National Epic.* Gainesville: University of Florida Press, 2002.

Valente, Joseph. *James Joyce and the Problem of Justice.* Cambridge: Cambridge University Press, 1995.

Wexler, Joyce Piell. *Who Paid for Modernism?* Fayetteville: University of Arkansas Press, 1997.

Whittier-Ferguson, John. 'The Voice Behind the Echo: Vladimir Dixon's Letters to James Joyce and Sylvia Beach'. *James Joyce Quarterly* 29:3 (1992), 511–33.

Wilner, Joshua. *Feeding on Infinity: Readings in the Romantic Rhetoric of Internalization.* Baltimore: Johns Hopkins University Press, 2000.

Witemeyer, Hugh. '"He Gave the Name": Herbert Gorman's Rectifications of *James Joyce: His First Forty Years*'. *James Joyce Quarterly* 32:3–4 (1995), 523–32.

Wollaeger, Mark A. 'Reading *Ulysses:* Agency, Ideology, and the Novel'. In Mark A. Wollaeger, Victor Luftig and Robert Spoo, eds., *Joyce and the Subject of History.* Ann Arbor: University of Michigan Press, 1996.

Woolf, Virginia. *The Diary of Virginia Woolf, Volume V: 1936–1941.* Ed. Anne Olivier Bell. London: Hogarth Press, 1984.

Wordsworth, William. 'Essay Supplementary to the Preface' [1815]. *The Prose Works of William Wordsworth.* 3 vols. Ed. W. J. B. Owen and Jane Worthington Smyser. Oxford: Clarendon Press, 1974.

Yeats, W. B. *The Cat and the Moon.* Dublin: The Cuala Press, 1924.
Collected Letters of W. B. Yeats, Volume I: 1865–1895. Ed. John Kelly; assoc. ed.,
  Eric Domville. Oxford: Clarendon Press, 1996.
Collected Poems. Ed. Richard J. Finneran. New York: Collier Books, 1989.
Essays and Introductions [1937]. New York: Collier Books, Macmillan, 1968.
'More Memories', *The Dial* LXXIII (July 1922), 48–72.
'Plans and Methods.' *Beltaine: The Organ of the Irish Literary Theatre* I
  (May 1899), 6–9. Rep. *Beltaine.* London: Frank Cass and Co. Ltd, 1970.
The Yeats Reader. Ed. Richard J. Finneran. London: Palgrave Macmillan,
  2002.

Index

Index